PETE ROSE

PETE ROSE

A BIOGRAPHY

DAVID JORDAN

BASEBALL'S ALL-TIME GREATEST HITTERS

GREENWOOD PRESS
WESTPORT, CONNECTICUT • LONDON

Library of Congress Cataloging-in-Publication Data

Jordan, David M., 1935–
    Pete Rose : a biography / David Jordan.
      p. cm.—(Baseball's all-time greatest hitters)
    Includes bibliographical references and index.
    ISBN: 0–313–32875–7 (alk. paper)
    1. Rose, Pete, 1941– 2. Baseball players—United States—Biography. I. Title. II. Series.
GV865.R65J67 2004
796.357'092—dc22   2004053048
 [B]

British Library Cataloguing in Publication Data is available.

Library of Congress Catalog Card Number: 2004053048
ISBN: 0–313–32875–7

First published in 2004

Greenwood Press, 88 Post Road West, Westport, CT 06881
An imprint of Greenwood Publishing Group, Inc.
www.greenwood.com

Printed in the United States of America

The paper used in this book complies with the
Permanent Paper Standard issued by the National
Information Standards Organization (Z39.48–1984).

10 9 8 7 6 5 4 3 2 1

TO CHARLIE

CONTENTS

Contents

SERIES FOREWORD

The volumes in Greenwood's "Baseball's All-Time Greatest Hitters" series present the life stories of the players who, through their abilities to hit for average, for power, or for both, most helped their teams at the plate. Much thought was given to the players selected for inclusion in this series. In some cases, the selection of certain players was a given. **Ty Cobb, Rogers Hornsby**, and **Joe Jackson** hold the three highest career averages in baseball history: .367, .358, and .356, respectively. **Babe Ruth**, who single-handedly brought the sport out of its "Dead Ball" era and transformed baseball into a home-run hitters game, hit 714 home runs (a record that stood until 1974) while also hitting .342 over his career. **Lou Gehrig**, now known primarily as the man whose consecutive-games record Cal Ripken Jr. broke in 1995, hit .340 and knocked in more than 100 runs eleven seasons in a row, totaling 1,995 before his career was cut short by ALS. **Ted Williams**, the last man in either league to hit .400 or better in a season (.406 in 1941), is widely regarded as possibly the best hitter ever, a man whose fanatical dedication raised hitting to the level of both science and art.

Two players set career records that, for many, define the art of hitting. **Hank Aaron** set career records for home runs (755) and RBIs (2,297). He also maintained a .305 career average over twenty-three seasons, a remarkable feat for someone primarily known as a home-run hitter. **Pete Rose** had ten seasons with 200 or more hits and won three batting titles on his way to establishing his famous record of 4,256 career hits. Some critics have claimed that both players' records rest more on longevity than excellence. To that I would say there is something to be said about longevity and, in both cases, the player's excellence was the reason why he had the opportunity to keep playing, to keep tallying hits for his team. A base hit is the mark of a successful plate appearance; a home run is the apex of an at-bat. Accordingly, we could hardly have a series titled "Baseball's All-Time Greatest Hitters" without including the two men who set the career records in these categories.

Joe DiMaggio holds another famous mark: fifty-six consecutive games in which he obtained a base hit. Many have called this baseball's most unbreakable record. (The player who most closely approached that mark was Pete Rose, who hit safely in forty-four consecutive games in 1978.) In his thirteen seasons, DiMaggio hit .325 with 361 home runs and 1,537 RBIs. This means he *averaged* 28 home runs and 118 RBIs per season. MVPs have been awarded to sluggers in various years with lesser stats than what DiMaggio achieved in an "average" season.

Because **Stan Musial** played his entire career with the Cardinals in St. Louis—once considered the western frontier of the baseball world in the days before baseball came to California—he did not receive the press of a DiMaggio. But Musial compiled a career average of .331, with 3,630 hits (ranking fourth all time) and 1,951 RBIs (fifth all time). His hitting prowess was so respected around the league that Brooklyn Dodgers fans once dubbed him "The Man," a nickname he still carries today.

Willie Mays was a player who made his fame in New York City and then helped usher baseball into the modern era when he moved with the Giants to San Francisco. Mays did everything well and with flair. His over-the-shoulder catch in the 1954 World Series was perhaps his most famous moment, but his hitting was how Mays most tormented his opponents. Over twenty-two seasons the "Say Hey Kid" hit .302 and belted 660 home runs.

Only four players have reached the 600-home-run milestone: Mays, Aaron, Ruth, and **Barry Bonds**, who achieved that feat in 2002. Bonds, the only active player included in this series, broke the single-season home-run record when he smashed 73 for the San Francisco Giants in 2001. In the 2002 National League Championship Series, St. Louis Cardinals pitchers were so leery of pitching to him that they walked him ten times in twenty-one plate appearances. In the World Series, the Anaheim Angels walked him thirteen times in thirty appearances. He finished the Series with a .471 batting average, an on-base percentage of .700, and a slugging percentage of 1.294.

As with most rankings, this series omits some great names. Jimmie Foxx, Tris Speaker, and Tony Gwynn would have battled for a hypothetical thirteenth volume. And it should be noted that this series focuses on players and their performance within Major League Baseball; otherwise, sluggers such as Josh Gibson from the Negro Leagues and Japan's Sadaharu Oh would have merited consideration.

There are names such as Cap Anson, Ed Delahanty, and Billy Hamilton who appear high up on the list of career batting average. However, a number of these players played during the late 1800s, when the rules of baseball were drastically different. For example, pitchers were not allowed to throw overhand until 1883, and foul balls weren't counted as strikes until 1901 (1903 in the American League). Such players as Anson and company undeniably were the stars of their day, but baseball has evolved greatly since then, into a game in which hitters must now cope with night games, relief pitchers, and split-fingered fastballs.

Ultimately, a list of the "greatest" anything is somewhat subjective, but Greenwood offers these players as twelve of the finest examples of hitters throughout history. Each volume focuses primarily on the playing career of the subject: his early years in school, his years in semi-pro and/or minor league baseball, his entrance into the majors, and his ascension to the status of a legendary hitter. But even with the greatest of players, baseball is only part of the story, so the player's life before and after baseball is given significant consideration. And because no one can exist in a vacuum, the authors often take care to recreate the cultural and historical contexts of the time—an approach that is especially relevant to the multidisciplinary ways in which sports are studied today.

Batter up.

ROB KIRKPATRICK
GREENWOOD PUBLISHING
FALL 2003

ACKNOWLEDGMENTS

A writer always piles up some obligations in doing a work of this kind, and I am no exception. Gabe Schechter, Claudette Burke, Pat Kelly, and Bill Burdick at the National Baseball Library in Cooperstown were extremely helpful, as were the staffs at the Public Library of Cincinnati and Hamilton County, the Free Library of Philadelphia, and the Urban Archives at the Temple University Library. My daughter Diana did her usual keen editorial job with the manuscript, for which I thank her. Finally, my wife Barbara contributed patience and encouragement.

CHRONOLOGY

1941   Pete Rose is born in Cincinnati, Ohio, on April 14.

1960   Rose is signed by the Cincinnati Reds and plays for the Geneva, New York, farm club in the New York-Penn League.

1961   Plays at Tampa, Florida, in the Florida State League.

1962   Plays at Macon, Georgia, for Cincinnati's Class A farm club in the South Atlantic League, more commonly known as the Sally League.

1963   Rose is named National League Rookie of the Year for the Cincinnati Reds; Rose meets his future wife, Karolyn Engelhardt, in July at River Downs racetrack.

1964   Rose marries Karolyn on January 25, but leaves his wife at the wedding reception that evening to attend the Cincinnati baseball writers' "Parade of Stars" dinner.

1968   Rose wins National League batting title with a .335 average.

1969   Rose repeats as National League batting champ with a .348 average.

1970   Rose is named the first team captain in the long history of the Cincinnati Reds; the team wins the National League pennant, but the Reds are defeated in the World Series in five games by the Baltimore Orioles.

1972   The Reds lose the World Series to the Oakland A's in seven games.

1973   Rose wins a third batting title with a .338 average and is named the National League MVP; the Reds win the National League West division, but fail to reach the World Series.

1975   The Reds win the World Series, defeating the Boston Red Sox in seven games; Rose is named the Series MVP and *Sports Illustrated*'s Sportsman of Year, and also wins the Hickok Award as Professional Athlete of the Year.

1976   The Reds repeat as World Series champs, defeating the New York Yankees in a four-game sweep.

1978   Rose's forty-four-game hitting streak extends from June 14 to August 1, when it is snapped in a game against the Atlanta Braves; after the season, Rose becomes a free agent and signs with the Philadelphia Phillies on December 5.

1979   Rose is named Player of the Decade by the *Sporting News*.

1980   Karolyn Rose is granted a divorce from Pete; the Philadelphia Phillies win the World Series, defeating the Kansas City Royals in six games.

1981   Rose breaks Stan Musial's National League hit record; the Phillies win the "first-half" championship of the strike-shortened 1981 season, but are eliminated in five games in the National League Divisional Series by the Montreal Expos.

1983   Philadelphia wins the National League pennant but loses the World Series in five games to the Baltimore Orioles; Rose is released by the Phillies after the World Series.

1984   Rose signs with the Montreal Expos as a free agent on January 20 but is traded to the Cincinnati Reds and becomes the team's player-manager on August 16; Rose marries Carol Woliung as his second wife.

1985   Rose breaks Ty Cobb's all-time hits record, getting hit number 4,192 on September 9 in a game at Cincinnati against the San Diego Padres.

1986   Rose ends his career as an active player but continues as manager of the Reds.

1988   Rose is suspended thirty days for pushing umpire Dave Pallone.

1989   For gambling on baseball, and particularly on Reds games, Rose is suspended from baseball for life by Commissioner Bart Giamatti.

1990   Rose goes to prison for five months for income tax evasion.

1997   Rose makes an unsuccessful application to Commissioner Bud Selig for reinstatement.

2004   After fourteen years of denying that he bet on baseball, Rose publicly confesses that he did, thus reopening the debate over whether or not he should be reinstated to baseball and elected to the Hall of Fame.

INTRODUCTION

October 21, 1980. Game 6 of the World Series, with the Philadelphia Phillies on the verge of winning the first world championship ever in their ninety-seven-year history. In Veterans Stadium, 65,838 victory-starved Phillies fans are screaming encouragement to their heroes. One out in the ninth, and the inside perimeter of the ballpark is being patrolled by mounted police and policemen with guard dogs, presumably to prevent the long-suffering Phillies fans from committing unspeakable acts in their moment of triumph. But Phillies fans know all too well that terrible things can happen with one out in the ninth. Their team holds a 4–1 lead over the Kansas City Royals, but the Royals have the bases loaded, and left-handed reliever Frank "Tug" McGraw is just about at the end of his tether. McGraw had barely squirmed out of a bases-loaded jam in the eighth, and now the Royals are at him again.

Frank White, the Kansas City second baseman, a .264 hitter with 70 runs batted in during the regular season but hitting only .083 in the World Series, is at the plate, aching to redeem himself. He swings at McGraw's offering and lofts a pop foul over near the home dugout, on the first base side. Bob Boone, the Phillies slow-footed but sure-handed catcher, sprints toward the dugout, a little bit out of control, and calls for the ball. Boone would later say that it should have been the first baseman's catch but that Pete Rose was slow in getting over to the dugout. As the ball comes down, Boone stretches his arms out, gets his mitt under it, and then watches in horror as the ball bounces off his glove, into the air. Rose, the first baseman, whose ball it should have been had Boone not called him off, watches the ball clank off the catcher's mitt, then calmly sweeps it up in his own glove before it can hit the ground, just as if they had practiced the play. He quickly turns, to make sure McGraw is covering the plate, and runs the ball back to the pitcher, jubilantly putting two fingers in the air to signify to his teammates that there are now two outs.

Phillies fans watching the play had a momentary sickening feeling with Boone's miscue, succeeded immediately by a sensation of exhilarating relief when Rose gathered the ball in. Memories of the four-straight loss in the 1950 World Series, the awful ten-game skid that cost the 1964 pennant, the playoff disasters of 1976, '77, and '78, as well as all the other losing teams from years past flared up, to be banished again with Rose's alert improvisation. Many fans felt for the first time, with that play, that the baseball gods were finally looking upon them with benevolence, that the Phillies were finally, really, going to win. After Rose caught that pop-up, they knew that McGraw would fan Willie Wilson to win the game and the Series, as indeed he did. And they knew that, no matter what, come what may, they would always have to cut Peter Edward Rose a little slack. What they never expected was how much slack Pete Rose would require over the years to come.

Rose played major league baseball for twenty-four seasons, mostly with the Cincinnati Reds, and his longevity helped him capture some of baseball's most respected records. When he finally stepped down as an active player, he had played in more games, had more plate appearances, and had more base hits than any other player in major league history. Rose had been named Rookie of the Year in 1963 and Most Valuable Player in 1973 by the baseball writers, Player of the Decade (for the 1970s) by the *Sporting News*, Sportsman of the Year for 1975 by *Sports Illustrated*, Hickok Award winner as best professional athlete of 1975, and six times to the major league All-Star team. A street in Cincinnati had been named Pete Rose Way, he had been appointed manager of the Reds in 1984, and baseball fans across the country adored him as "Charlie Hustle," the personification of what they expected a big-league ballplayer to be.

By the early 1990s, the glow was gone. Rose was banned for life from baseball for his gambling, he was no longer permitted to manage the Reds, and he went to jail for tax evasion. He was revealed to be a serial philanderer, an addicted gambler who welshed on his debts, a bad father, and a less than stalwart friend. In January 2004, he publicly admitted to betting on baseball, something he had been denying for fourteen years. However, through it all, Rose retained the allegiance of a great many of his fans, leading to a silent (and sometimes not-too-silent) pressure to let up on him, let Pete back in the game, and give him his rightful place in the Hall of Fame at Cooperstown. This allegiance baffled many in the press who felt that they could see Pete Rose all too clearly.

Rob Neyer, for example, a well-respected baseball writer, wrote in late 2002, when the pressure for Rose's reinstatement was mounting, that he was truly puzzled by "the public love for a man who's firmly established himself as one of the more despicable people to wear a major league uniform." Rose, he said, "is a convicted tax cheat and a crummy husband and father who has, for many years, surrounded himself with drug dealers and various other unsavory types." None of us is perfect, Neyer wrote, "but it seems to me that Pete Rose is significantly farther from perfection than just about anybody you would want to know."[1]

That's a pretty harsh indictment, especially when one realizes that it is just a baseball player Neyer is talking about, not a Middle Eastern dictator. Baseball is a simple game: nine guys to a side facing nine others (or ten, if it happens to be an American League game), four bases arranged in a diamond, one guy throwing the ball, another trying to hit it and score a run, three outs to a team's at-bats, nine innings, most runs wins. Pete Rose has played in more winning games than anyone else in the game's history. He played in 3,662 games, counting post-season and All-Star games, and he played for winning teams most of the time. The fact that Rose happened to play on so many winning teams is not coincidental; "as a player for 24 years," it has been said, "Rose was a relentless overachiever who played with unmatched abandon."[2]

Rose's longtime teammate Joe Morgan wrote, "Pete played the game, always, for keeps. *Every* game was the seventh game of the World Series. He had this unbelievable capacity to literally roar through 162 games as if they were each that one single game."[3]

In addition, baseball is about numbers because it is a game that invites statistical analysis. Individual statistics have been kept since the game's professional inception, and here too Pete Rose's name and his numbers keep rising to the top. Rose was always well aware of his statistical achievements, and he went out of his way to make sure that others were too, to an extent that often became tiresome.

Pete Rose may have had more written about him, pro and con, than any other baseball player of modern times. There is little difficulty in turning up material on Pete Rose; the problem is sifting through it all, sorting the wheat from the chaff, figuring out the axe a particular writer (including Rose himself) may have to grind, and coming to solid conclusions about the man. And, of course, behind everything are the numbers, the legendary statistics that Pete Rose left behind when he hung up his glove and bat for the last time. Even those numbers, of course, are subject to interpretation; those numbers, and what they mean, will mark the place Rose will finally assume in the history of the game. The thing to remember about those numbers is this: most of them represent line drives that found landing places in unoccupied sections of major league outfields. They were big league hits, and Pete Rose had more of them than anyone else ever accumulated.

Pete Rose the scrapping ballplayer and Pete Rose the gambling man are two sides to the same complex human being, greatly admired and widely reviled. This work will try to bring readers a greater sense of the real Pete Rose.

NOTES

1. Rob Neyer, ESPN.com, December 9, 2002.

2. Craig Neff and Jill Lieber, "Rose's Grim Vigil," *Sports Illustrated*, April 3, 1989, 56.

3. Joe Morgan and David Falkner, *Joe Morgan: A Life in Baseball* (New York: W.W. Norton, 1993), 285.

THE RIVER RAT FROM ANDERSON FERRY

To know Pete Rose, it helps to know something about Cincinnati. Cincinnati is an old town, old and rather conservative. Located across from where the Licking River empties into the Ohio, it was settled in 1788 by three land speculators. Originally called Losantiville, which the founders said meant "city opposite mouth of Licking River," the town's name was changed to Cincinnati by Governor Arthur St. Clair in 1790, when he made it the capital of the Northwest Territory. The new name was in honor of the organization of former Continental Army officers established by Henry Knox and George Washington, the Society of the Cincinnati, of which St. Clair was a member.[1]

There were 2,540 people in the town by 1800, and it was incorporated two years later. Most of the early inhabitants came from Pennsylvania and New Jersey, but by 1860 the population of Cincinnati had grown to 161,044, 45 percent of them foreign-born, largely Germans and Irish, displaced by political turmoil and the potato famine, respectively. A thriving meatpacking industry conferred on the town the name of "Porkopolis," although this eventually gave way to the more sedate title of "Queen City of the West," taken from a poem by Henry Wadsworth Longfellow. And Cincinnati, with its commanding location on the Ohio, ranked for a while third in manufacturing among American cities, enjoying a dominant position in both southern and western markets.

In 1837, two men who had stopped off in Cincinnati for medical reasons—William Procter for his dying wife and James Gamble for himself—were brought together by a strange coincidence. The widower Procter and the bachelor Gam-

Pete Rose's boyhood home at 4404 Braddock Street in Anderson Ferry. *Photo courtesy of David Jordan.*

ble married sisters, and their mutual father-in-law urged them to go into business in Cincinnati. The two men opened a soap and candle manufactory, which they shortly incorporated as Procter and Gamble. Lucrative contracts for the Union Army during the Civil War put the new business on a firm footing, and the company's introduction of Ivory soap in 1879 led to riches. Procter and Gamble became a mainstay of industrial Cincinnati.

While Procter and Gamble flourished, however, the country's westward shift and the supplanting of steamboats by railroads reduced Cincinnati's commercial pretensions; it settled back into the second tier of American cities, gritty and hard-working but often with little to show for the effort. The town still had Procter and Gamble, as well as breweries and small manufacturing outfits, machine tool shops and the like, but these were just enough to keep Cincinnati's communal head above water. Two other Ohio cities surpassed it in population,

Cleveland and Columbus, while Cincinnati relaxed into a comfortable Republican torpor.

Along the way, the city annexed a series of slightly down-at-the-heels communities which stretched westward along the Ohio River from downtown, with names like Sedamsville, Riverside, and Anderson Ferry, the Ohio terminus of a ferryboat operation to the Kentucky side of the river. Once fashionable residential areas, these small towns became less desirable as railroad tracks were laid out, storage tanks sprang up, and a steel mill became part of the skyline. Now gritty little hamlets along River Road, they were rural backwaters even though within the city limits. The men who lived there worked mostly for the New York Central Railroad, Ashland Oil, Indiana Grain, or Morton Salt, or for the company that operated the ferry across the river to Kentucky.

It was in Anderson Ferry that Peter Edward Rose spent his childhood and youth, and the community left its mark on him. Rose was born on April 14, 1941, at the Deaconess Hospital in Cincinnati, the third child (and first son) of Harry Francis and LaVerne Bloebaum Rose.

His father, who was called "Pete" for most of his life—a nickname he picked up from a local vegetable huckster's horse that he admired—was a legend of sorts in the rundown West Side of Cincinnati, an athlete for all seasons into his forties. Harry Rose had once been a boxer, and for years he played baseball, softball, and semipro football, spending his spare time on the ball fields between the New York Central tracks and the riverbank. There was a well-known athletic field in Sedamsville called Bold Face Park, and Harry Rose could often be found there. His best sport was football, and at five feet, eight inches tall, and about 170 pounds, he was renowned for carrying the ball on weaving, shifty runs of sixty or seventy yards. He played at a frenetic pace, risking life and limb for the sake of an extra two or three yards for the Tressler Comets, the Riverside A.C., or Captain Al's Trolley Tavern. It was a characteristic he would pass on to his older son, whom he usually took to the games with him.

In his day job, Harry Rose worked downtown for the Fifth Third Bank, starting as a messenger while he was still in high school and working his way up to a mid-level position—supervisor of the calculating department—by the time he died, forty-two years later. Harry Rose was dependable, "never late to work," his son said.[2] He was a quiet man who did not drink and rarely smoked, and he had a sense of dignity about him. Harry provided for his family, though certainly not lavishly; with a little scrimping here and doing without there, the Roses managed well enough in their two-story clapboard home at 4404 Braddock in Anderson Ferry, just a few hundred yards up from the river. They certainly did not live in poverty, although in later years Pete sometimes tried to give the impression that they had. To daughters Caryl and Jacqueline and son Pete was added another boy named David seven years later. Pete and his siblings had a good family life.[3]

LaVerne, Pete's mother, usually called "Rosie" by her friends, was much more outgoing, volatile, and cocky than her husband. Her language was colorful, and if challenged she could respond in kind. While Harry did not discipline the children, LaVerne said, "If they sassed me, then I would crack their little butts for them."[4]

Harry often took his children camping out by the river on summer nights, not in tents but sleeping on newspapers, and in the winter they would all go sledding down Intersection Street. Harry gathered together chunks of wood and rubbish for a bonfire, while LaVerne brewed up hot chocolate for everyone there. Sometimes, on a Saturday, Harry took his whole family to the local horse track, River Downs, east of Cincinnati, where he was an enthusiastic bettor. Harry had enjoyed gambling since his youth, when he learned to shoot dice.

On their own, the Rose children played along the riverbank, digging foxholes and elaborately interconnected tunnels, and they swam in the river, sometimes heading across to the Kentucky side, ending up a half-mile downstream thanks to the Ohio's strong current. Pete's brother and sisters were better swimmers than he, but with fierce determination and all-out effort he would keep up. The neighbors called the kids who played along and in the Ohio "river rats," and this description certainly fitted Pete Rose.

His dad frequently took little Pete to Crosley Field, to watch the hometown Reds play. He would buy Pete a kid's ticket for fifty cents. Then, said Pete, "I'd go mooching through the crowd asking if anybody had an extra ticket and I never missed. My father and I always got in that way together."[5]

Young Pete was small growing up, often smaller than the girls in his school classes, and he had a small boy's readiness to fight to prove his worth. He was a plain-looking child, with freckles and gaps in his teeth—nothing out of the ordinary, nothing to mark him out as different from his peers.

One thing Pete Rose had that others lacked was a father who was determined to make an athlete of his elder son. Harry Rose, the frustrated jock, the man who played hard into his forties, made sure that Pete was a player, with the same drive that he had always shown. His father made it clear to young Pete that when you played a game—any game—you played to win. You played hard and you played clean, but you played to win. Sometimes you lost, and that was all right, but winning was much better. Harry Rose had played ball at Bold Face Park, as had his father before him. Now young Pete would follow in line.

There was more to it than that, of course. There was the constant encouragement from his father, as well as from his mother's brother Buddy Bloebaum.

Uncle Buddy had played professional baseball in his youth and was now a "bird dog," or unpaid scout, for the Reds. He may have seen something in young Pete, perhaps just the fierce grit and determination, and he did what he could to help. Buddy Bloebaum's greatest success as a player had come after he learned to switch hit, so, as Pete later wrote, "Uncle Buddy and my father put their heads together and taught me to do the same. . . . And," he added, "I never had to face a curveball coming at me from the wrong side."[6]

What he did have to do from time to time was fend off coaches who tried to discourage him from switch hitting. With help from his father, Pete was able to keep on batting from both sides of the plate. He worked on fielding by bouncing a ball off the wall of Schulte's Fish Garden, a local saloon, for hours on end, playing the various caroms. His father shouted at him from the sidelines during games and grilled him constantly on game situations and the proper reactions to them, so that those reactions would become second nature to Pete. And Pete Rose played ball, just about as much as he could.

One day, Pete was playing ball in Schulte's parking lot when a man who worked there introduced him to big Joe Adcock, the Reds slugger. He said to the nine-year-old, "Pete, maybe Mr. Adcock can give you some tips on hitting." Rose looked up at the massive Adcock and replied, "My dad tells *me* how to hit."[7]

The western end of Cincinnati had a proud baseball history. Don Zimmer, Jim Frey, Russ Nixon, Dick Drott, Art Mahaffey, Herman Wehmeier, and Clyde Vollmer all came out of this area, and in Rose's time he played with Eddie and Chuck Brinkman, both of whom had respectable big league careers, though neither one could hit major league pitching very well.

Pete also played football at Western Hills High, where he was a quick but undersized halfback at 130 pounds. There was talk that he might someday be able to play in a small college program, but academically Pete Rose was not college material. He made the team in his second crack at ninth grade, which he had to repeat when his father forbade his going to summer school after his first year at that level. Harry Rose felt that it was more important for Pete to spend his summer playing baseball, because Harry decided there was more future for Pete in baseball than in academics. Pete was never much of a student, although repeating a grade was embarrassing to him, and he hung out with what were considered the tough kids in the neighborhood. School was simply not very important to him.

Pete played baseball at Western Hills, of course, where the coaches saw him as a small kid who was very determined. They probably had no idea just how determined that was. Pete's younger brother David said, "At night he'd come home from a date and swing a heavy, leaded bat Uncle Buddy gave him, swing

150 times right-handed and 150 times left-handed in front of a mirror . . . perfecting his swing." David went on to say, "He didn't become a great ballplayer because of size, or because it was born in him. He worked."[8]

Pete had another uncle, named Curley Smart, who worked with the Reds' clubhouse custodian, and from time to time Smart was able to get Pete into Crosley Field during batting practice. The scrawny teenager from Anderson Ferry would get himself out onto the field and, on occasion, have a catch with his idol, Cincinnati second baseman Johnny Temple, or with shortstop Roy McMillan. These forays only increased Pete's already burning ambition to play baseball.

All the summers of baseball and the work and the switch hitting helped, but Paul "Pappy" Nohr, the legendary coach at Western Hills who had developed so many future big leaguers, saw Pete as "a good ball player, not a Brinkman." Eddie Brinkman was his highly regarded superstar, and Pappy Nohr preened when the Washington Senators signed Eddie for $75,000 in 1959. As for Pete Rose, Nohr said, "I don't think I would have recommended him for the big leagues when he was in high school. . . . Pete Rose could not have made the minors on his own, but his uncle was a scout."[9]

Indeed, Pete's uncle was a scout, and Buddy Bloebaum was nothing if not a good family man. He made it his business to get the Reds to sign his nephew, if only so young Pete could have the satisfaction of getting paid to play baseball, at least for a year or so in the low minor leagues. Buddy owed that much to LaVerne and Harry. But Buddy had a selling job to do; Pete was still only 155 pounds, and the Reds' people were unenthusiastic about him. But Buddy Bloebaum worked on one of the Reds' regular scouts, Buzz Boyle, telling him all about the latent possibilities of Pete Rose, stressing the no-risk factor of signing the youngster for minimum dollars, selling, cajoling, persuading.

Because of the repeated ninth grade, Pete was ineligible to play at Western Hills in his senior year. Instead, he hooked on with an amateur team in Lebanon, Ohio, and played three games a week in a pretty fair league, a league that was watched by the professional scouts. Pete played poorly at first, but as he settled in he started to hit and attracted some attention, notably from a scout with the Baltimore Orioles. There was also the long-shot possibility of getting a scholarship to play college football at Miami of Ohio, based on his play at Western Hills.

On the day Pete graduated from high school in June 1960, Buddy Bloebaum came to the house to tell Harry and LaVerne that the Cincinnati Reds were prepared to offer Pete a minor-league contract for $7,000. The selling job on Buzz Boyle had worked. Harry wondered about the Orioles scout who had been talking to him about Pete, but Uncle Buddy replied, "A bird in the hand is worth two Orioles in the bush."[10]

Buddy Bloebaum did not want to see any hesitation on the Roses' part, because he had had to do a real sales pitch with the Reds, finally convincing Boyle and their minor league people, based on his inside knowledge of the family, that the Rose men did their growing late and Pete would ultimately be bigger than he appeared now. The Reds were a bit sensitive on this point because they had recently lost out on a couple of prospects after hesitating over the young men's size.

The next day Bloebaum took Harry and Pete to the team offices in Crosley Field, and the three of them sat down with farm director Phil Seghi. Seghi offered Pete the $7,000 that he had agreed on with Bloebaum, with another $5,000 if and when Pete Rose ever made it to the majors for at least thirty days. (No doubt Seghi, looking at the scrawny kid in front of him, figured that *that* money was safe.) After Harry hemmed and hawed about his promise to talk with the Orioles scout, Pete said he wanted to sign then and there. Gone was any thought of trying to interest Baltimore or of playing college football. And that is how Pete Rose became a Cincinnati Red.

Seghi then suggested that, while Pete could go to the Geneva, New York, farm club in the New York-Penn League—the lowest of the low minors—and start right away, he might be better off to wait until the following spring training, report to Tampa, and start off on an even keel with everyone else. Seghi doubted that Pete was in real baseball shape playing two or three times a week. Phil Seghi quickly learned the futility of telling Pete Rose that he couldn't play ball. Pete was adamant that he wanted to start in as soon as possible. So, a couple of days later, fresh from his first ride in an airplane, Pete Rose arrived in Geneva to play in the Class D minor leagues.[11]

It may have been the low minors, but to Pete Rose it meant that he was a professional baseball player, no longer just a river rat. Even more, it meant that he was a professional ballplayer when everyone had said he couldn't make it. The normal standards, the ones applied to everybody else, did not apply to Peter Edward Rose. Years later, he said, "I don't remember ever wanting to be anything but a professional athlete and it's a good thing I became one because I never prepared for anything else."[12]

Rose talked to Eddie Brinkman, too. "Pete always kidded me that the Washington Senators brought me my bonus in an armored truck," Brinkman said. "Pete said he cashed his at the corner store."[13]

NOTES

1. St. Clair's main claim to fame came in November 1791 when his ill-prepared army was soundly defeated by Indians in west-central Ohio.

2. Pete Rose and Roger Kahn, *Pete Rose: My Story* (New York: Macmillan, 1989), 56.

3. Pete later went around telling people, "We were so poor when I was a kid I had a sister who was stamped 'made in Japan.'" Milton Gross (NANA) in (Philadelphia) *Evening Bulletin*, May 14, 1967.

4. Michael Y. Sokolove, *Hustle: The Myth, Life, and Lies of Pete Rose* (New York: Simon and Schuster, 1990), 29.

5. (Philadelphia) *Evening Bulletin*, May 14, 1967.

6. Pete Rose and Peter Golenbock, *Pete Rose on Hitting: How to Hit Better Than Anybody* (New York: Perigee Books, 1985), 30.

7. John Erardi, *Pete Rose* (Cincinnati: Cincinnati Enquirer, 1985), 11. Emphasis in original.

8. Rose and Kahn, *Pete Rose: My Story*, 69.

9. James Reston Jr., *Collision at Home Plate: The Lives of Pete Rose and Bart Giamatti* (New York: Edward Burlingame Books, 1991), 14.

10. Ibid., 27.

11. When the *Sporting News*, on July 27, 1960, listed the two players recently signed by the Reds, one was simply "Pete Rose, 19, second baseman of Cincinnati," while the other, right-handed pitcher Doug Proffitt, was noted as having "hurled two no-hitters and compiled a 31–3 record in high school."

12. Rose and Kahn, *Pete Rose: My Story*, 74.

13. Erardi, *Pete Rose*, 13.

ON THE WAY UP

It was June 21, 1960, and Pete Rose had his first airplane ride, from Cincinnati to Rochester, New York. Like most first-time fliers, Rose was uneasy, but he soon overcame any concern in his eagerness to start his new career. From Rochester he took a bus the forty-six miles to Geneva, at the northern tip of Seneca Lake, and from the bus terminal he caught a cab to Shuron Park, the old ballpark that the Geneva Red Legs called home.

Geneva was a small town, with a population hovering around 15,000, in the heart of New York's Finger Lakes. It prided itself on its beautiful setting on Seneca Lake, its surrounding wine country, and its history. Supported by an early glass industry and local agriculture, the town also housed the Geneva Medical College, which produced Elizabeth Blackwell, the first woman doctor in the United States. The college subsequently became Hobart and William Smith Colleges.

It is doubtful that Pete Rose was aware of or cared about Geneva's attractions, past or present; to him, Geneva was a place to play ball. When Pete got to the ballpark, he came across a man just inside the front gate and asked, "Hey, mister. I'm Pete Rose. Where do I get my uniform?"

The man, who happened to be Asa Brooks, the team's general manager and also the local chief of police, looked at the scrawny kid wearing a Cincinnati cap and carrying a battered-looking suitcase with a couple of bats strapped to it and snapped, "Who the hell do you think you are?"

"Well, I'm your new second baseman, mister." This was Geneva's introduction to Pete Rose.[1]

Minor league baseball in the 1960s was a glorious mixture of hope, anticipation, struggle, success, failure, and dark reality. From their halcyon days after World War II, when there were nearly sixty leagues spread from sea to shining sea, the minors had been forced to trim down to a more manageable twenty or so leagues. Television had brought big league ball into the homes of millions of people, many of whom lost interest in the bush league variety of the game. Most minor league franchises were locally owned but totally dependent on a major league connection for players, guidance, and sometimes financial help. Few if any clubs made any money, and most club owners found baseball to be a constant matter of juggling creditors and the priority of their claims: the electric bill had to be paid ahead of the bus company's bill because the ballpark lights needed to be turned on sooner than the next out-of-town bus trip.

The players, particularly in the low minors, were overwhelmingly young men, single, far from home, and desperately hoping to make a place for themselves in the national pastime. Some few would succeed, while most would find after a season or so that their preeminence in high school baseball did not translate into a professional career. So, back home they would go, still young enough to start another kind of job, knowing that baseball would not be their life's work.

Minor league baseball was a lonely life, especially for a young man who had seldom strayed far from his hometown. Pete Rose rented a room from the Charles Hickey family for about ten bucks a week, but his real digs were at the ballpark. "The minors were good days," Rose would say later. "Maybe a little nervous. Maybe a little lonely."[2] Your friends, the people you got to know best, were your teammates, the guys you were with every day. But even with them, there was a bit of an edge, because after all there were twenty or so of you competing for a couple of spots at the next level on the minor league ladder. You tried not to dwell too much on this as you went about your day-to-day activities, but it was always there.

And there were always girls. It was in the minor leagues that ballplayers learned to take for granted the fact that there were always young ladies available to take care of their needs, physical and emotional, what Pete Rose phrased as "a fringe benefit of being a ballplayer." "Baseball Annies," as they were called, seemed to be a fixture of the game, from the big leagues to the lowest minors. Rose, however, claimed that he did not get too involved with girls at first. "In the minors," he said, "I was a straight young guy."[3]

Rose introduced himself to the Geneva manager, Reno diBenedetti, a minor league lifer who was on his last legs with a bad ballclub. DiBenedetti was under instructions from Cincinnati to stick the new kid in the line-up, so he wrote Pete Rose in at second base.[4] The manager would later be fired and replaced on August 1 by Reds' scout Jack Cassini, who had once had an eight-game "cup of coffee" with the Pittsburgh Pirates, "a hard-bitten, pistol of a guy, but a pure baseball man," according to Johnny Bench.

The incumbent second baseman, Atanacio "Tony" Perez, a tall, 18-year-old Cuban, was none too happy about having to move to third base to make room for the newcomer from Cincinnati. But second base was no place for Perez; in sixty games there, he had twenty-three errors, for an abysmal fielding average of .933. "Tony was a *terrible* fielder," said one teammate. "He couldn't pick up a ground ball. It was a far-out thing for him." Perez was even worse at third, but eventually someone moved him to first base and there he settled down, going on to a twenty-three-year career that landed him in the Hall of Fame.[5]

Pete Rose, it turned out, was no improvement on Tony Perez at the keystone sack. In 72 games, Rose made 36 errors, for a fielding average of .916. "The truth is," Rose admitted, "that I wasn't a good fielder. I may have been pressing. I knew I wasn't what you'd call a natural." He was better at the plate. He batted .277, with 89 hits and 43 runs batted in in 321 times at bat, although most of his hits came right-handed.[6]

The New York-Penn League was way down the minor league ladder, and the Geneva Red Legs were the worst team in the league, finishing 29 games behind league-leading Erie, a Washington Senators farm club. The day before Rose arrived, the Red Legs had ended a five-game losing stretch during which they had committed an astonishing 28 errors. Wellsville, Auburn, Corning, and Elmira were the other towns with teams in the league, and there were just a few players in the league who would make it to the big time: Elrod Hendricks, Rollie Sheldon, and a shortstop at Elmira named Richie Allen, who led the league with 48 errors. Surprisingly, the biggest names would come out of the sorriest team: Geneva's Rose and Perez, as well as their teammate Art Shamsky, who was the only Red Leg chosen for the league's All-Star team.

The new Geneva second baseman was loud, vulgar, and cocky, and some fans were upset with the obscenities he shouted on the field, which could easily be heard in the grandstands. "He used to come out with some pretty good terms," recalled Charles Hickey, his landlord, "and that's what upset a lot of people." But he made a hit with most of the followers of the club, few though they were, who voted him the team's most popular player.[7]

Pete was homesick, so he asked his mother to come to Geneva for a couple of weeks, and she dutifully took a bus from Cincinnati and stayed in a tourist home to cheer him on. His aunt and uncle, the Bloebaums, showed up for a while too, to offer more encouragement.

All in all, Pete's first season in pro ball was so-so; he hit a little better than expected but his fielding was terrible. Harry Rose made the mistake of asking a Reds executive to see the scouting report on his son. "Pete Rose," the report

read, "can't make a double-play, can't throw, can't hit left-handed and can't run."
When the stunned father asked if it said Pete did anything right, the Reds' man
replied, "Well, it does say that Pete seems to have a lot of aggressiveness." It
seemed like little on which to build a baseball career.[8]

Pete Rose left Geneva at the end of the New York-Penn season with a direction to report the following spring to Tampa for spring training. He returned
to Cincinnati determined to build himself up over the winter, so he got a job
with the Railway Express Agency, unloading boxcars in the railroad yards. It was
hard work, heavy work, but it paid off. With the help of his mother, who kept
him well fed on a daily basis, Pete grew two inches and put on twenty pounds,
mostly of muscle, by the time he reported to Al Lopez Field in Tampa.

The Cincinnati Reds certainly expected little of Pete Rose when training for
the 1961 season began, but they had agreed with Bloebaum and Harry Rose
when they signed Pete that he would at least get the chance at Tampa. The Reds'
minor league people were surprised at the physical appearance of the young man
who reported in Tampa; he was no longer the scrawny-looking misfit who had
played at Geneva. And he no longer played like him. His fielding improved, and
he began hitting the ball with authority. "He was unbelievable," said a teammate. "I couldn't believe it was the same Pete Rose I played with in Geneva."[9]

Harry Rose came down to Tampa to help out, and after practice he hit
grounders to Pete to help him with his fielding. Ground balls, one after another,
until the lateral move, the stoop, the pickup, became a matter of muscle mem-
ory. After hours, Harry took Pete to the dog track or the jai alai fronton to get
down a few sporting wagers, just as he had done taking the family to River
Downs back home. Pete, who adored his father, could see that an evening of
pari-mutuel betting was just the thing for a serious adult.

For the 1961 season, Pete Rose was moved up to the Tampa Tarpons in the
Florida State League, still Class D but considered a tougher league than the New
York-Penn. There were six other teams in the league, Palatka, St. Petersburg,
Daytona Beach, Orlando, Sarasota, and Leesburg, mostly in the central or west-
ern part of the state, except for Daytona Beach. After a few weeks in the league,
one thing a player knew was the geography of the state of Florida.

Pete's manager at Tampa was Johnny Vander Meer, who had, after his glory
days of throwing back-to-back no-hitters in 1938, put in another eleven years
of big league pitching, interrupted by wartime military service. Vander Meer,
unlike the managers at Geneva, was vastly impressed with his new second baseman. Originally Pete Rose was consigned to the second-stringers, the ones considered to have little chance of hanging on. But he showed the Reds a lot more
than he had the year before. Vander Meer told the front office it had to keep
him.

Pete Rose started out the year with the Tarpons as a hitting machine, batting a gaudy .376 well into May, but he still had fielding deficiencies. Vander Meer said, "The way he pivoted on a double play . . . he wouldn't *ever* get a good major league runner. And then his range was limited, particularly to his right." Vander Meer was particularly impressed with Pete's drive and hustle. "Hitting and speed are not his greatest assets," Vander Meer commented. "It's aggressiveness." A .376 hitter has to be in the line-up, regardless of his shortcomings in the field. Vander Meer did try to switch Rose to third base or the outfield, but Phil Seghi and the big club insisted the young man was a second baseman.[10]

Vander Meer said, "Every time I looked up he was driving one into the alleys and running like a scalded dog and sliding headfirst into third. He hit thirty triples for me that year." A writer for the *Sporting News* called Rose a "tripling terror." Early on Harry Rose had taught Pete that triples were made by running hard right out of the batter's box, not just between second and third, and that training paid off at Tampa. The 30 triples Rose hit stood for many years as a Florida State League record. When Topps, the chewing gum and trading card company, named a "player of the month" for each of the existing nineteen minor leagues, the winner of the engraved watch for the Florida State League for May was Pete Rose.[11]

Pete hit an inside-the-park home run in both games of a double-header on June 10, each ball rolling to the right-center-field wall, about 425 feet from the plate. For good measure, Rose added a pair of singles to his day's output.

It was with the Tarpons that Rose developed the headfirst slide that would become almost a signature for him. Rose himself got a rush from hurling himself forward into the air, his arms outstretched in front of him, and the fans loved it. "Those headfirst slides were kind of a joke with the other players," a teammate remarked, but Pete Rose did things his way, even when he hurt his wrist doing it. He missed only a few days, and he kept on sliding headfirst.[12]

The Tarpons dominated the league that season, finishing with a 90–44 record, thirteen and one-half games ahead of the next team; Pete Rose, hitting .331 for the year, finished second in batting behind Leesburg's Jim Livesey. On August 27, Tampa beat Sarasota 4–0 to win the fifth and deciding game of the Florida State League championship playoff. It was the first such title for Tampa since 1957, and it was a perfect cap for Pete Rose's breakout season.[13]

Pete Rose's accomplishments in the Florida State League changed his status in the parent club's minor league books to one of "prospect," a young player who needed more careful tending than he had heretofore received. At the end of the season Pete returned to Cincinnati, resumed his job unloading railroad boxcars, built his body up a little bit more, and looked forward to what the Reds had in mind for him for 1962.

The next year meant a season in Macon, Georgia, where Cincinnati now had its Class A farm club in the South Atlantic League, more commonly called the Sally League. Macon had been in the Southern Association the year before, but when that venerable league folded the Columbia, South Carolina, club in the Sally League was transferred to Macon. This was a couple of steps up from the Florida State League, and the competition was a good bit stiffer.

Dave Bristol, the Macon manager, was a young man who had given up his dream of playing in the big leagues fairly early in his twenties when the Reds offered him another alternative, that of managing in their minor league system. It turned out to be an inspired choice, both for the Reds and for Dave Bristol. He was moving up in the organization and was happy to be placed in 1962 in his hometown, Macon, Georgia.[14]

Bristol's Macon Peaches were not the best club in the Sally League that year—they finished third, twelve games behind Savannah—but they produced a lot of offensive firepower. Pete Rose was right in the middle of it. On April 24, Macon beat the Greenville Spinners by a score of 32–5, with Rose going 6 for 8, with a triple, home run, and 6 RBIs. In a series against Savannah June 1–4, Rose had 9 hits in 14 at-bats, along with 8 walks. On August 11, Pete went 5 for 5. He was one of seven Macon players named for the midseason All-Star game.

For the year Pete hit .330, with 31 doubles, a league-leading 17 triples, and 9 home runs. His 125 runs scored broke a club record that had stood since 1927. He was named the second baseman on the Topps Class A Minor League All-Star team, winning an engraved silver bowl. Bob Bonifay, the Peaches' general manager, later told Michael Sokolove, "By the end of his season with us, anyone could tell he was a very special player." Tommy Helms, who batted .340, was considered by the Reds' front office to be the team's top prospect, but, as Bonifay recalled, "as good as Tommy was, he didn't have the charisma Pete had. Pete put out electricity when he played. . . . [Y]ou knew that this boy was not going to be denied from reaching his goal." One manager in the league said that Rose was the only player he had ever seen who got down to first base after a walk before the catcher could throw the ball back to the pitcher.[15]

Pete was nicknamed "Hollywood," for his flashy style of play, but he soon demonstrated that there was substance behind the flash. Rose still had difficulty with the double-play pivot, but with constant practice on ground balls he made himself into a decent second baseman. In concert with the groundskeeper at the Macon ballpark, Pete kept the area around second a little soft, sometimes even a bit muddy, to slow ground balls as they went through, giving himself a little better shot at getting to them. Pete was getting a feel for the position. Revealingly, when a Macon sportswriter asked Rose who his baseball hero was, Pete named the Cincinnati second baseman he'd watched while he was growing up,

Johnny Temple, another player who was not a natural, who had to go hard all the time, who had to look for an edge here or there.[16]

His season at Macon was a great success for Pete Rose. It was still the bush leagues, of course, and overnight trips were made in station wagons packed eight to a car. "We slept sitting up," Rose later recounted. Meal money of $3.50 a day didn't go too far, either. "I'd eat a two-dollar breakfast," Rose said, "and have a buck and a half left for the rest of the day. I always wound up spending my own money [in addition to the per diem] because I've always believed it's important to eat good meals." The year before, when Pete once ran out of meal money on a three-town road trip, he ate table scraps off the plates left by other customers. Because he did not smoke or drink, Pete was able to avoid expenditures for cigarettes and booze. He and Art Shamsky, living together at the local YMCA, kept the pretty girls of Macon busy.[17]

The team scored a lot of runs and won eighty games, losing only fifty-nine. The Peaches swept three straight from Savannah in the first round of playoffs, then knocked off Knoxville, three games to one, to win the league championship, with Rose slugging a grand slam in the deciding game. Pete finally made an impression on the Cincinnati front office. He was one of six Macon players named to go to the Reds' Winter Instructional League club at Tampa, and in February 1963, he would go to spring training with the big league club. Although there were still a couple of rungs on the ladder between the Sally League and the majors, Pete Rose was now considered a prime prospect.

NOTES

1. Sokolove, *Hustle: The Myth, Life, and Lies of Pete Rose*, 44; Kevin Oklobzija, "Geneva, N.Y., Doesn't Much Care That Rose Used to Play There," *Cincinnati Enquirer*, September 8, 1985, A-12.

2. Rose and Kahn, *Pete Rose: My Story*, 86.

3. Ibid., 87.

4. Johnny Bench and William Brashler, *Catch You Later: The Autobiography of Johnny Bench* (New York: Harper and Row, 1979), 19.

5. Erardi, *Pete Rose*, 14. Emphasis in original. Even at Cincinnati, the Reds tried playing Tony Perez at third base from 1968 to 1970 because they had slugger Lee May at first; Tony led the National League in errors at the position each season.

6. Rose and Kahn, *Pete Rose: My Story*, 91.

7. Oklobzija, "Geneval N.Y., Doesn't Much Care That Rose Used to Play There," A-12.

8. Reston, *Collision at Home Plate: The Lives of Pete Rose and Bart Giamatti*, 30. Art

Shamsky said later, "Looking at Pete in 1960, there was no way he was going to make the big leagues" (Erardi, *Pete Rose*, 14).

9. Erardi, *Pete Rose*, 15.

10. Rose and Kahn, *Pete Rose: My Story*, 96; *Sporting News*, July 19, 1961.

11. *Sporting News*, May 17, 1961, and "Topps to Honor 19 Minor Standouts," *Sporting News*, June 21, 1961.

12. Erardi, *Pete Rose*, 15.

13. Rose and Kahn, *Pete Rose: My Story*, 97.

14. Dave Bristol would ultimately reach the major leagues and manage there for parts of eleven seasons, with the Reds, Brewers, Braves, and Giants. He would also coach in the majors for thirteen seasons, with the Reds, Expos, Giants, and Phillies.

15. Sokolove, *Hustle: The Myth, Life, and Lies of Pete Rose*, 46; Harley Bowers, "Reds to Harvest Prime Peaches," *Sporting News*, October 20, 1962.

16. Temple played second base for the Reds as a regular from 1954 through 1959.

17. Earl Lawson, "Rookie Rose Silenced Cincy's Skeptics," *Sporting News*, October 26, 1963, 3.

THE ROOKIE

The Cincinnati Reds squad with which Pete Rose went to spring training in February 1963 was composed largely of the members of the pennant-winning team of two years earlier. The 1961 Reds won the National League pennant by four games over the Los Angeles Dodgers, gaining the first league championship for the Queen City since the teams led by Frank McCormick, Bucky Walters, Billy Werber, and Eddie Joost in 1939 and 1940. It had been a high old time in Cincinnati in 1961, with 1,117,603 fans crowding into ancient Crosley Field for the season, only the third time the Reds had gone over a million in home attendance. The Yankees of Mickey Mantle and Roger Maris had taken some of the wind out of Cincinnati's sails with a five-game World Series victory, but the Reds still felt they had something special in their club.

In 1962 the Reds, still under manager Fred Hutchinson, had dropped to third place, behind the Giants and Dodgers. Nevertheless, the Reds players who reported to spring training in Tampa in February 1963 felt that they had as good a chance, with their tested, veteran line-up, as anyone in the National League to win that season's pennant.

First baseman Gordie Coleman, second sacker Don Blasingame, shortstop Eddie Kasko, and third baseman Gene Freese had made up the Reds' infield in the pennant-winning year, and its members were still part of the inner core of the club. Utility man Leo "Chico" Cardenas had played a lot of shortstop in 1962, because Freese was hurt with a broken ankle and Kasko had to move over to third, but Freese was ready to take his job back. Coleman and Blasingame,

Rose as a rookie second baseman in a none-too-graceful double-play pivot. *National Baseball Hall of Fame Library, Cooperstown, N.Y.*

on the right side, 28 and 31 years old respectively, looked like fixtures for the next couple of seasons.

Blasingame, the second baseman, had been a big league regular with the Cardinals, Giants, and then the Reds since 1956. He had batted a solid .289 in 1959 when Fred Hutchinson was his Cardinal manager, so he went back a long way with Hutchinson. A native of Corinth, Mississippi, the "Blazer," as he was called by one and all, was a popular figure on the baseball scene, well regarded by both fans and his peers on the playing field. A .281 hitter for the Reds in 1962, just in the prime of his career, Blasingame had no reason to feel that his job was in any kind of jeopardy when he arrived in Tampa for spring training in February 1963.

Pete Rose played for the Reds in the winter instructional league after the 1962 season, in the course of which he hit .324 and mightily impressed Don Heffner, the longtime major league infielder who ran the Reds' instructional league club, and Hutchinson, the big club's manager, with his hustle, intensity and drive. Heffner said, "Pete Rose and Tommy Helms definitely are big leaguers of the future, whether they make it in '63 or not." Another player working out in the instructional league was a Cuban kid named Chico Ruiz; Ruiz buttonholed a reporter to tell him, "That Rose, he's got a line-drive bat."[1]

Earl Lawson, the baseball beat writer for the *Cincinnati Post*, said, "As soon as Hutch saw Pete play, he fell in love with him. At the winter meetings that year, he told me, 'If I had any guts, I'd stick Rose at second base and just leave him there.' "[2]

That, of course, was just off-season rumination; Hutchinson knew he had a perfectly adequate second baseman in Don Blasingame. But the thought had clearly taken up residence inside the manager's head. A most surprising spring training lay ahead, and the Reds had invited eleven nonroster prospects, including Rose, to camp with them.

There was considerable press speculation about Cincinnati's infield situation for the season coming up. The club had a lot of infielders to be fitted into the two slots on the left side of the diamond—Kasko, Freese, Cardenas, Don Zimmer, Chico Ruiz, Cookie Rojas (who was shortly traded to Philadelphia), Tommy Harper—and much would apparently depend on the state of Freese's ankle. Pete Rose was seldom mentioned. Nor did he appear in a rundown on the Reds' top rookie prospects in the *Sporting News*, which featured Harper, catcher Jesse Gonder, and pitchers Sammy Ellis, George McWilliams, and John Tsitouris.[3]

Blasingame noted the surfeit of infielders on the Reds and joked that "I read in *The Sporting News* about all of these kids who were coming to camp to take my job away from me [and] I got a little worried." Don would soon find that he had real reason to worry, and from someone who was not even on the Cincinnati roster.[4]

When the Reds players reported to Tampa, they were startled to note that Freddy Hutchinson gave as much time at second base to the rookie Rose as he did to Blasingame, who was nursing a mild groin injury. The veteran members of the team could not understand what was in Hutchinson's mind and why Blasingame, one of *them* who certainly did not deserve such treatment, was getting such short shrift. And for whose benefit? Pete Rose was cocky, abrasive, self-assured, indiscreet—all the things a rookie should not be. And Rose was up from Class A ball, not even Double-A or Triple-A! The veterans assumed he soon would be sent out to Macon (the Sally League had been elevated to Double-A for 1963, so Macon was now the Reds' second tier farm club) or San Diego, the Triple-A farm, but why should he be getting such attention in the meantime?

One day, during batting practice, Rose took one too many swings. John Edwards, the Reds' regular catcher, snapped, "Can't you count?" Rose quickly retorted, "I didn't go to Ohio State like you did." Hutchinson, listening, said, "He's lucky big John didn't punch his head off," but clearly he was taken with his rookie second sacker. "There isn't a harder worker in camp," said Hutchinson, "but to Pete, it really isn't work, just fun."[5]

Rose was nothing if not confident. One evening, Coach Dick Sisler, driving back to the club's training headquarters at the Causeway Inn, passed a pedestrian who looked familiar. Later on, back at the hotel, Sisler asked Rose if he had been the man on the road. Pete admitted that it was and that he was coming from a place five miles away. "And you walked?" asked Sisler. "Sure," Rose replied. "I didn't have money for a cab and you wouldn't expect a major league player to hitch-hike, would you?"[6]

When the club's first exhibition game came up, Rose worked out on a separate field with the other players not in the day's line-up and, when he was finished his running, prepared to go into the dressing room and shower. Mike Ryba, a Reds' scout who was working as an instructor in camp, saw Pete and suggested that he hang around for a while, on the chance that Hutchinson might use him. Sure enough, late in the game, Hutch sent Rose in as a pinch-runner for Wally Post and kept him in the game at third base. In the eleventh inning, Pete smacked a double to left center field and then, after another two-base hit in the fourteenth, scored the game-winning run. It was a surefire way of getting the boss's attention.[7]

As training camp went on, it became clearer that Blasingame was truly in danger of losing his job. Pete Rose kept pounding out line drive hits, and it seemed as if he was always on base, taking the extra base, sliding in headfirst in a cloud of dust. Hutchinson was obviously delighted with Rose, just as much as the veteran players on the club were disgusted with him. Earl Lawson wrote that "rookie second baseman Pete Rose continues to impress Hutch, who plans to give him a 'long look.'" Hutchinson said, while denying that he was favoring the rookie over the veteran, "It's more or less a case of seeing what the kid can do. He's an aggressive youngster and he has a lot of ability."[8]

Even players on other teams noticed him. In an exhibition game against the New York Yankees, Rose drew a base on balls and sprinted down to first, as was his custom. Whitey Ford, the Yankees' great lefthanded pitcher, sneered, "Charlie Hustle!" Mickey Mantle guffawed, and the press picked up the epithet. Rose was delighted; after all, what could be a more valuable trademark for a ballplayer than hustle? His teammates were not pleased. What Ford clearly meant, they knew, was that Rose was "showboating," even showing other guys up, and they had seen it from the beginning of spring training.

They were aghast at Pete's performance one night in Mexico City. Half the Cincinnati squad had gone south for several exhibition games, March 22–24, and one evening a group of them, including Rose, went to a local strip club. That was nothing out of the ordinary for a bunch of ballplayers; what was unusual was Pete Rose climbing up on stage and getting tangled up with one of the naked performers.[9] His teammates were appalled at his lack of discretion, and the Mexico City incident solidified their sour opinion of Rose. None of it fazed Pete Rose. When he was needled by players on other teams about his Mexico City performance, Pete just grinned.

Earl Lawson liked to tell the story of an evening late in spring training when he asked ten veteran Reds to list on a piece of paper who the twenty-eight members of the squad would be after cutdown time. He passed out paper and pencils to the players and then collected the finished products. Of the ten players, only one listed Rose's name on the season-opening squad. That one player was Don Blasingame.[10]

Just before the Reds left Tampa for home, their trip to include four games with the Chicago White Sox on the way north, Gene Freese, a former member of the Sox, got together with Nellie Fox, Chicago's second baseman, and suggested that the White Sox pitchers might want to feed Rose a steady diet of high fastballs in their games, figuring the rookie would have trouble with them. Fox and his pitchers knew just what was going on, and they were happy to oblige. "I was just trying to help Blazer make the team," Freese said later. Whatever the motive, it did no good. Pete Rose kept belting line drive base hits into various parts of the outfield, and the starting second base job was his. He had realized his dream: he was a major leaguer.[11]

Veteran sportswriter Joe King wrote, "Pete Rose was an unknown when the

Cincinnati Reds opened their training camp; he wasn't even on their roster. However, Rose was playing second base on opening day and the veteran Don Blasingame was seated on the bench." Lefty Jim O'Toole pitched for the Reds as they beat Pittsburgh 5–2 in their April 8 opener. O'Toole was aided by four double plays, three of them with Rose as the pivot, the play that the experts and his teammates said he couldn't make. In his big league debut, Pete walked in his first at-bat against Pirate pitcher Earl Francis, grounded out, reached on an error, and struck out. He scored one run, ahead of Frank Robinson's home run, and made an error.[12]

The next day, in Philadelphia, Rose was 0 for 4 against Art Mahaffey, another Western Hills High School alumnus, who fanned him all four times, and he was 0 for 4 in his third game. Pete got his first major league hit on April 13, a triple off of Pittsburgh's Bob Friend at Crosley Field; Friend later said "he hit a pretty good pitch down the left field line." But when Rose's slump reached 3-for-23, Hutchinson sat him down, reasoning that a stay in the dugout would ultimately help the young second baseman. The Reds had lost four of six games at that point, and Freese and Harper were benched as well.[13]

Luckily for Rose, Blasingame did not hit much better when given his chance, so Pete went back into the line-up on April 27 at Houston, where he went 1 for 3. Don Blasingame became a father for the second time on April 29 when his wife gave birth to a baby boy, but he had by then definitely lost his second base job.

Rose later admitted that he had been pressing early in the season and, as Hutchinson surmised would happen, benefited from the benching. "I just wasn't myself," Pete told reporters. "That spell on the bench did me a lot of good. I watched the pitchers, saw how they set up hitters." Back in the line-up, Rose knew he was really a big leaguer, and he began to act the part. "I guess I must have spent about $500 on clothes the first month of the season," he said, reflecting on the sports coats, natty shirts and ties, and spiffy shoes with which he dressed himself.[14]

On May 3, Rose hit a triple and his first major league home run against the Cardinals' Ernie Broglio, and in the eight games played after he was reinserted into the line-up Pete was 10 for 28. After the home run, Hutchinson remarked dryly, "I just hope Rose doesn't get the idea he's supposed to hit like Robby [slugger Frank Robinson]."[15]

Pete Rose knew that he could hit an occasional home run, but he was very aware that his future as a baseball player was in singles, doubles, and triples—lots of them. One of Rose's strengths over the years ahead was the coldly realistic appraisal he could make of his own ability, what he was doing, what he could be doing, and what he should be doing. The long balls would come from time to time, but in between there would be a great many line drives into the outfield.

As Rose's hitting picked up, others began to notice him. Late in May, Marty Marion, the old Cardinal shortstop, now a scout for the team, said that Rose "was the best-looking youngster I saw."[16]

The Cincinnati team, however, was not doing too well. Tabbed as a possible pennant-winner in preseason reckoning, the Reds were labeled by the *Sporting News* in early June as the biggest disappointment of the season in the National League thus far. The main reason for this was a lack of hitting. Freese had not done well and had been sent down to San Diego to work on getting his stroke back, and the club's two big hitters, Frank Robinson and Vada Pinson, were mired in batting slumps, though Pinson started to hit in mid-June. Without the slugging counted on from Robinson and Pinson, the Reds simply could not provide enough firepower for their pitchers.[17]

Pete Rose was still an outcast in the Reds' clubhouse. While the white players shunned him as a brash and cocky kid who had not paid his dues before taking a job from one of them, the black players, Robinson and Pinson, took him under their protection. The two black stars had originally shared their teammates' resentment at a rookie taking away Don Blasingame's job. Soon, though, they recognized that some of what Rose was going through as an unpopular rookie was akin to what they had suffered in their early baseball days because of the color of their skin.[18]

Robinson later wrote: "When I saw that Pete was being ostracized by most of my teammates—guys hardly talking to him, never inviting him out with them—I asked Pete one night if he would join Vada and me for dinner." Notably, until this time, Robinson had never invited a white player to go out with him after a game. "No other players warmed to Rose all season," Robinson said, "so Vada and I became his friends and showed him the ropes around the league." It was not long before Pete Rose was spending most of his off-field time with the two of them, or with fellow rookie Tommy Harper, another black man.[19]

For many of the white players on the Cincinnati club, Rose's clear preference for black men's company became one more reason why they disliked him. A guy should stick with his own kind, they believed, whites with whites, blacks with blacks, overlooking the fact that no one was having much to do with Pete Rose before Robinson and Pinson took him up.

With many of its players, managers, and coaches having grown up in the segregated South, baseball in the early-to-mid-1960s was not particularly enlightened in the area of racial relations. The Cincinnati Reds' management was certainly not integrationist; Phil Seghi called Harry Rose at his bank job and asked him to talk to his son, to warn him away from his black associates. Harry followed up on this, telling Pete, "Let the coloreds go; leave them alone." But Pete told him these were his friends, and that was the end of that.[20]

Club president Bill DeWitt told Rose to cut off the friendship with Robinson and Pinson, and pitcher Jim O'Toole tried his hand at it, too, telling Pete, "I don't know who taught you the facts of life, but there are certain things you do and certain things you don't do. . . . You know, like talkin' that nigger talk. Not if you want to have people accept you." Pete's response? "I kept hanging out with Frank and Vada."[21]

And while this little drama was being acted out in the Cincinnati clubhouse, Pete Rose kept banging out hits on the ballfield. On June 9, he hit his second home run, an inside-the-park job in Philadelphia that hit the 447-foot sign on the Connie Mack Stadium wall on the second bounce. At the All-Star break, the Reds were stuck in fifth place, six games out, and Hutchinson told the press, "The only player who has been hitting the ball hard is Pete Rose," who was at .271.[22] On July 1, the Reds sold Don Blasingame to Washington.

On July 26, Rose had a single, double, and home run in Milwaukee before coming up in the ninth inning. His long shot to left center was hauled down by Braves' outfielder Bob Taylor just shy of the fence. Pete was anxious to talk to the reporters afterward: "I was standing on second base when he made that catch. I'd had a triple for sure. You know what it would have meant if I had hit a triple—the cycle. Why, it takes a guy twenty years to do that!"[23]

Even without the cycle, Rose was attracting attention all around the National League. An August 17 front-page article in the *Sporting News* said there were only three possible candidates for the league's rookie-of-the-year award at that point, Rose and Harper of the Reds and pitcher Ray Culp of the Phillies. At about the same time, Rose was assuring the press that he would raise his average in the last weeks of the season. "I've always been a strong finisher," he said. "A lot of the older players will be a little tired during the last few weeks. I'll still be strong, and that'll give me a little advantage." One more quote to endear Rose to his teammates, as well as to other players around the league.[24]

Among other things, Rose was receiving acclaim for his fielding, something which was a surprise to many observers as well as to Pete himself. His double-play pivot was still no thing of beauty, but it was effective. His hitting, however, would always be Pete Rose's strong point. On August 25, in Candlestick Park, after warning Willie Mays, "Better play me deeper," he smashed a ball over the head of the Giants' center fielder. "Man, you just ain't that strong," Willie shouted, and then was astonished to learn that the Reds' rookie was three pounds heavier than he was.[25]

The Reds had just about packed it in by the end of August, conceding that they had no chance for the pennant, which was won by the Los Angeles Dodgers. Season-long batting slumps by Robinson, Freese, and Coleman and disappointing pitching by Bob Purkey, Joey Jay, and even O'Toole were cited as prominent reasons for the club's failure. And there was more. Beat writer Earl

Lawson said, "This year you don't see the one-for-all all-for-one spirit" which had marked the '61 Reds. " 'We're a team of strangers,' is the way one Red player put it. And that very well could be a capsule explanation for a lot of the Reds' difficulties this season." No one was impolite enough to say it, but the Rose-Blasingame imbroglio in spring training—and how the team reacted to it—may have started a lot of the trouble.[26]

Pete Rose went blithely on his way. On Labor Day Jim Maloney notched his twentieth win of the year, beating the Mets 1–0 at the Polo Grounds, when Rose hit a mammoth home run to the upper deck in right field on Jay Hook's first pitch of the game. "That was definitely my best shot," Rose crowed afterward.[27]

Shortly before the end of the season, the *Sporting News* named Pete Rose its National League Rookie Player of the Year (Culp was the Rookie Pitcher of the Year), and in early December the baseball writers handed Rose their Rookie-of-the-Year designation for the senior circuit by a nearly unanimous vote, with seventeen of the twenty ballots cast.[28]

Bill DeWitt, president of the Reds, said he was "mighty happy" over Rose's selection but not "too surprised." "Frankly," he went on, "I didn't see any other young players who measured up to him. . . . The fact that he's a local Cincinnati boy makes it all the better."[29]

For the year, Pete Rose hit .273, with 170 hits, 25 of them doubles, 9 triples and 6 home runs. He drove in 41 runs, scored 101, stole 13 bases, and was caught stealing 15 times. He had some problems in the field, particularly on balls hit to his right, and his double-play pivot still looked awkward. He made 22 errors. But Pete Rose looked like a polished performer when he stood at the plate. All in all, it was quite a season for a kid up from Class A ball.

Rose soon had to put baseball behind him, temporarily, anyway. In order to avoid the draft Pete had joined the Army Reserve and he was soon off to Fort Knox, Kentucky, to put in his required six-months active duty, which in Pete's case was shortened to five so he could report to spring training. Basic training was no problem for a young man hardened by a season of big-league baseball, although he later admitted he couldn't make his bed the way the army liked it. He had a buddy do it for him and then slept on top of the covers for the rest of his tour so as not to disturb the bedding.

Rose's life did take a dramatic turn on January 25, 1964, when he married Karolyn Ann Engelhardt in St. William's Catholic Church in Cincinnati. Rose had met Karolyn in July 1963, on an afternoon when he was taking in the ponies at River Downs. He spotted her through his binoculars, took a second look, liked what he saw, and walked down and introduced himself. Karolyn was a beauty with a lush figure and knew very well how to present herself. Brassy and earthy, she too had grown up in the streets of Cincinnati, around the Findley

Market downtown—"I was born in the slums," she often said, proudly—and she and Pete hit it off from the start, despite Karolyn asking him if he didn't play football for a local tavern team. They began dating and within a couple of months started planning to marry, the event pushed along by Karolyn's refusal of premarital sex.[30]

Pearl Engelhardt, Karolyn's mother, approved of the marriage, saying, "If there's such a thing as a match made in heaven, this is it. No one else could stand either one of them." Pete's father, though, was opposed to the marriage; he felt his son should become established as a big leaguer before permitting himself the distraction of a wife. He worried about the "sophomore jinx."[31]

Harry tried to sabotage the affair and had to be virtually blackmailed into attending the wedding, which he had threatened to boycott. Phil Seghi of the Reds called Harry and said the reporters and photographers covering the nuptials of Cincinnati's newest star would make a huge thing out of the absence of the player's father. So Harry and his wife reluctantly attended the ceremony, which took place during Pete's two-week leave after basic training.

"Here goes nothing," Pete Rose told his parents as he prepared to meet his bride at the altar. The ceremony went off without a hitch, but Pete left Karolyn at the wedding reception to attend that evening's annual "Parade of Stars" dinner, sponsored by the local baseball writers and the Cincinnati Chamber of Commerce. Rose, who was honored as the Reds' rookie of the year, told the assembled guests he was going for doubles in 1964; "after all," he said, "I'm no longer a single man." He then returned to the wedding reception, his bride, and their 1,200 guests. Karolyn had received her first taste of life in the fast lane with Pete Rose.[32]

NOTES

1. Fred Lieb, "Rose, Helms Cut Didees as Slick DP Duo," *Sporting News*, November 17, 1962, 28; Earl Lawson, " 'That Pete Rose—He's Got a Line-Drive Bat,' " April 20, 1968, 3.

2. *Cincinnati Post and Times-Star*, April 8, 1963; Sokolove, *Hustle: The Myth, Life, and Lies of Pete Rose*, 51.

3. *Sporting News*, December 1, 1962; January 12, 1963.

4. *Cincinnati Post and Times-Star*, February 26, 1963.

5. *Cincinnati Post and Times-Star*, March 11, 1963; Earl Lawson, "Brash Kid Rose Can Use Needle along with Bat," *Sporting News*, March 23, 1963, 34.

6. *Sporting News*, September 3, 1966, 19.

7. *Cincinnati Post and Times-Star*, March 11, 1963.

8. *Sporting News*, March 30, 1963; *Cincinnati Post and Times-Star*, April 2, 1963.

9. Sokolove, *Hustle: The Myth, Life, and Lies of Pete Rose*, 53.

10. Lawson, "Rookie Rose Silenced Cincy's Skeptics," 3.

11. Sokolove, *Hustle: The Myth, Life, and Lies of Pete Rose,* 113.

12. *Sporting News*, April 20, 1963.

13. *Cincinnati Enquirer*, April 13, 1984.

14. Lawson, "Rookie Rose Silenced Cincy's Skeptics," 3.

15. *Sporting News*, May 18, 1963. Rose almost got a third hit in the May 3 game, just missing beating out an infield grounder. After he was called out, Rose said to umpire Jocko Conlan, "I need those close ones. I'm hitting only .170." Conlan retorted, "You'd been out if you were hitting .470. You want gifts?" "No, just the truth," Rose said, and Jocko replied, "That's what you got."

16. *Sporting News*, June 1, 1963.

17. *Sporting News*, June 8, 1963.

18. Frank Robinson and Berry Stainback, *Extra Innings* (New York: McGraw-Hill, 1988), 55. Robinson said, "Being black and having gone through some hard times with aloneness myself, I felt for Pete."

19. Ibid. Robinson later told a Philadelphia writer, Mark Whicker, "Those were Don's friends. They didn't like him very much because they thought he was cocky. But Vada Pinson and I got along with him, maybe because no one else had much to do with him" (Philadelphia) *Evening Bulletin*, May 14, 1981.

20. Sokolove, *Hustle: The Myth, Life, and Lies of Pete Rose*, 58.

21. Ibid., 56–58; Rose and Kahn, *Pete Rose: My Story*, 109.

22. *Sporting News*, July 20, 1963.

23. *Sporting News*, August 3, 1963.

24. Earl Lawson, "Reds' Rose Rapid Climber in Dash for Rookie Honors," *Sporting News*, August 17, 1963, 6.

25. Lawson, "Rookie Rose Silenced Cincy's Skeptics," 3.

26. *Sporting News*, August 31, 1963. There had also been reports of Robinson and Pinson forming a "Negro clique" on the club (Robinson and Stainback, *Extra Innings*, 54). Club president DeWitt told a local luncheon group, "You'll need a scorecard to tell the names of players next year" (*Sporting News*, August 31, 1963).

27. *Sporting News*, September 14, 1963.

28. *Sporting News*, September 21, 1963; Hy Hurwitz, *Sporting News,* December 7, 1963. In the writers' voting, Ron Hunt of the Mets drew two votes and Culp of the Phillies one.

29. Hy Hurwitz, December 7, 1963.

30. (Philadelphia) *Evening Bulletin*, December 10, 1978.

31. Reston, *Collision at Home Plate: The Lives of Pete Rose and Bart Giamatti*, 116.

32. Sokolove, *Hustle: The Myth, Life, and Lies of Pete Rose*, 182; Earl Lawson, "Rose Wins Wisecrack Honors at Cincy Writers' Banquet," *Sporting News*, February 8, 1964; Sandy Grady, "Hustling Rose Runs on Walks," in (Philadelphia) *Evening Bulletin*, March 25, 1964. The cost of the reception exhausted the couple's funds; they sold their wedding gifts so Karolyn could afford to go to spring training (Reston, *Collision at Home Plate: The Lives of Pete Rose and Bart Giamatti*, 116).

Pete Rose as a young star of the Cincinnati Reds. *National Baseball Hall of Fame Library, Cooperstown, N.Y.*

ESTABLISHED STAR

Rose was released from active duty at Fort Knox on March 14. He immediately made his way to Tampa, leaving his new bride behind on her twenty-second birthday and arriving in southern Florida late that night. He was ready to work out with his Reds teammates the next day. Rose was in solid shape after his military tour, and it did not take him long to round into baseball condition. He checked into camp at 192 pounds, one pound less than he weighed at the close of the 1963 season. "They see that you're well fed, plenty of meat and potatoes," he said about the army cooks.[1]

Rose played in his first exhibition game on March 19, against the Cardinals, and picked up three hits, so no one in the Cincinnati organization worried about him. What they did have grave concern about was the health of manager Fred Hutchinson. Hutchinson had commenced a two-month radiation treatment for a cancer in his chest on January 9. Hutch finished the treatment, reported to camp early in March, and said, "My doctors have given me no reason not to be optimistic," but his cancer was a shadow hanging over the club.[2]

Hutchinson was concerned about his young second baseman associating primarily with the black players on the team, so he brought back Johnny Temple, let go by Houston after the 1963 season; the manager's plan was for the white veteran to room with and smooth the rough edges of Pete Rose. Hutchinson told Temple, who was hired as a player-coach but was no longer much of a player, "Pete Rose is your project." Temple described it to Michael Sokolove: "He said, 'The first thing I want you to do is teach him to use a knife and fork.' The second thing Hutch told me is, 'I want you to keep him away from the goddamn niggers.' " Temple worked with Rose on his fielding, told him to watch Pittsburgh's Bill Mazeroski play the hitters, encouraged him to bunt more, tried to polish up Pete's social graces, and failed utterly at changing the people with whom Pete hung around.[3]

Temple said, "I did try to counsel him in a fatherly way. Every time we ate, we would talk about things, and I let him know that he didn't have the respect of any of the white players. But Pete was a cornpone, tough kid, and very head-strong. His answer was, 'I'll do what I want to do. These people are my friends.' " Soon, Temple found that Rose was not listening at all. "I couldn't go to the places Pete went," Temple said. "They were too lowbrow." The Johnny Temple Experiment failed.[4]

Nevertheless, there were high hopes for the Reds heading into the new season. With power from Frank Robinson, Vada Pinson, Gordy Coleman, and new-comer Deron Johnson, and more offensive fire by Rose, Tommy Harper, John Edwards, Leo Cardenas, and third-base hopeful Chico Ruiz, the Reds knew they would score runs. The pitching staff, led by Jim O'Toole, Bob Purkey, Jim Maloney, Joey Jay, and Joe Nuxhall, looked ready to go as well. The defending champion Dodgers had fine pitching, but their hitting was suspect. The Cardinals and Giants were regarded as contenders, and perhaps the Phillies also, but Cincinnati looked as good as any of them.

The season opened, as always, in Cincinnati, on April 13, with the home players wearing their names on the backs of their uniforms for the first time. Recognizable or not, the Reds lost to the Houston Colt .45s, 6–3, and Pete Rose was 0 for 4. He was hitless in the second game of the season as well and was 0 for 12 before he got his first base hit in the third game.

Few of the Reds were hitting as the campaign got underway, and on the evening of April 23 they nearly wasted a great effort by the veteran Nuxhall. He and Houston's Ken Johnson, a right-hander who had pitched for Cincinnati's 1961 pennant-winner, hooked up in a classic pitcher's battle before a small crowd of 5,426 Houston fans.

The game was scoreless and the Reds were hitless with one out in the ninth when Rose pushed a bunt down the third base line. The Colt .45s were look-ing for a bunt, and Johnson was on it in a hurry, fifteen or so feet in front of the plate. "A halfway decent throw and I would have had him," Johnson moaned, later, but his throw to first was low—"a perfect sinker to [first base-man Pete] Runnels"—and Rose wound up at second base. Rose thought he had a base hit, but the official scorer called it an error. Ruiz hit a low line drive which caromed off Johnson's shin to third baseman Bob Aspromonte, who threw the batter out as Rose took third. Vada Pinson then hit a ball to second base that the Colts' Nellie Fox bobbled, and Rose scored. The Reds won, 1–0, in an hour and fifty-six minutes, and Ken Johnson lost despite pitching a no-hitter.[5]

In his first eleven games, Pete Rose hit only 8 for 46, for an ugly-looking .174 average, and Hutchinson said he was considering putting rookie Bobby Klaus at second base. Then he thought better of it and said he would let Pete work his way out of the slump. When Rose still failed to hit, however, he was replaced by Klaus in the second game of a May 3 double-header. At that point, 12 for 66, Rose was batting .181.

Two days later, though, the Reds beat the Pirates, 5–4, with three runs in the ninth inning, winning the game on Pete Rose's bases-loaded, two-out single up the middle. Pete's hitting picked up a little, and he got over the .200 level on May 11 with a three-run homer at Pittsburgh's Forbes Field, his first major-league home run from the right side. By May 18, Rose's average was up to .215, but there it stayed.

On June 7, Hutchinson took a leave of absence for further treatment, and one of the first things interim manager Dick Sisler did was bench Rose. Bobby Klaus, given a chance, hit a couple of home runs but was otherwise not up to National League pitching. Pete Rose, about to go back into the line-up, made a visit to Dayton to his uncle Buddy Bloebaum. Uncle Buddy told him he was swinging defensively. "Lower your hands, Pete," he said, "and attack the ball."[6]

On June 27, at Pittsburgh, Rose was 4 for 4 against the Buccos' Steve Blass, and then he went 5 for 9 in the next day's twinbill. "I think my Uncle Buddy straightened me out," Pete said. Earl Lawson wrote that Rose, "after a spell on the bench, came back to give the club a shot in the arm by going on a hitting binge during which he rapped out 19 hits in 45 at-bats over an 11-game span." The Reds won seven of nine preceding the All-Star break, one on Rose's tenth-inning home run against Chicago's Dick Ellsworth on July 1. On July 18, Rose had six RBIs as he went 4 for 4 against Philadelphia, including the only grand slam he ever hit, a line shot into Crosley's right field bleachers off Dallas Green.[7]

Still, even with Rose hiking his average up to .270, the team muddled along in third or fourth place, behind the Giants, Cardinals, and Phillies. Toward the end of July, Cincinnati brought up infielder Tony Perez, Rose's old Geneva team-mate, from San Diego, along with Chico Ruiz, who had earlier been sent down, and Bobby Klaus was sold to the Mets. Freddy Hutchinson was hospitalized again on July 22, and on August 13 he was given a leave of absence for the rest of the season, with Sisler taking over once again.

Rose was benched again on August 15, after a stretch of hitting 2 for 28. As August came to an end, his average had dropped to .259. Catcher John Edwards was hurt in August, Don Pavletich took over his duties, and Rose became the emergency backup catcher. Sisler had him catch batting practice on August 22.

"I caught a couple of games when I was with the Geneva club," Pete volunteered. The club then purchased veteran catcher Jim Coker from Denver, and the chance of Rose winding up behind the plate evaporated.[8]

As August passed into September, it looked as if the Reds would be playing out the string. Hutchinson was mostly out of the picture, there were fisticuffs in the clubhouse on August 28 between two Reds' coaches, Temple and Reggie Otero, which ended in Temple's departure, and the race looked to be over. Gene Mauch's Phillies took a commanding lead and appeared to have the pennant nearly wrapped up. On September 20, when the Reds beat St. Louis 9–6 to tie the Cardinals for second place, the Phillies had a lead of six and one-half games with but twelve to play.

What transpired next seared an unhealing sore into Philadelphia's baseball consciousness, and it left a considerable scar on Cincinnati's as well. It all started on September 20 in Philadelphia, when Chico Ruiz broke from third base for home on his own, with Frank Robinson at bat and two out in the sixth inning of a scoreless game. No one expects a base runner to try to steal home with his team's best hitter at bat. A startled Art Mahaffey, seeing Ruiz running, threw the ball in the dirt, Ruiz scored, and the Reds won, 1–0. The next night Jim O'Toole won, 9–2, with Rose going 2 for 4. The third game of the series with the Phillies went to the Reds, 6–4, behind superb relief pitching by Sammy Ellis. Rose was 2 for 5, including an RBI single in the seventh to tie the score. The Reds left Philadelphia for New York only three and one-half games back, although the Cardinals were keeping pace with them.

Rose told a reporter, "I think we'll catch 'em. The pressure is on them now, not us. Those three straight games we took from them has got to start them thinking."[9] Sisler's team swept five games from the hapless Mets, while the snakebitten Phillies were losing four to the Milwaukee Braves, and suddenly the Reds were in first place. Pete Rose was 9 for 22 in the Shea Stadium series. The Phillies moved on to St. Louis, where they continued losing, but the Reds now began to treat the league lead like a very hot potato.

On September 29, Billy McCool of the Reds lost at home to Bob Friend of the Pirates, 2–0, when Mazeroski singled in the only runs of the game with two out in the ninth. Rose had 3 of the Reds' 11 hits in a losing effort. This loss ended a nine-game winning streak and dropped Cincinnati into a first-place tie with the Cardinals. On September 30, before a sparse crowd of 8,188 in Crosley Field, the Pirates won 1–0 in sixteen innings. Bob Veale dueled Maloney for the first eleven frames. Pete Rose was 0 for 7 as the frustrated Reds left 18 men on base. St. Louis now had a game lead, narrowed to a half-game when the Reds salvaged one win over Pittsburgh on October 1.

Mauch's Phillies came into Cincinnati for the final two games of the season.

On Friday night October 2, the Phillies won, 4–3, when Cardenas misplayed a pop-up behind shortstop and opened the door for the visitors. It was the end, finally, of Philadelphia's ten-game losing streak; Rose was 0 for 3. When the Cards lost to the Mets on Friday night and again on Saturday, while the Phillies and Reds had an off-day, the stage was set for dramatics on the last day of the season.

Sunday October 4 dawned with the Reds and St. Louis tied for first place, and the Phillies one game back. The Cards had another game with the Mets, while the Reds and Phils squared off against each other in Cincinnati.

The game at Crosley Field quickly lost its competitive glow. The Phillies, with rookie star Richie Allen contributing a double and two homers, battered Red starter John Tsitouris, while his teammates could do little against the Phils' ace, Jim Bunning, who held the Reds to six hits, one of them by Rose. The result was a 10–0 Philadelphia victory, which meant both teams had to root for a Mets triumph, which would produce a three-way tie for the championship. Casey Stengel's Mets gave it a shot, taking a 3–2 lead into the fifth inning, but the Cardinals' superior firepower took over and St. Louis won the 1964 pennant with its 11–5 victory.

For Pete Rose and the Reds it was a dreadful way to end the season—four losses in the last five games, shut out in three of them—after they had had the pennant in their hands when they left New York. It was a disappointing season for Rose on a personal level as well; his average for the year slipped to .269, and his numbers were down from his rookie year in every category. It wasn't a bad year—no "sophomore jinx"—but it wasn't what he had anticipated. Certainly, a "sophomore slump."

During the off-season, Pete went to Venezuela, where he played a little third base on a team managed by Reds' coach Reggie Otero. The club wanted to see if Rose might be the answer to a problem there. The Venezuelan fans fell in love with Rose's hustling style of play—running out walks, head-first slides, and a bat that kept producing line-drive hits.

While Rose was in Venezuela, he got word that Fred Hutchinson had died in Florida on November 12. Rose cried at learning of the death of the brave, tough man who had believed in him so completely, who had given him a shot that very few others would have. Pete was established now, but who knew where he might have been without Freddy Hutchinson's willingness to roll the dice with him in spring training 1963. "Hutch had faith in me. He gave me my chance," Rose said, later. "I just wish he coulda lived to see me hit .300."[10]

In 1965, Pete Rose answered any remaining questions there might have been about his ability. With work and lots of practice, his fielding at second became big league quality. He batted .312, fourth in the league, led the majors with 209 hits, was third in the league in both runs scored and doubles. Rose finished sixth in the voting by the writers for the National League's Most Valuable Player. He received the nod as the league's Player of the Month in July, and he played second base for the Nationals in the All-Star game. It was a super season for the kid from Anderson Ferry, and the local fans loved him.

"This year," he told a reporter, "I feel like I really belong in the majors. I've confidence both at the plate and in the field. That 'rookie feeling' is gone." By the end of the year, Gene Mauch, the intense Phillies manager, said, "Rose is being recognized now for the things he does, not the way he does it."[11]

And Pete Rose was settling into the good life of a big league ballplayer, including the availability of "baseball Annies" on the club's road trips. He was still no favorite of the white players, and he upset them on occasion by taking his wife to nightspots where some of his married teammates took their girlfriends. But Karolyn tried to tell the boys that they should not be concerned about her being there. She told Jim O'Toole she knew Pete had sex regularly when the team was on the road, but "as long as he doesn't do it at home, I don't care." Karolyn was unusual in other respects; none of the white wives of Cincinnati players were friendly to the wives of the black players until Rose made the team and married. Karolyn, Frank Robinson said, "was friendly with everyone."[12]

Pete Rose became a Cincinnati favorite, but the fans were not as happy with the team's performance overall. Dick Sisler, the "interim" removed from in front of his name, led the Reds to a winning 89–73 mark, but it was good only for fourth place, behind the Dodgers, Giants, and Pirates. The Dodgers' pitching, led by Sandy Koufax, Don Drysdale, and Claude Osteen, was just too much to overcome. The Los Angeles staff earned run average, at 2.81, was more than a full run better than Cincinnati's. After the season, Sisler was let go and replaced by Don Heffner.

In the off-season, Rose got a job selling cars at Glenway Chevrolet and was turned down by Bill DeWitt when he wanted to play in a local touch football league. The car job backfired on him slightly when he drove the convertible bearing the University of Cincinnati's homecoming queen to the Bearcats' football stadium. When the queen was introduced to Pete, she inquired sweetly, "Do you do anything else besides sell cars?"[13]

New manager Heffner won Rose's ill will by trying to make a third baseman of him. "Suddenly, in spring training," Rose said, "the manager *told* me, he didn't *ask* me, that he was moving me to third." After all the work he had put in to become a competent second baseman, Rose was outraged to be moved to another position. With a new $25,000 contract, he was now too big a star to be moved around like that, even if the manager thought it would help the team. Pete Rose decided, "I didn't think the switch would help the team." So he sulked. He didn't work at becoming a third baseman, thereby assuring that the experiment would fail. Before April had ended, he was back at second, after sixteen games, and his old buddy Tommy Helms was playing third. By mid-season Heffner was gone, fired on July 13, and Pete Rose's old manager from Macon, Dave Bristol, was running the Reds.[14]

Rose personally had another fine season in 1966. He hit .313, with 205 hits and a career-high 16 home runs (which he matched in 1969). He was second in the league in hits and doubles, and he finished tenth in MVP voting. He won another Player of the Month award in August and finished up strongly in September.

Rose was a particularly tough out for Gene Mauch and his Phillies, so Mauch decided to try to get inside Pete's head. One day Rose came to the plate in Connie Mack Stadium, and the Phils' catcher, Mike Ryan, said, "Gene told me to tell you what pitch is coming." For the next three times up, Ryan told him what the next pitch would be, Rose disbelieved him, and Rose made an out. He began grumbling to the umpire to make Ryan shut up, because "I don't want to know what's coming." Finally, in the ninth inning, with the game tied and a runner in scoring position, Rose came up and Ryan muttered, "Curve." At this point, Pete finally decided that the Phillies were really telling him what the pitch would be, they'd been getting away with it, and they wouldn't change now. He set himself for a curve ball and lined it off the scoreboard to drive home the winning run. When Rose came up to lead off the next day, Mike Ryan said, "Gene told me to tell you to go to hell."[15]

Helms, his roommate, said, "I've never seen a guy with his energy." Rose, he said, "bounces out of bed in the morning . . . goes into a hitting stance and takes one swing lefthanded with an imaginary bat and then another righthanded. I'm lying there, rubbing my eyes and wishing I could sleep a couple of more hours."[16]

But the Reds team fared poorly, even with Rose's heroics. With a losing record, it finished a dismal seventh in the ten-team league. The pitching was off, and without Frank Robinson (traded to Baltimore for righthander Milt Pappas; Robinson proceeded to win the American League triple crown and Most Valuable Player award in 1966), the hitting was not enough to make up the difference. The team played marginally better under Bristol but not enough to move up very far.

Pete Rose figured he was due for another substantial pay raise after his successful 1966 season. "They're always saying a guy can't make big money playing for the Reds," Rose said. "Well, I'm going to show everybody you can. All you have to do is play every day and do the job." As good as his word, Rose wheedled a $46,000 salary out of the usually tight-fisted Cincinnati management.[17]

Despite the disappointment of 1966, the 1967 season was more of the same. With Bristol as manager, the Reds were once again a winning team, with a mark of 87–75, but they were still fourth, fourteen and one-half games behind the pennant-winning Cardinals. After a great start, Bristol's men were in first place at the end of May. But they fell flat in June and never did regain their pace.

The Reds now relied on Pete Rose's hitting as a constant, and they were entitled to do so. About his fielding, there were still questions. Writer Allen Lewis called him "a winning player, although some downgrade his ability to make the double play" and said "there is an outside chance that Rose might move to the outfield." In fact, Rose was switched to left field in 1967, moving Deron Johnson, a bad outfielder, to third base, with Helms taking over second. This time Pete acquiesced in the position change, presumably because Bristol proposed it to him in the proper manner. Gene Mauch called the switch a "stroke of genius," predicting that Rose would make more spectacular outfield plays than anyone "because of his enthusiasm." Regardless of where he was playing, Rose hit. In 1967 he batted .301, leading the team, and again finished tenth in the most valuable voting.[18]

Rose reversed his usual method and started the season hitting well, putting together a twenty-five-game hitting streak, and thinking about a possible batting title. He was happy in the field, too. Then, on June 16, shortstop Leo Cardenas broke his hand when he was hit by a pitch, and Rose moved again. Helms switched to shortstop and Rose came back in to play second base. By July 7, Pete had his average up to .331. When Cardenas came back, Helms had a two-week Marine Corps reserve stint to serve, so Rose stayed at second. He could hardly wait for Helms to return, though. "I love the outfield now," Rose said. "I don't feel right at second base any more."[19]

Despite his new position, or perhaps because of the switching around, Rose's hitting tailed off in the latter part of the year. His .301 average represented a disappointment to him, as did his failure to reach 200 hits. He collected only 176 safeties in 1967, although he blamed that failure on injuries. Sidelined early when hit on the right elbow by a Turk Farrell pitch, Pete missed more than two weeks in mid-June after hurting his shoulder making a diving catch.

Aside from Tony Perez, who hit 26 home runs and drove in 102 runs while playing third, there was not much pop in the Reds' line-up. Pinson hit only 18 home runs, while Johnson hit 13 and Rose and May hit 12 each. After the good start, finishing a distant fourth did not make for a very satisfying season in the Queen City.

NOTES

1. Earl Lawson, " 'Watch Reds in '64' Rose Replies to Ribs by GI Pals," *Sporting News*, January 11, 1964, 9.

2. *Sporting News*, January 18, 1964.

3. Sokolove, *Hustle: The Myth, Life, and Lies of Pete Rose*, 60; Sandy Grady, "Hustling Rose Runs on Walks," (Philadelphia) *Evening Bulletin*, March 25, 1964.

4. Sokolove, *Hustle: The Myth, Life, and Lies of Pete Rose*, 61.

5. Dick Peebles, "This Was One Hit Pete Rose Didn't Get," *Baseball Digest*, September 1978, 35. Peebles, a Houston writer, was the official scorer that day.

6. Rose and Kahn, *Pete Rose: My Story*, 116.

7. *Sporting News*, July 18, Earl Lawson, "Pete Rose Real Thorn in Side of Redleg Foes," August 1,1964, 15.

8. *Sporting News*, August 23, 1964.

9. United Press International, (Philadelphia) *Evening Bulletin*, September 25, 1964.

10. Rose and Kahn, *Pete Rose: My Story*, 118.

11. Earl Lawson, "Reds' Rose Blooms into Spring Dandy after Winter Drills," *Sporting News*, June 5, 6, 1965, and Earl Lawson, "Reds' Rose Gets Bouquets—With Big Pay Hike in Store," *Sporting News*, September 4, 1965, 6.

12. Sokolove, *Hustle: The Myth, Life, and Lies of Pete Rose*, 53; Robinson and Stainback, *Extra Innings*, 53.

13. *Sporting News*, November 27, 1965.

14. Rose and Kahn, *Pete Rose: My Story*, 119–20. Emphasis added. During the winter, when asked by a writer about a move to third base, Rose had responded, "It's okay with me if it happens" (Earl Lawson, "Flash Bulbs Pop on Cincy Celebrities Rose, Cardenas," *Sporting News*, January 29, 1966, 17). Presumably Heffner read this quote and must have been puzzled by Rose's subsequent reaction.

15. Reston, *Collision at Home Plate: The Lives of Pete Rose and Bart Giamatti*, 60.

16. Earl Lawson, "Speaking of Hustle, Start with Red Rose," *Sporting News*, September 3, 1966, 19.

17. "Rose Licks Chops, Time to Start Talking Turkey," *Sporting News*, December 3, 1966, 53.

18. Allen Lewis, "How the Big League Teams Shape Up for 1967," *Baseball Digest*, April 1967, 40; Earl Lawson, "Transplanted Rose Gains Fresh Bloom in Cincy's Garden," *Sporting News*, June 10, 1967, 9. Leo Durocher, managing the Cubs, said Rose played the outfield "as if he were born out there."

19. Earl Lawson, "Reds' Rose Quick-Pedals along Road to 200 Singles," *Sporting News*, August 19, 1967, 13.

BATTING CHAMP

In November 1967, Rose visited U.S. troops in Vietnam. A group made up of Rose, former Yankees great Joe DiMaggio, Yankees infielder-turned-broadcaster Jerry Coleman, Red Sox slugger Tony Conigliaro, and Yankees publicity man Bob Fishel, sponsored by the government, toured via helicopter, stopping at outposts where U.S. Army "advisors" were working with South Vietnamese troops.

Rose was always good at dealing with his public. He was already famous for signing all requested autographs at the ballpark, and he usually carried a stack of signed photos to give to the curious who waited outside the players' gate at Crosley Field after a game. He had no difficulty in relating to the mostly 19- or 20-year-old young men he found in his tour of Vietnam. Still, he was happy to get back home, looking forward to another baseball season.

Pete Rose soon got a lesson in baseball economics. Shortly after the beginning of the year, the Reds mailed out contract offers to their players, and when Rose read his he gaped in disbelief. He was dismayed to be offered the same $46,000 he had signed for in 1967. He contacted Phil Seghi, who was handling contract matters for Bob Howsam, the new general manager of the Reds, and reminded Seghi of his .300 batting average and 200 hits. When Seghi responded, "You're supposed to do that making your salary," Rose said, "I got 209 hits my third season in the majors. Was I supposed to do *that* making $12,500?" He said he wanted $70,000, and he sent the contract back unsigned.[1]

He was worth it, Rose reasoned. "I'm one of the two most exciting white guys in baseball," he proclaimed, "me and Carl Yastrzemski."[2]

In the meantime, Rose played basketball to stay in shape over the winter. He played in four different basketball leagues in order to burn off his excess energy as well as any calories he might have picked up along the way. Howsam and Seghi shuddered at the possibility of their young star sustaining a crippling injury on the hardwood, but Rose himself dismissed the thought. "I'm careful," he said.[3]

On March 5, Rose agreed in a telephone conversation with Seghi to a 1968 contract for $55,000, a raise of $9,000 over the year before. During the 1967 season, Rose told some baseball writers, "I'm going to be the first ball player who doesn't hit homers to make $100,000." He was now more than halfway there. With his excellence thus recognized, Pete headed off to Tampa for another spring training.[4]

Rose played mostly right field in 1968, the third different position he had played regularly in his six years with the Reds. His primary role on the team, though, was as a hitter. The club as a whole hit well, with rookie catcher Johnny Bench, Perez, Lee May, and Alex Johnson all putting up good numbers. Still, with mediocre pitching and a bunch of injuries, Bristol's Reds finished a distant fourth, fourteen games behind the Cardinals.

The 1968 season was dubbed the "Year of the Pitcher" because of the increasing dominance of pitching over hitting. This dominance was reflected in such statistics as 339 shutouts, 185 of them in the National League (there were 274 in 1967 and 246 in 1966), 82 1–0 games, a major league batting average of .237 (the lowest ever), 300 fewer home runs than in 1967 and 700 fewer than in 1966, and a record low 1.12 earned run average for St. Louis pitcher Bob Gibson, breaking the mark set by Grover Cleveland Alexander in 1915. Cincinnati's pitchers, however, bedeviled by arm miseries, put together a league-worst ERA of 3.56.

On July 5, amid the numerous physical problems with which the Reds were afflicted, they lost Rose with a broken thumb, suffered at Dodger Stadium in Los Angeles. On a ball hit by the Dodgers' Paul Popovich, Rose landed on his left thumb, the ball fell for a double, and Pete wound up on the disabled list. Dr. Robert Kerlan, the Dodgers' team doctor, after looking at the X-rays, said, "An injury like this usually keeps a player out of the line-up about four weeks. But knowing Rose, I'd say he'll be out only three weeks." Three weeks to the day Pete was back on the field for the Reds, ready to go.[5]

He missed the All-Star Game in Houston, for which he had been the National League's top vote-getter, an honor he achieved for the first time. Rose chafed at the inactivity and went on a hitting tear when he returned. His teammates were relieved when Rose came back. "When he isn't playing," Tommy Helms said, "he has too much time to agitate. He was driving everyone crazy."

The Reds were never in contention in 1968, but that was not the fault of Pete Rose. The converted infielder even led all National League outfielders in assists.[6]

In the midst of all that—the team's mediocrity and his own damaged thumb—Pete Rose went out and won himself a batting title, the first for Cincinnati since Ernie Lombardi's in 1938. Rose hit .335 for the season, beating Matty Alou of the Pirates by three points. Pete also had 210 hits for the year, tying him for the league lead in that department with Matty's brother Felipe of the Atlanta Braves. Twice during the season, on June 18 against the Braves and on September 28 against San Francisco, Rose went 5 for 5. In seven other games, he had 4 hits.

In mid-August, Rose was greeted at Wrigley Field in Chicago with a barrage of garbage and seat cushions as he stood in the outfield. Leo Durocher's Cubs were challenging the Cardinals for first place, and their rabid fans were particularly keyed up. They should have known better than to stir up Pete Rose. With 11 hits in 20 times up, Rose led his club to a four-game sweep which effectively terminated the Cubs' pennant hopes.

The last two weeks of the season were dramatic for Rose, as he and Matty Alou waged their fight for the league batting crown. He fought a slump on the club's final western trip and watched anxiously as Alou crept ever closer. Even worse, he was alone in his hotel rooms, because roomie Helms had broken his wrist and gone home.

"Tommy's good for Pete," Bristol said. "When you're in a slump as Pete was, you need a guy like Tommy around. Rooming alone and staring at four walls can drive you batty." Rose was also pestered by advertising account executives, proposing various endorsement offers, all contingent on his winning the batting title.[7]

When the club returned home for its final three games, Rose's twelve-point lead in the batting race was gone, and he and Alou were tied at .331. Helms showed up from his home in North Carolina, "so I could get Pete back on the ball." He watched Rose go 1 for 7 in a fifteen-inning loss to the Giants on Friday, September 27 (while Alou was 0 for 4 against the Cubs), then told Pete "he swung the bat like a girl." Helms's needling and twenty-five minutes extra batting practice on Saturday morning were apparently what Rose needed: he put together a 5-hit game that day, against Gaylord Perry and his spitter. Pete figured that the crown was his, only to be told by Giant second baseman Hal Lanier after the fifth hit that Alou had gone 4 for 4 at Wrigley Field. "Those Alous, they're hard to shake," Rose said.[8]

The fight came down to the last games of the season: Rose and the Reds against the Giants, Alou and his Pirates versus the Cubs, Pete with a two-point lead after Saturday. Before a roaring crowd of 27,464 in Crosley Field, Rose led off the first inning with a double against the Giants' Ray Sadecki, and that was what he needed to clinch the title. Alou went 0 for 4 at Chicago, and Rose was the winner. Dave Bristol said, "I've never seen anyone who coveted that batting title more than Pete."[9]

Not surprisingly, the Cardinals' Gibson won the honors as the Most Valuable Player in the National League. Second in the voting, and far ahead of third-place finisher Willie McCovey, was Pete Rose. It was a fitting ending to an excellent season for Rose, who led all major leaguers in hitting. Over the winter, though, when asked about his salary expectations for 1969, Rose was surprisingly cautious. On the Reds' annual good-will caravan, someone brought up his quest for a $100,000 contract. Not this year, Pete said. "I'll be close to it, but our 1968 attendance [733,354] does not justify a $100,000 contract at this time."[10]

He did expect a raise, however, and he had to hold out briefly before signing a 1969 contract for $85,000, the highest figure ever paid to a Cincinnati ballplayer. But Pete Rose would give the Reds their money's worth.

One of the highlights of Rose's season came in spring training, when the Washington Senators came to Tampa for an exhibition game. The biggest attraction the Senators had was their new manager, the legendary Ted Williams. After the game, Williams was giving hitting instruction to Eddie Brinkman, Rose's old Western Hills teammate, and while he was at it he gave autographs and a few words to several Cincinnati players.

"Do you know what he told me?" Rose asked. "He told me I could be the next .400 hitter, that it was possible because I switch-hit, make good contact and can run." Pete Rose was no starry-eyed rookie; he was 28, a six-year veteran, and defending batting champion. Still, a few words from the old Boston star were enough to set off his imagination once more.[11]

Unfortunately for manager Dave Bristol, the Reds, and the Crosley Field faithful, the 1969 season was very much like the 1968 season. The team hit well, but a crippled and often ineffective pitching staff doomed it to also-ran status once more, with a third place finish in the newly-created western division of the National League, four games out, behind Atlanta and San Francisco.

The season started auspiciously for the Reds when Rose led off the traditional home opener with a home run off Dodger star Don Drysdale, but the Reds still lost. Bristol's team went 9–11 for April, despite a Maloney no-hitter against Houston on April 30. Maloney did not win again until July 15.

The Reds had their moments, as in a June 27 game with San Francisco, when they beat Juan Marichal for the first time in four years on a two-run homer by

Rose. On July 19, they staged an incredible comeback, rallying from a 9–0 deficit to beat the Astros 10–9 in eleven innings. And there was the slugfest of August 3, when the Reds piled up 25 hits to beat Philadelphia, 19–17. Alex Johnson, Lee May, Perez, Bobby Tolan, and Bench supplied a great deal of offense to Bristol's team.

Through it all, day in and day out, no one hit any better than Pete Rose, who won a second consecutive batting championship with a sterling .348 average. He started a bit slowly, batting .287 at the end of May, when he took off for his two-week stint with the Army reserve, but he was up to .329 by the All-Star break.

Hitting at .326 on August 2, Rose batted .379 the rest of the way, with 96 hits in his last 253 times up. He piled up 218 hits for the year, although this was second in the league to Matty Alou's 231. On September 24, Rose moved into a tie with the New York Mets' Cleon Jones for the batting lead, after Jones had led for most of the season. The next night, against Houston's Denny Lemaster, Rose put together a 4-for-5 game to take a four-point lead.

Once he had the lead, Rose just kept hitting. Jones slipped to third, and the main challenge came from the Pirates' Roberto Clemente. Going into the last game of the season, at Atlanta, Rose held a six-point lead over the Pittsburgh outfielder, and someone suggested that Pete sit out the finale. "Hell, no," he replied, as he prepared to hold off Clemente's try for his fifth batting crown.

The Braves started a 19-year-old rookie lefthander named Mike McQueen, whom Rose had never seen, and Pete grounded to short to start the game. He walked in the third, lined out to left in the fifth, and hit into a fielder's choice in the seventh. As Rose came to bat in the eighth, there were runners on first and second, two outs, and the Reds were ahead, 5–3. A fan sitting in the front row called out to Rose that Clemente was 3 for 3 in Pittsburgh.

"I've never been more nervous in my life than I was when I went to the plate in the eighth inning," Rose said later, as he described the perfect bunt he laid down to the left of the mound for a single that won him his batting championship. "It's the first time I've ever bunted with two out and a runner in scoring position," he said, "but this time I was willing to let someone else drive home the runs." Rose's 1 for 4, combined with Clemente's 3 for 4, gave Rose the title by three points.[12]

It was another top-grade year for Pete Rose. He scored 120 runs, tied for the league lead with the Giants' Bobby Bonds, and drove in 81; his hit total included 33 doubles, 11 triples, and 16 home runs, matching his career high. He finished fourth in the MVP voting, which was won by Willie McCovey, and he won a surprising Gold Glove for his outfield play.

Pete put it all in perspective after the last game: "When you're making $85,000, you're expected to have a good year. That's another reason why I wanted that batting title. I figured I had to win it to get another good raise."[13]

NOTES

1. *Sporting News*, January 27, 1968. Emphasis added.

2. Erardi, *Pete Rose*, 25.

3. Earl Lawson, "Rose Dazzles as Playmaker in Four Cincy Cage Loops," *Sporting News*, February 24, 1968.

4. Lawson, "'That Pete Rose—He's Got a Line-Drive Bat,'" 4.

5. Earl Lawson, "Reds Heave Sigh as Pete Returns," *Sporting News*, August 10, 1968, 7.

6. Ibid. The All Star Game in the Astrodome, which fittingly occurred in the "Year of the Pitcher," was won by the National League, 1–0, the unearned run scoring on a double-play grounder.

7. Earl Lawson, "Swat King Rose Handled Pressure Like a Champion," *Sporting News*, October 12, 1968, 19.

8. Ibid.; Rose and Kahn, *Pete Rose: My Story*, 126–127.

9. Lawson, "Swat King Rose Handled Pressure Like a Champion," 19. It is interesting to contrast Rose's .335 average with the figure of the American League leader, Boston's Carl Yastrzemski, whose .301 average made him the only .300 hitter in that league.

10. A. L. Hardman, "Gate Down, So Pete Won't Ask for $100,000," *Sporting News*, February 15, 1969.

11. Earl Lawson, "'You Can Be Next .400 Hitter,' Williams Tells Starry-Eyed Rose," *Sporting News*, April 5, 1969, 13.

12. Earl Lawson, "Safe Bunt Carries Rose on Last Step to Batting Crown," *Sporting News*, October 18, 1969, 31.

13. Ibid.

A Spark for Cincinnati

A predictable result of the Reds' disappointing performances of 1968 and 1969 was the dismissal of Dave Bristol as manager. He was replaced by a virtual unknown named George Lee Anderson, who bore the nickname "Sparky." Anderson, a short and slight second baseman as a player, had put in one season in the majors, with a dismal Phillies team in 1959, for whom he hit an equally dismal .218. He then spent five years managing in the minors, as well as selling used cars in the off-season, before being named third base coach for the San Diego Padres in 1969. It was here that Bob Howsam spotted him and selected him to run the Reds.

Sparky Anderson, 35 years old when he got the Reds' job but already silver-haired with leathery brown skin, had grown up in the Dodgers' organization before being traded to Philadelphia in December 1958, and he was well-schooled in the fundamentals. He named former Pirates manager Larry Shepard as his pitching coach, Alex Grammas as third base coach, and Cincinnati legend Ted Kluszewski as first base coach. Bringing "Big Klu" back to the Reds was sure to be popular with the club's fans, as was another of Anderson's moves.

He appointed Pete Rose the first team captain in the Reds' long history. "Pete deserves the right to be recognized in the same manner as a Willie Mays, a Henry Aaron, a Ron Santo or a Maury Wills," Anderson said. "We're not giving him anything he hasn't already earned." Rose responded, "It's just a great honor and I'm also flattered a new manager has enough faith to appoint me to such a position."[1]

Not everyone on the team was pleased that Rose was named captain. Johnny

Rose crashes into catcher Ray Fosse during the 1970 All Star Game at Riverfront Stadium in Cincinnati. © *Bettmann/CORBIS.*

Bench wrote that, even though Rose had "been with the team for eight years, and was a bona fide performer . . . still, his being captain bothered me." Bench felt that he was supposed to be "the team's general, the leader," directing things from his post behind the plate, with the whole field spread out in his view. When he wrote his book, eight years later, Bench admitted, "even now it affects me."[2]

Pete Rose had come a long way from being the scorned outcast of the Reds' clubhouse to captain of the team. He had by now put in seven seasons in the National League and played 1,064 big league games, which would have come as a shock to Phil Seghi back in 1960, when he signed Pete as a favor to Buddy Bloebaum. Rose had 1,327 hits, a .309 career average, and two National League batting titles. He even had 75 home runs and 433 runs batted in, not bad for a singles hitter leading off most of the time. His crouched-over batting stance, from either side of the plate, the big number 14 on his back, was familiar to National League fans from Jarry Park in Montreal to San Diego Stadium.

Pete was an established star, making big money, and living in a big league way. He and Karolyn had a four-year-old daughter, Fawn, born in 1965. He had just bought a big new house in an upscale part of Cincinnati, he was able to indulge his love for shiny, expensive cars, and he was the toast of his town. In fact, Pete Rose was beloved, admired, or respected by baseball fans all over the country as the exemplar of every guy with a bit of talent who stretched that talent into stardom through constant, unremitting effort. He was the guy who gave 110 percent of himself all the time. He was cocky, brash, out in the open for all to see. There was no pretense about Pete Rose; he said what was on his mind, and he was available to sportswriter and baseball fan alike.

If there was perhaps one exception to the universal admiration for Rose, it was with the "bleacher bums" of Wrigley Field. These loud and often crude spectators had had it in for Rose since July 1, 1967, when he accidentally spiked beloved first baseman Ernie Banks in trying to beat out a bunt. Banks' foot was on the middle of the bag, and Rose came down hard on Ernie's ankle, resulting in a gash requiring ten stitches. The long-suffering Cubs fans, seeing their idol writhing on the ground in pain, gave vent to their anger with boos, beer cans, bottles, and other assorted debris, all directed at Rose when he took up his station in the outfield. After the game several fans tried to get at Rose physically but were prevented from doing so. Thereafter, Rose was always greeted with boos, catcalls, garbage, and various chants, printable and unprintable, in Wrigley. "Rose is a fairy! Rose is a fairy!" was a favorite. Pete didn't mind bantering back and forth with these fans, and he usually answered the abuse with base hits.[3]

Rose was proud of being a major leaguer, and he made sure that he looked the part. When he appeared on the field, his uniform was always crisp and neat, although he would soon have it soiled from diving for a ball or sliding into a base. When, later in his career, he played for the Phillies, who wore pinstripes on their home uniform, Rose always made sure that the pinstripes on his shirt aligned with those on the pants below his belt. He took care to see that his baseball shoes were given the utmost shine that polish, a buffing rag, and a little saliva could give them.

Rose was well aware that the source of all the fine things he had come to enjoy in life was his baseball bat and the hits it accumulated for him. He was especially careful to lavish attention on his bats. "Every night after the game," he said, "I take a clean towel and some alcohol, and I clean off the barrel of my bat. Some of my teammates think I'm crazy." But he had a well-thought-out reason for doing so. "It is crucial to me that I begin the game hitting with a clean bat. Ninety-nine times out of a hundred when I hit the ball, it leaves a mark on the bat, so that starting with my first time up, I can come back to the dugout and actually study my bat to see whether I was judging the speed of the pitches properly."[4]

If he hit the ball at the signature on the bat, he knew he was meeting it squarely. If the mark of the ball was down near the trademark, he knew the pitcher was throwing harder than he thought, and if the mark was out near the end of the bat this told him he swung too quickly. "By the end of the game," he said, "I've noted every single one of the marks on my bat and understood how they got there"—and made appropriate adjustments in order to bang out a couple more base hits.[5]

To help keep in shape over the winter, Rose organized a Reds' basketball team, with Gerry Arrigo, Jim Maloney, Jimmy Stewart, and Johnny Bench among its members. To the surprise of all, Bob Howsam, who did not generally like his players playing the hoops game, gave his approval and even saw to it that the club paid for uniforms. Rose's squad played its games in packed high school gyms against teams of high school faculty members and coaches; Howsam figured that with that kind of competition, rather than organized league teams, "there was a lot less chance of their getting injured." With halftime autograph sessions, Rose's hoopsters generated a lot of good will for the Reds.[6]

There was change in the air in baseball's world early in 1970. The Reds' new ballpark, to be called Riverfront Stadium, was scheduled to be ready by mid-season, with Crosley Field being abandoned. The entire field was to be covered with Astroturf, except for small areas of dirt around the bases and the pitcher's mound.

During the off-season, the Cardinals and Phillies had made a major trade, involving seven players: St. Louis received Dick Allen, Jerry Johnson, and Cookie Rojas, for Curt Flood, Tim McCarver, Byron Browne, and Joe Hoerner. It became an even bigger story when Flood announced that he had no intention of reporting to Philadelphia and that he planned to challenge the reserve clause, which permitted him to be bought and sold like a piece of property. Players, with the notable exception of Carl Yastrzemski, applauded Flood's move, while waiting cautiously to see how it turned out. Management deplored it, blaming Marvin Miller, the new executive director of the players' union. Miller confessed, however, that Flood's rebellion was Curt's idea alone.

Rose was not particularly concerned at that point with Flood's stand, or the lawsuit he initiated. Pete was about to enter into negotiations with the Reds, backed by two straight batting crowns and his newly acquired captaincy. In January, he met with Sheldon "Chief" Bender, Howsam's assistant, who explained, as Rose remembered, "the ball club would like for me to be the first player signed since I'm now the team captain." After another meeting, with Bender and Howsam, Rose signed for $105,000, thus achieving his goal of becoming the first singles hitter to reach the century mark.[7]

In the third week of February, Rose and Johnny Bench celebrated the grand opening of their Lincoln-Mercury agency in Kettering, Ohio, just south of Dayton. The kid from Anderson Ferry was becoming an entrepreneur. The car dealership was an impressive addition to the endorsements that were already adding more dollars to the ever-growing Rose bank account. Bench, the sensational young catcher, said, "Pete has had a great influence on me. Win, lead the league in hitting and make money. That's Pete."[8]

Unfortunately, the city of Dayton was second in the country in unemployment at the time, and the town was suffering a run of labor strikes. There was little inclination in the area, and less money, to purchase upscale automobiles. Before too long, the agency closed down.[9]

On March 15, Sparky Anderson winced as he watched Rose score the winning run in a meaningless exhibition game with a headfirst slide. "I watch Pete," Anderson said, "and I say to myself, 'I wish he wouldn't do things like that now.' But that's Rose. That's the way he plays the game. It's why people buy tickets to watch him play."[10]

Pete Rose's credo, he told syndicated columnist Milton Gross, was simple: "If I have to slide head-first into home, I'll do it. If I have to run through a wall, I'll do it. The money I'm making, I'd be willing to take any chances. My whole career has been taking chances." He went on: "The man gives me a pot of money. I got to give him something in return."[11]

Sparky Anderson was happy with his team and expected great things from it. C. C. Johnson Spink, publisher of the *Sporting News,* saw things a little differently and picked the Reds to finish fourth in the West, with Atlanta on top again. In the same issue, beat writer Earl Lawson predicted, "Same old story. Team will go as far as pitching carries it. Hitting is pennant caliber."[12]

The 1970 Reds lined up with Lee May at first, Helms at second, Perez at third, and Woody Woodward at shortstop, although, as the season went on, he wound up splitting the job with a rookie from Venezuela named Dave Concepcion. They had Rose in right, Tolan in center, and another rookie named Bernie Carbo in left. Bench was a fixture behind the plate. Pitching as usual was the big question mark. Rose liked the looks of the freshman shortstop Concepcion. The 21-year-old was a skinny six feet, two inches and 155 pounds. When Pete saw the trainer taping Concepcion's thigh, he said, "Hey, kid, with those legs of yours, how can you get a pulled muscle? It's gotta be a pulled bone." Concepcion grinned self-consciously in response; whether he understood Rose's jibe is questionable.[13]

The Reds played moderately well in April, though without too much help from their slow-starting captain. Rose was hitting only .247 on May 2, but Anderson said, "You know that's not going to last." Rose captured attention with a couple of fielding plays. On May 5, Dick Allen of the Cards hit a fly to right field, which Rose caught after staggering around under it. "It hit a pigeon and changed direction," Pete said; it was actually a nighthawk, which fell dead into the seats along the foul line. And on May 19, Rose made one of the most spectacular catches ever seen at Crosley Field, hauling down a drive by the Cubs' Jim Hickman while crashing at full speed into the right-field fence. Sparky Anderson, sure that Rose had broken his shoulder, raced out to his captain, only to find him undamaged. "Sparky got there so fast," Rose said, grinning, "he could have thrown out Hickman at the plate if I had dropped the ball."[14]

There was a nasty incident in the May 5 game with St. Louis. After Reds pitcher Wayne Simpson knocked Lou Brock down in the first inning, the Cards' lefty Steve Carlton threw his first pitch behind Rose's head. Rose, furious, headed toward the mound, shouting at Carlton, before he was intercepted. After he grounded out, Rose shouted again at the St. Louis pitcher. Umpire Augie Donatelli quickly summoned the two managers, Anderson and Red Schoendienst, and made sure there would be no beanball war.

In mid-May, the Reds had moved into first place, although Rose was still hitting only .254. Bench and Perez were leading the offense, with Gary Nolan and Jim Merritt showing the way for the pitchers. "I wasn't worried," Rose said later, "but I sure was plenty disgusted with myself. Me hitting .250. And for what they're paying me." On May 16, facing the Atlanta knuckleballer Phil Niekro, Rose changed bats, for the first time in five years. "I switched from a skinny-handled bat to one with a thick handle," he related. "It felt good in my hands that night and I decided to stick with it."[15]

With his new lumber Pete Rose went on a hitting tear. In three and one-half weeks, he added 51 points to his batting average. Between May 16 and June 11, he hit in 22 of 24 games, picking up two or more hits in thirteen of them. "That's the thing about Pete," crowed his manager. "When he's hot, the hits come in clusters." Pointing out that Rose had scored in eight straight games until being shut out on June 11, Sparky added, "That's another thing about Pete. Once he gets on base, he has just one thing in mind—score."[16]

By June 16, the high-flying Reds were eleven games ahead of the second-place Braves. On June 7, Rose was presented with the Lou Gehrig Award for good citizenship by Phi Delta Theta fraternity, and late in June the team was preparing to say goodbye to Crosley Field.

The last game in the old park was played on June 24, and the Reds won, 5–4, beating Juan Marichal of the Giants on eighth-inning homers by Bench and May. Rose was in on the fun, running through Coach Alex Grammas' stop sign at third in the fifth inning and bowling over catcher Dick Dietz to score the run that pulled the Reds to within one. "I had to come in standing up," he said, in words that would soon have an echo, "because Dick Dietz had the plate blocked."

After the game, a helicopter flew home plate to the site of the new stadium. Well-behaved Cincinnati did not have the riotous tear-up-the-place ending that some other towns did when their old ballparks closed. Rose told the press, "What a great ending for the last game to be played at Crosley Field. We beat the highest-paid pitcher in baseball and we came from behind to do it."[17]

Riverfront Stadium opened on July 1, and it would shortly be in the national spotlight. In the meantime, Pete Rose already was. The All Star Game issue of the *Sporting News* carried on its cover a full-page portrait of the Reds' captain, wearing a batting helmet and a determined look, and a headline "PETE ROSE in Full Bloom." Inside was a lengthy article on Pete, written by Earl Lawson. "I was a kid once myself," Rose was quoted, explaining his accessibility, "and I still can remember how thrilled I was when I had a chance to meet a major league player. And I can remember, too, how disappointed I was when I asked a player for an autograph and he refused." And he was suitably humble: "I feel I'm very lucky. Most guys who fooled around the way I did in high school don't wind up making $100,000. And, without baseball, I wouldn't be."[18]

As the All Star break approached, Anderson's Reds maintained their big lead in the NL West (the major leagues having turned to two-division alignments the year before), with the Dodgers now second. The pitching, led by Merritt, was much better than expected, Bench and Perez were slugging at a prodigious pace, and Rose was now cruising at .323.

The All Star Game was played on July 14 in the new Cincinnati stadium, before a capacity crowd including President Richard Nixon. The game itself was a good one, featuring good pitching, particularly for the American League. Jim

Palmer, Sam McDowell, and Jim Perry combined to hold the Nationals to one run and three hits in eight innings, with the Americans holding a 4–1 lead going into the last of the ninth. Then the Giants' Dietz led off with a home run against Catfish Hunter, and hits by Bud Harrelson, Joe Morgan, and McCovey, plus a sacrifice fly by Clemente, tied the score. With two on and two out, Rose had a chance to win the game but was fanned by Mel Stottlemyre.

The tie game moved on, into the twelfth inning. With two out, now against Angels' lefthander Clyde Wright, Rose singled to center and moved to second on a hit by Billy Grabarkewitz. Jim Hickman lined a hit to center which reached outfielder Amos Otis on the second bounce. Off with the hit with two out, Rose headed toward third and, waved on by third base coach Durocher, home. Cleveland catcher Ray Fosse awaited Otis' throw, which tailed slightly to the right, a couple of feet up the third-base line. Fosse crouched, straddled the foul line, and watched the throw coming toward him. He was never to touch it.

Pete Rose, coming at full speed, prepared to slide headfirst into the plate but apparently decided, at the last split second, that this might be dangerous, with the catcher's spiked shoes and shinguards in his path. Instead, with his upper body now rising, he chose to crash into Fosse with his left shoulder at maximum force. Fosse was obliterated from the path of the ball as Rose scored the game-winning run. Fosse was bowled over backward and lay on the ground, writhing in agony. Rose leaped to his feet, stood for a moment over the prostrate catcher, then made his way to the dugout and his victorious teammates.[19]

A groundswell of controversy developed from the collision with Ray Fosse, heightened in succeeding years as it became clear that the crash had permanently damaged Fosse, regarded at the time as one of the bright young catchers of the game. Fosse, taken to Christ Hospital, had his injury erroneously diagnosed as a bad bruise of the left shoulder. In fact, he had a separated shoulder, which was not diagnosed until the following spring. Worse, the Indians convinced him to keep playing in 1970, which certainly did him no good. Fosse never again had the power he'd had before the collision; it changed his swing and probably shortened his career.

Initial reaction was mostly favorable to Rose, who said, "Fosse was about two feet in front of the plate. If I'd slid in there, I could have broken both legs," somehow overlooking the fact that players, himself included, slid into home plate all the time. "If I had slid head-first," he continued, "I could have broken my neck." Fosse said, "I know he didn't mean it. But who knows? Maybe he should have run around me. It all happened so quick. I never got hit like that before." Later, Fosse said, "if he had slid conventionally on his rear, he would have made it easily."[20]

Infielder Jim Fregosi of the Angels said, "I didn't particularly like the play.

All Rose has to do is slide and nobody gets hurt." Wright, the American League pitcher, had as good a view of what happened as anyone; he said, "I don't know why he had to hit him so hard. I guess it was instinct with Rose. That's the way he plays. But I was standing there and he could have gone around Fosse."[21]

But few players were willing to criticize Rose publicly. The play was within the rules, Fosse was technically in error for occupying the base line without the ball, and Rose's body block had succeeded. Very few observers called it a cheap shot. But there was an uncomfortable feeling about it, a feeling that Pete Rose's "enthusiasm" had become something a bit more dangerous. From this time on, a feeling grew that boyish, playful Pete Rose would do anything to win, even if it risked maiming another player.

Dallas Green, who was to manage Rose in Philadelphia years later, felt that Pete's style of play angered quite a few players. "I think there were plenty of times he was 'sent a message' by pitchers during his career," Green said.[22]

For Ray Fosse, the Rose collision was just something that had happened. As a couple of years went by, though, with his shoulder still achy, Fosse began to wonder. He heard of Rose boasting about the play, about proving his manhood, showing his greatness as a competitor. Rose started telling of how he and Fosse had been out carousing together till two in the morning the night before but he had still been willing to slam into a good friend the way he had. Fosse had never met Rose until the night before the All Star Game when, after a press conference, Rose, Fosse, his teammate Sam McDowell, and their wives had gone out to dinner. They returned briefly to the Rose home to talk a little baseball before the Indians players and their wives returned to their hotel. Fosse resented Rose portraying him as a bosom buddy.

Finally, Fosse read an article in 1974 in which Rose responded to a question about the collision by saying, "I could never have looked my father in the eye again, if I hadn't hit Fosse that day." This statement confirmed to Fosse that Rose had crashed into him with malicious intent. Later still, he read that Rose had said, "nobody told me they changed it to girls' softball between third and home." Nevertheless, Ray Fosse held no bitterness toward Pete Rose.[23]

Rose missed three games with a bruised thigh from the Fosse collision before getting back to the business of the National League West. Late in July, he was the first victim of the soon-to-be notorious Morganna Roberts, the "Kissing Bandit," a hugely-endowed blonde exotic dancer who ran onto baseball fields to kiss players during a game. Her kiss of Pete Rose was to be followed by similar on-field busses of Bench, Clete Boyer, Frank Howard, Billy Cowan, Nolan Ryan, and Wes Parker, among others over a quarter-century. But Rose was the first.[24]

Meanwhile, the Reds kept winning. People were starting to call the club the

Big Red Machine, and by the end of July it had a twelve-game edge on the Dodgers. By August, it appeared unlikely that Rose, his average hovering in the .320s, would win a third straight batting crown, with Atlanta's Rico Carty almost forty points ahead. Rose's primary goal now was 200 hits for the year. "If I get them," he said, "I'll be the only player active today who has had three straight 200-hit seasons." He needed 45 in his last 42 games, no very difficult task for Pete Rose.[25]

On August 29, at Montreal, Rose picked up the 1,500th hit of his career, a milestone that he recognized but rightfully considered a mere way-station along his career path. A more important event took place on September 17, when the Reds clinched their division title. By the time the season ended, almost two weeks later, Anderson's crew had a fourteen and one-half game lead over Los Angeles. Pete Rose ended the year at .316, with 205 hits.

Rose was not the only big hitter on the Cincinnati club. Bench led the league with 45 homers and 148 RBIs, to go with his .293 average, while Perez hit .317, with 40 home runs and 129 driven in. Lee May belted 34 homers, while Bobby Tolan and Bernie Carbo each hit well over .300. On the pitching staff, Jim Merritt was 20–12, Gary Nolan 18–7, Jim McGlothlin 14–10, and Wayne Simpson 14–3, though he was hurt and would miss the postseason. Wayne Granger had 35 saves and Clay Carroll 16 out of the pen. The Reds' home attendance, with half the season in their new digs, was 1,803,568. It had been a good year for the "Big Red Machine," which would face the Pittsburgh Pirates in a best-of-five playoff for the National League championship.

The playoff series was hard fought but ultimately one-sided. In the opener, at Pittsburgh's new Three Rivers Stadium, Gary Nolan and Dock Ellis dueled through nine scoreless innings. Ellis, hung-over when he arrived at the ballpark, "took about ten greenies [pep pills] to snap me out of it." He later remembered nothing of the first nine innings, but he did recollect Rose's run-scoring single in the tenth; "Rose muscled the ball," Ellis said. "The infield was playing in and he muscled it past them." Rose's hit was followed by May's two-run double, and the Reds had Game 1.[26]

In the second game, Merritt, Carroll, and young Don Gullett stopped the Pirates, while Tolan scored all three runs in a 3–1 Cincinnati victory. Finally, in Game 3 at Riverfront, with the score 2–2 in the eighth inning, pinch-hitter Ty Cline of the Reds walked and went to second on Rose's single. Tolan singled him home, and in the ninth Granger and Gullett struggled but retired the Pirates without scoring to bring the pennant to Cincinnati.

In the victorious locker-room Sparky Anderson exulted, "I've said it before and I'll say it again. I think I manage the best team in baseball." One of the

Reds players said the team won "because there were no cliques on this ball club. Everybody had a common purpose." Kudos were handed out to Bob Howsam for putting the team together, bringing in such integral parts as Tolan, Granger, Carroll, Merritt, McGlothlin, and of course Anderson.[27]

Sparky would get the chance to show how good his team was against Earl Weaver's Baltimore Orioles, who took the American League East by fifteen games over the Yankees and then swept Minnesota in the league playoffs. The Orioles were led by ex-Red Frank Robinson, third sacker Brooks Robinson, big Boog Powell, and a pitching staff with three twenty-game winners, Mike Cuellar, Dave McNally, and stylish Jim Palmer.

Game 1 of the World Series was played before 51,331 fans in Riverfront Stadium, the first Series game ever played on artificial turf. Beforehand, Rose told the assembled press that the Palmer-Nolan matchup was the key to the Series. "If we beat Palmer in the first game," he said, "we'll be doing a very important thing, because we will be beating the guy Earl Weaver thinks can beat us."[28]

The Reds scored three runs against Palmer before Baltimore came back with two in the fourth inning and one to tie in the fifth. The key play in the game came in the bottom of the sixth, with the Reds' Bernie Carbo on third base. Pinch-hitter Ty Cline hit a little chopper a few feet in front of the plate and down the third base line. As catcher Elrod Hendricks jumped out in front of the plate to grab the ball, umpire Ken Burkhart straddled the line to call the ball fair. Hendricks was ready to throw to first when pitcher Palmer screamed, "Tag him! He's coming!" Carbo, in a base running blunder, was trying to score from third. Carbo found the umpire in his way as he slid past the plate, Hendricks crashed into the umpire as he whirled around to try to tag Carbo, and Burkhart, from the ground, gave an emphatic "out" signal. Carbo and Anderson beefed, but the play stood. Replays and photographs of the controversial play revealed that Carbo missed the plate, Hendricks tagged him with his glove but had the ball in his other hand, and the only correct call Burkhart made on the play was when he first ruled the batted ball fair. Brooks Robinson's home run in the next inning gave the O's a 4–3 victory; he also contributed a couple of spectacular plays at third base.

Rose was 0 for 3 in Game 1 but reached base twice, once when catcher Hendricks tipped his bat and catcher's interference was called, and again in the ninth, when Palmer walked him with two out. Rose represented the tying run, but he was stranded as Pete Richert came in to get the final out on Bobby Tolan's soft liner to short. Rose snorted defiantly after the game, "The only thing today's game proved was there won't be any sweep."[29]

In the second game, Rose was 0 for 3 again, though he reached base in the first on shortstop Mark Belanger's error and later drew a walk from reliever Moe Drabowsky. Baltimore overcame a four-run deficit to win, 6–5, aided by more fielding wizardry at third by Brooks Robinson. Asked about pressure after the second loss, Rose said, "I don't feel no pressure. Two down is just two down."[30]

The third game, in Baltimore's Memorial Stadium, went to the Orioles, 9–3, despite Rose's 2-for-5 day. Brooks Robinson dazzled the fans and the Reds with one fantastic play after another. Referring to the new automobile which *Sport* magazine gave annually to the Series' most valuable player, Rose said, "If we knew Robinson wanted a car so badly, we'd have given him one before this thing started."[31]

For the fourth game, Anderson dropped Rose to the second spot in the line-up, with Tolan moving to leadoff. It must have helped, for the Reds finally won 6–5 on Lee May's three-run home run. Rose once more went 2 for 5, including a home run. Pete also picked up an assist when he threw out Robinson in the third, trying to score on Hendricks' single to right. Despite the win, the Reds were in deep trouble, and the Orioles put them away in a rainy Game 5, 9–3. Rose's bloop double helped his team get three runs off Mike Cuellar in the first, but the O's came right back with two runs and Cuellar settled down to blank Sparky Anderson's squad the rest of the way.

Pete Rose was 5 for 20 in the Series, batting .250, with a double, a homer, and two runs batted in. He told the press, "No excuses. But you weren't looking at the real Big Red Machine of the regular season. I can't explain it, but we didn't play the game we're capable of playing."[32]

The 1970 Reds won seventy of their first one hundred games, with strong hitting and a superb rotation of Simpson, Merritt, Nolan, and McGlothlin. Then the pitching broke down, as Simpson, Merritt, and McGlothlin went down with injuries, and the team struggled for the rest of the season. Anderson's task for 1971 was to recharge his pitching staff without giving up any of his batting power.

NOTES

1. *Cincinnati Enquirer*, October 24, 1969.
2. Bench and Brashler, *Catch You Later: The Autobiography of Johnny Bench*, 45.
3. Reston, *Collision at Home Plate: The Lives of Pete Rose and Bart Giamatti*, 60–61.
4. Rose and Golenbock, *Rose on Hitting: How to Hit Better Than Anybody*, 78.
5. Ibid., 79.
6. Earl Lawson, "Hustler Pete Rose: Baseball's Best Ad," *Sporting News*, July 18, 1970, 3.
7. *Cincinnati Post and Times-Star*, January 13, 1970.
8. *Sporting News*, March 21, 1970.

9. Bench and Brashler, *Catch You Later: The Autobiography of Johnny Bench*, 97.

10. Earl Lawson, "Perez' Booming Drives Jar Foes and Please Reds," *Sporting News*, April 4, 1970.

11. Milton Gross (NANA), "Ever-Blooming Rose Says He Still Hasn't Reached His Potential," (Philadelphia) *Evening Bulletin*, March 8, 1970.

12. *Sporting News*, April 11, 1970.

13. Earl Lawson, "Reds' Phenom Bears Out Latin Raves," *Sporting News*, March 28, 1970.

14. *Sporting News*, May 16, 23, 1970; Earl Lawson, "Reds Thank Angels as McGlothlin Flies High," June 6, 1970.

15. *Sporting News*, June 27, 1970.

16. Ibid.

17. *Sporting News*, July 11, 1970. Rose got the last hit in Crosley Field, and he would get the first hit in Riverfront Stadium.

18. Lawson, "Hustler Pete Rose: Baseball's Best Ad," 3.

19. Rose usually slid feet first at home plate, but perhaps because this was the All Star Game, before his Cincinnati fans, he initially chose to go head first.

20. Stan Isle, "Rose's Grid-Style Block Brings Praise, Brickbats," *Sporting News*, July 25, 1970; *Cincinnati Enquirer*, July 14, 1985.

21. *Cincinnati Enquirer,* July 14, 1985; (Philadelphia) *Evening Bulletin*, July 15, 1970.

22. Erardi, *Pete Rose*, 28.

23. Reston, *Collision at Home Plate: The Lives of Pete Rose and Bart Giamatti*, 68; Rose and Kahn, *Pete Rose: My Story*, 135; *Cincinnati Enquirer*, July 14, 1985.

24. Steve Rushin, "Morganna: The Final Kiss-off," *Sports Illustrated*, June 30, 2003.

25. *Sporting News*, August 29, 1970.

26. Rose and Kahn, *Pete Rose: My Story*, 137; *Cincinnati Enquirer*, October 4, 1970.

27. *Cincinnati Enquirer*, October 11, 1970.

28. Lowell Reidenbaugh, *Sporting News*, October 24, 1970.

29. Ibid.

30. Ibid.

31. Ibid.

32. Ibid.

PUTTING IT TOGETHER

Brooks Robinson, as everyone expected, won *Sport's* automobile as the Most Valuable Player in the World Series, and the Cincinnati Reds went home to figure out how to go that final step in the future. Each of the Reds' thirty-two full shares of Series proceeds came to $13,687.59, which softened somewhat the harshness of the five-game blowout.

Johnny Bench was voted the MVP in the National League, easily outdistancing Chicago's Billy Williams, while Rose finished seventh in the voting. Once again, Pete was one of three National League outfielders winning a Gold Glove for fielding, quite a turnaround for the once-awkward infielder who had trouble turning a double play.

Pete Rose, after eight solid years with the Reds, had by now become something of an institution in Cincinnati. The good conservative citizens of the Queen City admired his work ethic, his drive, his hustle, even his striving for the last dollar he could get. His was the classic "local boy makes good" story, and he had completed the move from down-at-the-heels Anderson Ferry to the more upscale Oak Hills. Pete's chunky body, square jaw, and crewcut had become the image of Cincinnati baseball, and the fans looked forward to many more years' relationship with their "Charlie Hustle."

They read items in the local papers about Pete's little girl, Fawn, and about Pete Jr., born in November 1969, which presented the picture of Pete Rose as a family man. They knew and admired Karolyn as a typical "baseball wife." The television cameramen at the ballpark liked to focus on Karolyn sitting in the stands, with her striking good looks, doing so to the extent that other players' wives complained that they were being ignored. The outspoken Karolyn became a minor celebrity in Cincinnati, working as a disc jockey in one of the town's popular clubs and using her gift of gab on her own radio sports show on WNOP in Newport, Kentucky. She became famous for telling her listeners regarding an ice hockey game that "Puck-off time is eight P.M."[1]

Everybody liked Karolyn Rose—breezy, witty, sometimes crude, almost always refreshing. "This is a marvelous woman," Sparky Anderson said. "I loved her. My wife loved her. I think everyone who ever came into contact with her loved her." Such a spouse is a not inconsiderable asset for a civic institution, and so she was for Pete Rose.[2]

In November 1970, Pete and Johnny Bench went into another business venture together, this time the Fairfield Bowling Lanes, a few miles northwest of Cincinnati. The forty-alley establishment was renamed the Pete Rose–John Bench Lanes. "The Reds stars expect to be on hand there many evenings," a friendly reporter wrote. Like the car dealership, this venture did not pan out very well, since Rose and Bench were not able to hang out at the lanes as much as they were expected to. Unlike the car dealership, they were able to get out of this venture at a slight profit.[3]

Not all went well for Pete Rose, however. On December 9, his father, Harry Rose, died of a massive heart attack, at the age of fifty-eight, after climbing the steps of his front porch. It came as a great shock to Pete, who thought of his father, the man who still played hard-nosed football in his forties, as indestructible. When he was told, while getting his hair cut in his barber shop, that his father was dead, Rose said, "My father? You must mean my mother."[4]

Pete Rose wept unashamedly at the news. "There's nothing wrong with crying when there's something to cry about and when Dad died so sudden, I musta cried for three days." A big league star who remembered the man who hit ground balls to him by the hour, who made sure his coaches in amateur ball let him switch hit, who showed up at spring training to make sure his son was doing everything the way it should be done, Peter Edward Rose said, "There's only one person that's *really* influenced me, and that was my dad."[5]

Not only was Rose's father gone, but Sparky Anderson tried to make another change in his off-season routine. The manager said, "no basketball," and he easily picked up Bob Howsam's backing for his edict. Pete Rose was accustomed to keeping in shape by playing organized or semiorganized basketball four nights a week over the winter. After the 1969 season, the Reds' management even provided equipment for Pete's team, although Howsam always worried about possible injuries.

Anderson, whose pitching staff had been crippled the second half of the 1970 season, chose to take no chances. When he heard that Lee May, Jim McGloth-

...feller, John D., Jr. *The Personal Relation in Industry.* New York: Boni and ...eright, 1923.

..., William E. *The Businessman and His Overflow.* New York: Association ...ss, 1919.

...as, Norman. *America's Way Out.* New York: The Macmillan Co., 1931.

SOME ANTISOCIAL GOSPEL TRACTS

...ow, Victor. *Mistakes of the Inter-church Steel Report.* Boston, 1920.

...nt, Judson E. *The Growing Menace of the Social Gospel.* Chicago: Bible ...stitute Colportage Association, 1937.

...ch, John. *Communism.* Chicago: Bible Institute Colportage Association, 1937.

...Henry B. *Our Pro-Socialist Churches.* Detroit, 1937.

———. *Reference Materials, with Reference to FCCCA, etc.* Detroit, 1938.

..., Marshall. *Analysis of the Interchurch World Movement Report on the Steel ...rike.* G. P. Putnam's Sons, 1922.

...ctuary, E. N. *Tainted Contacts.* New York: American Christian Defenders, 1931.

...th, Leroy, and E. B. Johns. *Pastors, Politicians, Pacifists.* Constructive Educa- ...onal Publishing Co.

SECONDARY WORKS

...ams, Ray. *Preachers Present Arms.* New York: Round Table Press, 1933.

...ins, G. G., and F. L. Fagley. *History of American Congregationalism.* Boston ...nd Chicago: Pilgrim Press, 1942.

...brey, E. E. *Present Theological Tendencies.* New York: Harper and Brothers, ...936.

...nes, Harry E. *The Twilight of Christianity.* New York: The Vanguard Press, 1929.

...lfrage, Cedric. *A Faith to Free the People.* New York: Dryden Press, 1944.

———. *South of God.* New York: Modern Age Books, 1941.

...achly, Clarence. *The Treatment of the Problem of Capital and Labor in Social- Study Courses in the Churches.* Chicago: University of Chicago Press, 1920.

...runner, Edmund. *Industrial Village Churches.* New York: Institute of Social and Religious Research, 1930.

...arter, Paul. *The Decline and Revival of the Social Gospel, 1920–1940.* Ithaca: Cornell University Press, 1956.

...ase, Adelaid. *Liberal Christianity and Religious Education.* New York: The Mac- millan Co., 1924.

...ole, Charles C. *The Social Ideas of the Northern Evangelists.* New York: Co- lumbia University Press, 1954.

...urti, Merle. *Peace or War.* New York: W. W. Norton and Co., 1936.

...ombrowski, James. *The Early Days of Christian Socialism in America.* New York: Columbia University Press, 1936.

...Douglass, H. Paul. *Church and Community in the United States.* Chicago: Willett, Clark and Co., 1938.

———. *The Protestant Church as a Social Institution.* New York: Harper and Brothers, 1935.

...*Five-Foot Shelf of Pacifist Literature.* Pamphlet. Philadelphia, 1942.

Fletcher, Joseph F., ed. *Christianity and Property.* Philadelphia: Westminster Press, 1947.

Hough, Lynn H., ed. *Whither Christianity?* New York: Harper and Brothers, 1929.

"Industrial Relations and the Church," *Annals of the American Academy of Social and Political Science,* CIII (September, 1922).

Johnson, F. Ernest, ed. *A Bibliography of Social Service.* Pamphlet. New York: Federal Council of Churches, 1918.

———. *The Social Work of the Churches.* New York: Federal Council of Churches, 1930.

Knox, Edward, ed. *Religion and the Present Crisis.* Chicago: University of Chicago Press, 1942.

Lewis, John, ed. *Christianity and the Social Revolution.* New York: Charles Scrib- ner's Sons, 1936.

Myers, James. *Churches in Social Action.* New York: Federal Council of Churches, 1935.

———. *Religion Lends a Hand.* New York: Harper and Brothers, 1929.

Niebuhr, Reinhold, ed. *This Ministry: Essays in Honor of H. S. Coffin.* New York: Charles Scribner's Sons, 1945.

Oxford Conference. *Christian Faith and the Common Life.* Chicago: Willett, Clark and Co., 1938.

———. *The Christian Understanding of Man.* Chicago: Willett, Clark and Co., 1938.

———. *The Kingdom of God and History.* Chicago: Willett, Clark and Co., 1938.

Page, Kirby, ed. *A New Economic Order.* New York: Harcourt, Brace and Co., 1930.

———, ed. *Recent Gains in American Civilization.* New York: Harcourt, Brace and Company, 1928.

Protestant Episcopal Church, Joint Commission of. *Reconstruction Programs: A Bibliography and Digest.* New York, 1919.

———. *Triennial Report.* New York, 1919.

Rall, H. F., ed. *Religion and Public Affairs.* New York: The Macmillan Co., 1937.

Read, Ralph, ed. *The Younger Churchmen Look at the Church.* New York: The Macmillan Co., 1935.

Sayre, John N., Kirby Page, and A. J. Muste. *Pacifism and Aggression.* Pamphlet. New York, n.d.

Schilpp, P. A., ed. *Theology and Modern Life.* Chicago: Willett, Clark and Co., 1940.

Smith, G. B., ed. *Religious Thought in the Last Quarter Century.* Chicago: Uni- versity of Chicago Press, 1927.

Swift, Arthur, ed. *Religion Today.* New York: McGraw-Hill Book Co., 1933.

Van Dusen, H. P., Francis Henson, and Sidney Hook. *Christianity and Marxism.* New York: Polemic Publishers, 1934.

Van Dusen, H. P., ed. *Ventures in Belief.* New York: Charles Scribner's Sons, 1930.

WORKS RELEVANT TO THE SOCIAL PASSION, BUT OF LARGER FOCUS

Atkins, Gaius G. *Religion in Our Times.* New York: Round Table Press, 1932.

Barclay, Wade C. *The Church and a Christian Society.* New York: The Abingdon Press, 1939.

Barth, Karl. *The Church and the Political Problem of Our Day*. New York: Charles Scribner's Sons, 1939.

Brightman, Edgar S. *Personality and Religion*. New York: The Abingdon Press, 1934.

Brunner, Emil. *Justice and the Social Order*. New York: Harper and Brothers, 1945.

Cadbury, Henry J. *The Peril of Modernizing Jesus*. New York: The Macmillan Co., 1937.

Calkins, Raymond. *The Christian Church in the Modern World*. New York: The Macmillan Co., 1924.

Case, Shirley Jackson. *Christianity in a Changing World*. New York: Harper and Brothers, 1941.

———. *Jesus Through the Centuries*. Chicago: University of Chicago Press, 1932.

———. *The Social Triumph of the Ancient Church*. New York: Harper and Brothers, 1933.

Coffin, Henry S. *Religion Yesterday and Today*. Nashville: Cokesbury Press, 1940.

Eddy, G. Sherwood. *Eighty Adventurous Years: An Autobiography*. New York: Harper and Brothers, 1955.

Fitch, Albert P. *Can the Church Survive in the Changing Order?* New York: The Macmillan Co., 1920.

Fosdick, Harry E. *Christianity and Progress*. New York: Fleming H. Revell Co., 1922.

Haroutunian, Joseph. *Wisdom and Folly in Religion*. New York: Charles Scribner's Sons, 1940.

Holt, A. E. *Christian Roots of Democracy in America*. New York: Friendship Press, 1941.

———. *The Fate of the Family in the Modern World*. Chicago: Willett, Clark and Co., 1936.

———. *Social Work in the Churches*. Boston: Pilgrim Press, 1922.

Holt, Ivan Lee. *The Search for a New Strategy in Protestantism*. New York: Cokesbury Press, 1937.

Homrighausen, Elmer. *Christianity in America*. New York: Abingdon Press, 1936.

Jaspers, Karl. *Man in the Modern Age*. London: G. Routledge and Sons, 1933.

Leiper, Henry S. *Christ's Way and the World's*. New York: Abingdon Press, 1936.

Lewis, Edwin. *A New Heaven and a New Earth*. New York: Abingdon-Cokesbury Press, 1941.

Luccock, Halford. *Christianity and the Individual*. Nashville: Cokesbury Press, 1937.

Macintosh, Douglas C. *Personal Religion*. New York: Charles Scribner's Sons, 1942.

Mathews, Shailer. *Christianity and Social Process*. New York: Harper and Brothers, 1934.

———. *Creative Christianity*. Nashville: Cokesbury Press, 1935.

McConnell, Francis J. *By the Way: An Autobiography*. New York: Abingdon-Cokesbury, 1952.

Niebuhr, H. Richard. *The Kingdom of God in America*. Chicago: Willett, Clark and Company, 1937.

———. *The Social Sources of Denominationalism*. New York: Henry Holt and Company, 1929.

Niebuhr, Reinhold. *Beyond Tragedy*. New York: Charles Scribner's Sons, 1937.

———. *The Contribution of Religion to Social W[...]* versity Press, 1930.

———. *Does Civilization Need Religion?* New Y[...]

———. *Leaves from the Notebook of a Tamed Cyn[...]* Colby, 1929.

———. *The Nature and Destiny of Man*. 2v. New [...] 1941, 1943.

Nixon, Justin Wroe. *The Moral Crisis in Christia[...]* Brothers, 1931.

———. *Protestantism's Hour of Decision*. Philadelph[...]

Page, Kirby. *Living Prayerfully*. New York: Farrar an[...]

———. *Religious Resources for Personal and Social [...]* Rinehart, 1939.

Rehwinkel, Alfred M. *The World Today—A Challe[...]* St. Louis: Concordia Publishing House, 1940.

Reisner, E. H. *Faith in an Age of Fact*. New York: [...]

Roberts, D. E., and H. P. Van Dusen, eds. *Liberal T[...]* York: Charles Scribner's Sons, 1942.

Scott, E. F. *The Ethical Teachings of Jesus*. New York[...]

———. *The Kingdom of God in the New Testament*. [...] Co., 1931.

Swift, Arthur. *New Frontiers of Religion*. New York: [...]

Tillich, Paul. *Interpretation of History*. New York: Cha[...]

———. *The Protestant Era*. Chicago: University of Chic[...]

———. *The Religious Situation*. New York: Henry Holt [...]

Van Dusen, H. P. *God in These Times*. New York: Char[...]

Wieman, Henry N., *et al*. *Religious Liberals Reply*. Bos[...]

SOME LAY EXPRESSIONS

Babson, Roger. *New Tasks for Old Churches*. New Yo[...] Company, 1922.

———. *Religion and Business*. New York: The Macmillan [...]

Davis, Jerome, ed. *Business and the Church*. New York: [...]

———, ed. *Christianity and Social Adventuring*. New Yo[...] 1927.

———, ed. *Labor Speaks for Itself on Religion*. New York [...] 1929.

Ellwood, Charles. *Christianity and Social Science*. New York [...] 1923.

———. *The Reconstruction of Religion*. New York: The Mac[...]

———. *The World's Need of Christ*. New York: Abingdon-C[...]

High, Stanley. *The Church in Politics*. New York: Harper and [...]

Hutchins, Grace, and Anna Rochester. *Jesus Christ and the [...]* York: George H. Doran Co., 1922.

Nash, Arthur. *The Golden Rule in Industry*. New York: Fle[...] 1923.

Fry, Luther. *The U.S. Looks at Its Churches.* New York: Institute of Social and Religious Research, 1930.

Hammar, George. *Christian Realism in Contemporary American Theology.* Uppsala: Appelberg, 1940.

Hopkins, Charles H. *The Rise of the Social Gospel in American Protestantism, 1865–1915.* New Haven: Yale University Press, 1940.

Huber, Milton J. "A History of the Methodist Federation for Social Action." MS. Boston University, 1949.

Hughan, Jessie W. *Three Decades of War Resistance.* Pamphlet. New York: War Resisters League, 1942.

Hughley, J. Neal. *Trends of Protestant Social Idealism.* New York: King's Crown Press, 1948.

Hutchison, John, ed. *Christian Faith and Social Action.* New York: Charles Scribner's Sons, 1953.

————. *We Are Not Divided.* New York: Round Table Press, 1941.

Hyma, Albert. *Christianity, Capitalism and Communism.* Ann Arbor: G. Wahr, 1937.

Kegley, C. W., and R. W. Bretall, eds. *Reinhold Niebuhr: His Religious, Social and Political Thought.* New York: The Macmillan Co., 1956.

Keller, Adolph. *Karl Barth and Christian Unity.* New York: The Macmillan Co., 1933.

Kincheloe, Samuel. *Research Memorandum on Religion in the Depression.* New York: Social Science Research Council, 1937.

Lee, Umphrey. *The Historic Church and Modern Pacifism.* New York: Abingdon-Cokesbury Press, 1943.

Lowrie, Walter. *Our Concern with the Theology of Crisis.* Boston: Meador Publishing Co., 1932.

Macfarland, Charles. *The Christian Faith in a Day of Crisis.* New York: Fleming H. Revell Co., 1939.

————. *Contemporary Christian Thought.* New York: Fleming H. Revell Co., 1936.

————. *Trends of Christian Thinking.* New York: Fleming H. Revell Co., 1937.

Matthews, Joseph B. *Odyssey of a Fellow Traveller.* New York: Mount Vernon Publishers, 1938.

May, Henry. *Protestant Churches and Industrial America.* New York: Harper and Brothers, 1949.

Mays, Benjamin. *The Negro's Church.* New York: Institute of Social and Religious Research, 1933.

McCown, Chester C. *The Search for the Real Jesus.* New York: Charles Scribner's Sons, 1940.

Melish, John Howard. *Paul Jones.* New York: Fellowship of Reconciliation, 1942.

Miller, Robert M. *American Protestantism and Social Issues, 1919–1939.* Chapel Hill: University of North Carolina Press, 1958.

Miller, Spencer, and Joseph Fletcher. *The Church and Industry.* New York: Longmans, Green and Co., 1930.

Mould, Ralph N. *Christianity Where Men Work.* New York: Friendship Press, 1947.

Nash, Arnold, ed. *Protestant Thought in the Twentieth Century.* New York: The Macmillan Co., 1951.

Nichols, James R. *Democracy and the Churches*. Philadelphia: Westminster Press, 1951.

Odegard, Holtan P. *Sin and Science: Reinhold Niebuhr as Political Theologian*. Yellow Springs: Antioch Press, 1956.

"Organized Religion in the United States," *Annals of the American Academy of Political and Social Science*, CCLVI (March, 1948).

Pope, Liston, ed. *Labor's Relation to Church and Community*. New York: Harper Brothers, 1947.

————. *Millhands and Preachers*. New Haven: Yale University Press, 1942.

Sanderson, Ross, and Norman Trott. *What Church People Think About Social and Economic Issues*. New York: Association Press, 1938.

Sharpe, Dores R. *Walter Rauschenbusch*. New York: The Macmillan Co., 1942.

Shelton, Arthur E. "The Methodist Church and Industrial Workers in the Southern Soft-Coal Fields." MS. Boston University, 1950.

Singer, Anna. *Walter Rauschenbusch and His Contribution to Social Christianity*. Boston: R. G. Badger Co., 1926.

Spaude, Paul W. *The Lutheran Church Under American Influence*. Burlington: Lutheran Literary Board, 1943.

Thelen, Mary F. *Man as Sinner in Contemporary American Realistic Theology*. New York: King's Crown Press, 1946.

Un-American Activities Committee. *100 Things You Should Know About Communism and Religion*. Washington, 1949.

Visser t'Hooft, W. A. *The Background of the Social Gospel in America*. Haarlem, 1928.

Wilder, Amos. *Eschatology and Ethics in the Teaching of Jesus*. Rev. ed. New York: Harper and Brothers, 1950.

Yinger, Milton. *Religion in the Struggle for Power*. Durham: Duke University Press, 1946.

Index

Index

lin, and possibly a few others were planning to join Rose's team, Sparky put his foot down. He had seen one game that Rose's team had played the year before, which turned into a brawl—Rose said "it was the roughest game we played all season"—and he had seen enough.[6]

Anderson phoned Rose with the news, then had Sheldon "Chief" Bender issue a statement banning basketball for the Cincinnati players. "We realize," Bender said, "players must keep active during the off-season to remain in shape. But basketball presents too much of a risk." The Reds, he said, would set up an organized conditioning program for players staying in the Cincinnati area. The same program would be sent to "those players who aren't wintering in Cincinnati," Bender said.[7]

It would take more than a front office edict, however, to bench Pete Rose. Claiming that fifteen games for his team had already been scheduled by the time Anderson said "no," Rose said they could hardly back out of playing them. Johnny Bench said, "Sparky doesn't want us to play basketball, but we've made some commitments, so I guess we will play a little." And so they played, even knowing that they were flouting the expressed policy of the baseball club. Sure enough, Bobby Tolan, whose success was based largely upon his speed, tore the Achilles tendon in his right heel playing on Rose's basketball team, putting his 1971 season, even perhaps his career, very much in doubt.[8]

In February, Rose changed a part of his image: he got a new hairdo, ditching the crewcut he had worn for so many years. The new hairstyle was called by experts on that sort of thing a "Prince Valiant" cut, after the long-running comic strip's title character. When asked about the change during training camp, Rose said, "Hustle always has been my trademark, not the crew cut."[9]

Pete was not happy with the club's salary negotiations. He was encouraged at first when Bob Howsam responded to Bench's request for a three-year contract for $500,000 by saying, "You can take it from me, the Reds will have only one $100,000-a-year player this season." Howsam added, "Consistency is the key. One or two good seasons don't make a career. Five or more in a row is a different story." He went on: "That is how Pete reached the $100,000 figure. Remember, too, Pete also led the league in hitting two successive years. He's also an exciting player. And he does extra things that enhance his value."[10]

When it came to dealing with Pete himself, however, the club tried to hold the line. Rose wanted a two-year contract in the range of $250,000, but he kept hearing from the club that he had reached a "plateau" where he was. Bob Howsam was not averse to a two-year contract with his team captain, but the number Rose mentioned was one the club considered way too high. Howsam was willing to give a "cost-of-living" increase, but even here there were differences. As so often happened, Rose was the last member of the team to sign, finally agreeing to a $2,500 raise rather than the $5,000 he was demanding. The increase brought his salary to $107,500. Rose said, "It was a hard fight. I've gotten a lot of mail and fans seem to be on me."[11]

With his contract taken care of, though, Rose was ready for camp. As always, Pete worked hard. Having played through 1970 at about 200 pounds, he wanted to get down to the 195 level for the new season, so he took extra hitting, extra fly-shagging, even lots of ground balls, as the sweat and the pounds poured off. Pete Rose wanted another winning season. He'd had a taste of the World Series, and he was ravenous now for a world championship. The baseball writers picked the Reds to win their division and to win the league pennant, but they picked Baltimore to win the Series again.

Anderson said he would keep Rose in right field, with Carbo in left and Hal McRae in center until Tolan was able to return. All looked fine until the season started, and the Reds promptly lost their first four games. The traditional opener at Cincinnati went to the Atlanta Braves, 7–4, with Rose going 0 for 5 and the Reds committing six errors, three by third baseman Woody Woodward.

In the early going, lack of hitting by their power men, Bench and Perez, crippled the Reds, even though Rose was at .327 after twelve games. Then Pete's average took a nosedive and fell below .300, and by May 3 the club was at 9–13, eight and one-half games behind the division-leading Giants.

In late May, Rose incurred the wrath of Philadelphia fans when he smashed into catcher Mike Ryan, trying to knock the ball out of the catcher's grasp. In customary Philadelphia fashion, the fans booed him consistently for the rest of the series. But, as *Philadelphia Inquirer* writer Frank Dolson pointed out, this was a great mistake. When the fans get on Pete Rose, Dolson said, "he plays even better." Rose told him, "I get ticked off. I get working." And the hits that rang off Rose's bat for the rest of the games showed the fans what a mistake they had made. The fans at Wrigley Field could have told them.[12]

But 1971 was to be a season of frustration for the Cincinnati ballclub, for its fans, and even for Pete Rose. Sparky Anderson struggled with his pitching all year, with sore arms and sore heads. By late May, Wayne Simpson had been farmed out to Indianapolis and Anderson was lamenting, "Our bullpen is shot, and it's only May." Bench had a miserable season, Perez had a so-so year, and Tolan missed the entire campaign. The team muddled along in fifth place for most of the season, and only a strong September enabled it to tie Houston for fourth place, with a record of 79–83, eleven games behind the division-winning San Francisco Giants. It scored 194 fewer runs than it had in 1970. The club's home attendance, despite the initial boost provided by the 1970 pennant, was off more than 300,000 from the year before, even with the first full year in the new ballpark. It was a very disappointing season for Cincinnati.[13]

For Pete Rose, too, it was less than a sensational year. He had some good things to talk about—a .400 average for the month of July, nine-game hitting streaks in August and September, a 4-for-4 game against the Dodgers in September—and he wound up the season with a .304 average. But he fell eight hits short of his annual goal of 200 hits, and there were some bad moments along the way. On June 15, Pete was thrown out of a game for arguing a called third strike by umpire John Kibler, the third ejection of Rose's career.

Rose also had a falling-out with Johnny Bench. The big catcher's MVP season in 1970 had been a challenge to Pete, who liked to think of himself as *the* Cincinnati Red, but he could not be really unhappy about something that helped the team win. The next year, though, they had a run-in over a fan newsletter called *Pete Rose's Reds Alert*, a sheet put out by a man named Bill Matthews, who paid Rose to allow his name to be used. That was all well and good, until Matthews started ripping some of the Reds players. "A lot of players," Bench said, "had hard feelings," and he went to management about it. "He and I went at it one day before a game," Bench said, and "Pete was pretty burned up about it and he went for a long time without saying a word to me." The front office told Rose his newsletter would no longer be tolerated, while Rose and Bench worked together in the dugout and clubhouse without speaking to one another.[14]

Pete also groused about scheduling twilight games starting at 5:30 or 6 P.M. "You just can't see the ball good in the twilight," he complained. "So, pretty soon you find yourself lunging at pitches. It's a habit, once formed, that's hard to break." He claimed that batting in the twilight was the quickest way to fall into a hitting slump.[15]

Twilight may not have been Rose's only problem. In the first week of September he went to see an eye doctor in San Diego and was told he had a virus in his left eye. "The eye had been watering a lot," Rose said. "That's why I requested the examination."[16]

On June 3, the Reds were held hitless by the Cubs' southpaw Ken Holtzman. They were subjected to the same indignity three weeks later by righthander Rick Wise of the Phillies, who added to their discomfiture by belting two home runs of his own in the game. Rose almost beat out a ball to deep short in the first inning, before anyone was thinking no-hitter, but a great play by Larry Bowa nipped him at first. Later, Rose's line drive to center fielder Willie Montanez was the hardest ball any Red hit. Ironically, Rose came to bat again with two outs in the ninth inning, when everyone was aware of the situation. Phillies catcher Tim McCarver groaned, "Oh no! Of all the guys to come up here, it has to be you in this situation." Rose worked the count to 3 and 2, then hit a fast ball on the outside corner on a line to third baseman John Vukovich, who caught it to clinch the no-hitter.[17]

Early in September, the club announced that Sparky Anderson would return as manager in 1972, despite the sour results in 1971. When the season ended, Bob Howsam informed Rose that there was to be no basketball during the off-season. Rose was less than enthusiastic about Howsam's proposed exercise program. "Some guys can keep in shape by exercising and running around a gym track," he said. "I have to do something that's competitive. You do that and you're always thinking about winning. And that's a spirit a guy should develop."[18]

Neither Bob Howsam nor Sparky Anderson ever worried about Pete Rose's dedication to winning. They were concerned about putting together a team that would work with him to win. On November 29, Howsam made a huge trade with the Houston Astros, sending Lee May, Tommy Helms, and Jimmy Stewart to Texas in exchange for infielders Joe Morgan and Dennis Menke, outfielder Cesar Geronimo, right-handed pitcher Jack Billingham, and utility man Ed Armbrister. The deal was unpopular in Cincinnati, where the fans were sorry to see favorites like May and Helms depart. Outfielder Hal McRae expressed a common feeling when he said, "The trade with Houston is going to hurt the morale of the team, unless the players we received are the same type we gave up."[19]

First returns on the big trade with Houston were favorable. Joe Morgan came to the Reds' camp with a reputation of being moody and hard to handle, a rap which he blamed on his Astros' manager, Harry Walker. When first Perez and then Rose started needling him, Morgan began to feel appreciated. Anderson made sure that Morgan was given a locker next to Rose's. Joe and Pete became a pair that Bench called "incredible. They like to get on each other like no two ballplayers I've ever seen." Morgan, he said, "likes to jab all the time . . . always jab, jab, jab at Pete. . . . They don't really argue, and they're not really malicious, but neither of them will let up. Like an all-day Ping-Pong match."[20]

Morgan recognized how they would fit together. "Pete will be getting on base about 300 times counting hits and walks," the left-handed hitter told a reporter. "And with the first baseman holding Pete on the bag, that should give me about 300 shots at a big gap on the right side of the infield."[21]

The Reds worked hard at Tampa, preparing for the season, getting the Big Red Machine back into running order, reading that the baseball writers had picked them for third place—then the players went on strike. The walkout, centered on player resentment of the restrictive reserve clause, lasted for two weeks, and the season did not open until April 15.

Rose and pitcher Gary Nolan flew back to Tampa on April 9, so they could continue to stay in shape working out in the Florida sunshine. Pete was being switched from right field to left for the 1972 season, and he would not risk coming into the campaign in anything less than tip-top condition. Rose calculated that he lost about $5,000 salary because of the walkout, which cost the club eight games.

The Reds, and Rose, started the season slowly, and by mid-May they were only at 12–13, in third place. During a Cincinnati luncheon appearance, Rose even took some verbal potshots at Sparky Anderson, questioning some of his platooning practices, most likely simply marking the depth of Pete's frustration to that point. Soon though, the Reds started winning, and Rose's batting average started rising. They swept four games from the Astros in Houston at the end of May, and by June 5, their record was 27–18, just a half game behind the Dodgers. A week later Cincinnati led by a full game.

Earl Lawson wrote in the *Sporting News* in mid-June, "Pete Rose is usually a slow starter. This season he's off to a slower than usual start and figures to have trouble attaining his perennial twin goals—a .300 average and 200 hits." Pete thought he would have something to say about that later on, even though he was hitting just .262 at the time.[22]

When the Astros came to Cincinnati on June 22, they were a half game behind the Reds, and observers were still weighing the balances on their big trade. Houston took the first game, 9–5, to move into first place, only to be bumped out of it the next day, as Ross Grimsley pitched a beauty for the Reds, winning 7–1. When the two clubs split the next two games, the Reds were still in first, although no one realized at the time that they would hold that spot for the rest of the season. Sparky Anderson said, "It's still early," but he knew he had a high-quality team.[23]

In early July, Rose, on fire at the plate, had a nine-game hitting streak, capping a month-long stretch in which he hit near .350. The Reds, with Clay Carroll and Tom Hall pitching fine relief, had moved six games ahead of Houston. Bench was having another great year, Joe Morgan was hitting as he never had before, and Rose had his average up in the .280 range.

In late August, Anderson discovered that he had an ulcer, an occupational hazard for a big league manager, but his club was doing its best to soothe him. Gary Nolan was getting stronger and healthier, and Jack Billingham and Don Gullett were also coming around from physical problems. By August 31, Rose was batting .303, with 157 hits. In mid-September, with his team comfortably in first place, Anderson was asked who should be MVP in the National League. Sparky said, "I'd say three guys on the club would rate serious consideration," naming Morgan, Bench, and Rose. Asked if Rose would make his twin goals, a .300 average and 200 hits, Anderson replied, "I'm betting he'll make it. It's like [coach] Alex Grammas said. He has never seen a player with more determination than Rose."[24]

The Reds clinched their division on September 22 with a victory, fittingly, in the Houston Astrodome. They would finish ten and one-half games ahead of the Astros, with a mark of 95–59. Home attendance, even with five dates lost to the strike, rose by 110,000 fans. Rose ended the year at .307 but went hitless his last two games, to finish with 198 hits, still good enough to lead the league. He knew that, with the eight games lost to the strike, he would have gone easily over two hundred. Rose's eleven triples finished second to Larry Bowa of the Phillies, so it was a good year overall, especially with the team's success.

Cincinnati faced the Pirates again in the National League playoff—two teams with good hitting, not quite so good pitching, playing in nearly identical ballparks. Rose looked forward to it, he told Philadelphia writer Ray Kelly: "I like to think I'm at my best when the money's on the line, and this is my kind of park—with lots of room for a line drive hitter."[25]

In the opener at Pittsburgh, Joe Morgan hit a home run in the first inning, but that was it for the Reds. The Pirates won, 5–1, as Steve Blass outpitched Gullett. The Pirates left only one runner on base, while the Reds stranded eleven. Rose was 2 for 5 but could score no runs. In the second game, Rose led off against Bob Moose with a first-inning single, touching off a four-run inning that was enough to win. Billingham and Tom Hall kept the Buccos in check for a series-evening 5–3 win.

Game 3, now in Cincinnati, went to the Pirates, 3–2, coming from behind. Rose, who had three hits, two of them doubles, in four at-bats, said, "I hate to lose. And I hate it even more when we lose after leading for six innings." The Reds were up against a wall in the best three-out-of-five series, but Ross Grimsley pulled them even again with a two-hitter, winning 7–1, as Pete Rose went 2 for 4.[26]

In the deciding fifth game, with Gullett starting against Blass, the Pirates led, 3–2, going into the bottom of the ninth. Bench led off against Pittsburgh's Dave Giusti, went to 1-and-2, then hit a palmball over the right-field wall to tie the score. After Tony Perez and Dennis Menke got hits and pinch-runner George Foster advanced to third on a fly ball, Pirates' reliever Bob Moose went to 1 and 1 on McRae before bouncing a slider that got past the catcher, allowing the winning run to score. Winning the pennant on a wild pitch may not have been how Sparky Anderson planned it, but no one offered to give that run back. The Reds were National League champions and would face Charles O. Finley's Oakland Athletics in the World Series.

The A's were accorded little chance against the Big Red Machine, but the baseball world was intrigued with the matchup, old-line Cincinnati versus Johnny-come-lately Oakland, the clean-shaven Reds against the hairy Athletics, who had been challenged by their iconoclastic owner to grow mustaches, goatees, and beards. The Cincinnati uniforms were classic white at home and gray on the road, and the A's wore wild combinations of green, yellow, and white. But while the country was well acquainted with the Reds' stars, it had yet to discover Catfish Hunter, Reggie Jackson, Joe Rudi, Sal Bando, Rollie Fingers, and the rest of Dick Williams' team, though Jackson, on crutches with a pulled hamstring, would miss the Series.

A crowd of 52,918 packed Riverfront Stadium for Game 1 of the Series, only to see Oakland's Ken Holtzman outpitch Nolan for a 3–2 win. Unsung catcher Gene Tenace belted two homers for the A's. With two out in the ninth, McRae at third base represented the tying run, and Rose tried to surprise the A's with a bunt to bring him in. "I was hoping for a curve that I could bunt," Rose said later, but reliever Vida Blue fed him fastballs. After one foul bunt, Rose grounded out to end the game.[27]

Rose, 0 for 4 in the opener, was 1 for 4 in the second game, as Catfish Hunter and Fingers beat Grimsley, 2–1, with the help of a spectacular catch by Joe Rudi in the ninth inning. An unhappy Rose told the press that Hunter was not in the same class as Tom Seaver or Bob Gibson: "He's a good pitcher, but hell, I'm not gonna make him out to be a super pitcher because he's not." Hunter commented that "I think the Reds underestimated my fast ball."[28]

Moving to the West Coast, the Series was interrupted by a torrential downpour in the Bay Area that rained out Game 3, leaving the field a quagmire. Rose told the press, "the rainout has to affect Oakland more than us. They had the momentum." Momentum in baseball, of course, is only as effective as the next starting pitcher, and Cincinnati's Jack Billingham, with ninth inning help from Clay Carroll, outpitched Johnny Lee "Blue Moon" Odom to win Game 3 for the Reds, 1–0. Pete Rose, greeted by the Oakland fans with a barrage of fruit, vegetables, and raw eggs, apparently for his comment about Hunter, was 0 for 3 with a walk and a stolen base.[29]

In the fourth game, Oakland rallied with two in the ninth against Carroll to win, 3–2. Tenace hit his third home run of the Series, but Rose went 0 for 4, leaving his Series average standing at .133. In Game 5, though, Pete hit Hunter's first pitch of the game out of the park, then went 3 for 5 as the Reds stayed alive with a 5–4 victory. Tenace hit his fourth home run, but it was the Reds' day, with Rose driving in the deciding run. Former Phillies manager Frank Lucchesi, covering the Series for a Philadelphia paper, raved about Rose, saying, "I'd pay four bucks to see that guy play till I ran out of money." Rose, he wrote, "was super. A home run, a game-winning base hit, a great catch in the outfield to rob Bert Campaneris. And he has magnetic qualities that really jack up the Reds and keep the other team on edge."[30]

The victory gave the Reds good things to think about as they flew back to Cincinnati, still trailing three games to two. Rose said, "I know we can take these guys. Don't forget, this is the kind of situation we like best—coming from behind."[31]

In the sixth game, the Reds got strong pitching from Nolan and the bullpen to win 8–1, and send the Series to a seventh game. Rose was 0 for 3 with two walks. With everything on the line, Anderson sent Billingham to the mound against Blue Moon Odom. The A's scored in the first when Tolan misplayed Angel Mangual's liner into a triple and Tenace singled him home. The Reds tied it in the fifth, but Oakland scored two in the sixth against reliever Pedro Borbon. In the eighth, Rose led off with a single, went to third on Morgan's double, then watched as Dick Williams ordered Bench walked, even though he represented the winning run. A sacrifice fly by Perez brought Rose in, but Menke flied out to end the inning.

With two out in the ninth, pinch-hitter Darrell Chaney was hit by a pitch. With Rose coming up, Williams came out to lift Rollie Fingers, until catcher Dave Duncan said, "Don't take him out, he's got great stuff." So Fingers stayed in and got Rose to fly out to left to end the game and the Series.[32]

Back home in Cincinnati, a few weeks later, discussing the possibility of the Reds making a major trade over the winter, perhaps for a third baseman, Rose was startled to be asked if he ever thought he might be traded. "Well," he said after some hesitation, "I honestly can say I hope I'm never traded." Asked again about that possibility, he said, "If I ever should be, you'll never hear me say I'm going to quit the game. That's not my makeup. I would, though, do everything I could to prove to the Reds that they made one helluva mistake if they should trade me."[33]

Sparky Anderson, sunning himself on Waikiki Beach in Hawaii a few days later, offered the thought that Rose would only be traded over his vigorous objection. "Rose is a manager's player," Anderson remarked. "In his way, he's a great leader and he doesn't know it. When spring training starts, he just puts on his uniform and goes."[34]

NOTES

1. Reston, *Collision at Home Plate: The Lives of Pete Rose and Bart Giamatti*, 117.

2. Sokolove, *Hustle: The Myth, Life, and Lies of Pete Rose*, 183.

3. *Sporting News*, December 5, 1970; Bench and Brashler, *Catch You Later: The Autobiography of Johnny Bench*, 97.

4. *Cincinnati Enquirer*, December 10, 1970; Rose and Kahn, *Pete Rose: My Story*, 44.

5. Rose and Kahn, *Pete Rose: My Story*, 45, 44. Emphasis in original.

6. Earl Lawson, "Basketball Touchy Subject to N.L. Champ Reds," *Sporting News*, November 28, 1970, 28.

7. Earl Lawson, *Sporting News*, November 21, 1970.

8. Ibid.

9. Earl Lawson, "Pete's Repeater Pistol Off to Red-Hot Start," *Sporting News*, April 3, 1971.

10. *Sporting News*, March 6, 1971. Bench signed for something in the range of $85,000 to $90,000. Howsam knew it was just a matter of time before Bench reached the salary stratosphere.

11. *Cincinnati Enquirer*, March 15, 1971.

12. Frank Dolson, "Lesson for Fans: Never Boo Rose," *Philadelphia Inquirer*, May 25, 1971.

13. Ibid.

14. Bench and Brashler, *Catch You Later: The Autobiography of Johnny Bench*, 98.

15. Earl Lawson, "Rose Always Loses His Batting Bloom at Twilight," *Sporting News*, August 7, 1971, 10.

16. Earl Lawson, "Bench Still Rates Super Tag, Despite .240 Bat Mark," *Sporting News*, September 25, 1971.

17. *Sporting News*, July 3, 1971.

18. Earl Lawson, *Sporting News*, November 6, 1971.

19. *Sporting News*, February 5, 1972.

20. Bench and Brashler, *Catch You Later: The Autobiography of Johnny Bench*, 86.

21. *Sporting News*, March 25, 1972.

22. Earl Lawson, *Sporting News*, June 24, 1972.

23. *Sporting News*, July 8, 1972.

24. *Sporting News*, September 30, 1972.

25. Ray Kelly, "Reds' Rose Likes Bucs' Roomy Park," (Philadelphia) *Evening Bulletin*, October 7, 1972, 11.

26. *Sporting News*, October 28, 1972.

27. Ibid.

28. Ibid.

29. *Sporting News*, November 4, 1972; Erardi, *Pete Rose*, 31.

30. Frank Lucchesi, "As Skipper Saw It, Pete Rose to Occasion," (Philadelphia) *Evening Bulletin*, October 21, 1972.

31. Ibid.

32. Ibid.

33. Earl Lawson, "'If I'm Ever Traded I Won't Quit'—Says Rose," *Sporting News*, December 9, 1972.

34. Earl Lawson, "Sparky Nixes Hair Tint . . . Players Should Be Sorry," *Sporting News*, December 16, 1972, 51.

CREAM OF THE CROP

Early in 1973, the ownership situation for the Cincinnati National League franchise was clarified, when Louis Nippert purchased the majority control of the club. Nippert, an original member of the DeWitt group that bought the team in 1966, had been a minority shareholder since then. Now he had full control. He announced that Francis Dale would continue as club president, and he gave Bob Howsam a new three-year contract as general manager. Howsam, with his aide Chief Bender, had the chore of handling the annual salary hassle with Pete Rose.

Rose asked for a salary of $120,000. Howsam balked at this figure, and the usual stalemate set in. One theory for the club's annual refusal to accommodate its most consistent and reliable player was that this was Howsam's payback for the winter basketball games. Howsam was strongly opposed to his players engaging in competitive basketball over the offseason, and Rose was the organizer and driving force behind the Reds' basketball team. Never far from management's consciousness was the entire season missed by Bobby Tolan because of basketball.

Rose finally signed his contract on March 6, but there was no increase in his admiration of the Reds' front office. Bench, having won in 1972 his second MVP award in three years, had passed Pete in salary, but Rose denied that his ego demanded that he had to be the highest paid player on the club. "What Bench makes doesn't concern me," he said, and then headed off to go to work.[1]

The defending National League champions were confident as they headed into a new campaign. Bench had undergone off-season surgery for a spot on his lung, but the spot had been harmless and the Reds' great catcher was back in form. Howsam said the 1973 squad was the best Reds team that he had put together. A rookie outfielder named Ken Griffey took the spring training camp by storm, as a kid named Rose had done ten years earlier. Joe Morgan told a reporter, "The guys on this club are the closest bunch a guy ever could play with." The Big Red Machine was ready to roll.[2]

The Reds got off to a good start but still trailed the San Francisco Giants by three and one-half games on May 7. Bench and Tolan were not hitting well, but Morgan, Perez, and Concepcion were, and Pete Rose, usually a slow starter, was well over .300. June was not a good month for Anderson's team, but it won ten out of eleven in early July.

Rose continued to dazzle, at the plate and in the field. Coach Alex Grammas said, "If Pete gave the Reds any more than he does now, we'd have to take blood from him." The team's first win of the season, against the Giants on April 8, was saved when Rose took a ball off the left-field fence and threw Dave Kingman out at second base to end the game. Charlie Fox, the Giants skipper, gaped in admiration and said, "There are some guys in this game who always make the great play when it's necessary and Rose is one of them."[3]

Larry Bowa, the Phillies shortstop, was another who talked about Rose. "Take Pete," Bowa said. "He can hit righthanded and lefthanded. And, like he told me when we were in Cincinnati a while back, he could hit standing on his head if he had to." Bowa had another story to tell, from his rookie year of 1970, when things were going badly for him and Rose took the trouble to come over and give him a pep talk. "Look, kid," Rose told him then, "anyone can quit when the going gets tough. It's the good ones who stay around and battle their tails off."[4]

On May 22, after Rose raised his average to .322 with three hits against Houston, Joe Morgan commented to a reporter, "Pete's swinging the bat super now. . . . Balls are jumping off his bat." The fans noticed: they voted Rose first among outfielders for the National League All Star team, even though, curiously, the simultaneous players poll ranked him only ninth.[5]

At the All Star break, the Reds trailed the Dodgers in the National League West by five and one-half games. Things looked bleak. Two days before the break, shortstop Dave Concepcion fractured his ankle. Rose was hitting .324, but Tolan's average was a weak .202 and Bench was hitting only .245. New York writer Dick Young commented, "Veteran Cincy players are convinced Bob Howsam is recycling the Reds and that all except Johnny Bench will be marketable next winter. Anybody want a full-blooming Rose?"[6]

Rose was 0 for 3 but scored a run in the All Star game, won by the Nationals, 7–1, at Kansas City. He always enjoyed the camaraderie with his fellow luminaries at the midsummer get-together, and winning the game made it even more worthwhile. Pete Rose never liked to lose, even in a game many felt was just a glorified exhibition.

When the pennant chase resumed, Rose stepped up his hitting, while the Reds fell farther behind the Dodgers. Going into August, Pete had 146 base hits, and Anderson said he thought Rose would get to his cherished 200 total. By August 9, Rose was hitting .342, with 164 hits, and the Reds picked up the pace somewhat.

A few days later, National League president Chub Feeney announced that Rose had been fined $25 for tossing a ball to a fan in the stands, an infraction which would seem ludicrous to a player in 2004. This was one of four times in 1973 that Rose was assessed this particular fine. Feeney said he was advised of the violation by Reds' executive Dick Wagner, a name significant in Rose's future.[7]

As August ended, Cincinnati was still four games behind LA, although Rose was quoted as saying, "The more you look at the Dodgers, the less you think of them." Rose was batting .345 at this point, with 193 hits. "Nobody will catch him," predicted Anderson, ". . . because there isn't another player in the league who grinds every day the way Pete does." Impressively, in 127 games leading off in the first inning, Pete was 37 for 111, along with ten walks and four times reaching base on an error; he had led off the game by getting on base more than 40 percent of the time.[8]

September was another story for Sparky Anderson and his men. They started the month with a seven-game winning streak, which put them in first place, two games up on the Dodgers. Then they just kept applying more pressure. By the 17th the Reds were six and one-half games ahead, and they clinched the division on September 24 with a 2–1 triumph over San Diego, finishing the season with a record of 99–63. For the first time in franchise history, they drew over two million customers at home.

When Rose got his 220th hit of the season on September 17, he broke Cy Seymour's Cincinnati record from 1905, the oldest record the club had. Pete commented, "I'd like to own every Cincinnati record. I mean, I live here. I grew up here. My children are going to live here." He then said the next record in his sights—Frankie Frisch's 223 hits by a switch hitter in 1923—was very important to him.[9]

The Reds celebrated their division crown with the customary champagne, but Anderson was glad to see the festivities a little subdued. "They know the job isn't done yet," Sparky said, "that there are still the playoff and World Series."[10]

Pete Rose won the batting title with a .338 mark, eighteen points ahead of runner-up Cesar Cedeno of Houston. He had 230 hits for the year, thirty more than anyone else, seven more than Frisch's switch-hitting record. In the other category that was most dear to Pete, he was third in the league in runs scored with 115. It was a most productive season for the Reds' captain.

In the National League East, the New York Mets, under manager Yogi Berra, managed to win the division with a startling mark of 82–79, the only Eastern team to go over .500. They had the lowest percentage ever to win a championship in the majors. Cincinnati was heavily favored in the National League playoffs, but the rules said the games had to be played nevertheless. Rose told the press, "Everyone thinks we should be worried about the Mets' pitching. Do you think they aren't worried a little bit about ours?"[11]

The first game was played at Cincinnati, starting at four P.M. to accommodate television. Not surprisingly, in the October twilight, the two excellent starting pitchers, Jack Billingham and New York's Tom Seaver, were hard to hit. The Mets got one run in the second when Seaver himself doubled, but it was still 1–0 when Rose came to bat in the eighth. Batting left-handed, Pete caught hold of a high fastball and hit it over the fence in right center field. When Bench took the tired Seaver deep in the ninth inning, the Reds had a walkoff 2–1 victory, despite Seaver's thirteen strikeouts.

In Game 2, the Mets' Jon Matlack pitched a beautiful two-hitter, mostly with breaking balls, and New York won 5–0. The two teams headed east with the best-of-five series all tied up. Rose, who had just the home run to show for the two games, said, "We're seeing the ball, but we're also seeing real good pitching."[12]

The third game of the series was the one that rocked Shea Stadium. The Mets pounded Ross Grimsley early and, with two home runs by Rusty Staub, boasted a 9–2 lead after four innings. Their fans—raucous and rowdy to begin with, energized by a division title they never expected—were riding high when Rose singled in the fifth inning with one out. Morgan followed with a ground ball to John Milner at first. Milner fired it to shortstop Bud Harrelson for one out, and Harrelson threw back to first for a double play to retire the side.

Rose, though, went high and late into Harrelson at second base and, according to the Mets shortstop, threw an elbow at him. Harrelson had been told by Morgan early in the series that Rose was going to get him at second because Rose thought Bud had demeaned the Reds' hitters, so Harrelson assumed Rose's crash into him was intentional. He shouted an obscenity at Rose, and then Rose picked him up and threw him to the ground. Rose, forty-two pounds heavier, landed on Harrelson. Wayne Garrett, the New York third baseman, ran over and began hitting Rose from behind. A general brawl broke loose, with both dugouts and bullpens emptying, "a free-for-all of sprawling immensity," as Arthur Daley of the *New York Times* put it. Bench pulled Rose up and dragged him out of the scrum; Mets pitcher Harry Parker tried to get at Rose but backed off when he saw Bench.[13]

Cincinnati reliever Pedro Borbon engaged in his own private battle beyond second base with Mets pitcher Buzz Capra, and when that was broken up Borbon found he had a Mets cap on his head. He tore it off, bit a hole in it, and spit out the swatch in his mouth. The umpires were finally able to separate all the combatants, and the Reds took the field for the bottom of the fifth. The fight was over, at least on the field.

The spectators still had their blood up. When Rose took his position in left-field, the fans in the left field stands started throwing anything they could find at him: garbage, beer cans, batteries, cups, programs, fruit, whatever. Rose picked up some of the trash and threw it back toward the fence, which further infuriated the spectators. When an empty whisky bottle whizzed past his head as he was catching a fly ball, Rose called time and started toward the dugout. Anderson came out to meet him, and Rose said, "Spark, they just threw a whisky bottle out." Anderson answered, "That's enough for us today. Let's go," and beckoned his players to leave the field. Umpire Chris Pelekoudas said, "We'll get this straightened out," and Anderson replied, "Let me know when you do." The Reds retreated to the clubhouse.[14]

National League president Chub Feeney and the umpiring crew felt the best way to bring the chaotic situation under control was to have manager Berra and Willie Mays, the future Hall-of-Famer who was then a back-up Mets outfielder, go out to left field and talk to the fans, to explain that the Mets' apparent one-sided victory was in danger of being forfeited. Seaver, Staub, and Cleon Jones joined the peace delegation, and eventually, after about twenty minutes, an uneasy truce was established that permitted the completion of the game with no further incidents, also thanks to New York policemen that were stationed in the left-field stands. After the 9–2 Mets win, the Reds' team bus required a police escort to get out of Shea Stadium.

Then, of course, the postmortems began. Sportswriter Jack Lang wrote that "it appeared that it was sheer frustration that caused Rose to go into Harrelson hard at second base," while Rose defended his actions: "I'll play the same way tomorrow. My job is to break up two. . . . I was trying to knock him into left field to be honest with you. . . . If I was a dirty player, I could have leveled him. The way I was brought up, if my dad was living, he'd kick my tail for not getting one in." Harrelson said, "I'm tired of being pushed around down there," and said Rose gave him the elbow. In the meantime, newspapers around the country carried the wire service photo of Rose on top of the frail Harrelson.[15]

The scrap was ironic in a way because Harrelson admired Pete Rose; he remembered Rose taking him aside seven years earlier, when the Reds star advised the Mets rookie to use a smaller glove playing the infield. Later, Harrelson described Rose: "Beneath the hustle and the perfection, there's a human being; beneath the great one, a simpler one who cares." He said they had had "a run-in. He couldn't handle it; I couldn't handle it."[16]

Rose, warned to stay out of sight, remained prudently in his hotel room that night. Even so, in a further insult, his room service steak was deliberately burned. The next day Shea Stadium was covered with bedsheets and cardboard signs, all with messages about the essential rottenness of Pete Rose; the fans began their anti-Rose chants well before the game started. M. Donald Grant, the Mets' owner, thought it would be a good idea to have Rose and Harrelson shake hands at home plate before the game. Harrelson agreed, reluctantly, but Rose refused, saying he was not into apologizing.

The game itself, a crucial one for the Reds, down 2–1 in the series, went into extra innings, tied 1–1. Every breath Rose took drew down more boos upon him, but he picked up two singles along the way. "Pete thrives on a fight," Bench said. "Make him mad, go ahead." Rose came to bat again with one out in the twelfth inning against Harry Parker, the Mets hurler who had tried to get him in the melee the day before. After going to two and two, Parker came in with a high fastball, and Rose crushed it. As one reporter put it, "The ball went out toward the right-field fence on a line and in a hurry and 50,768 people in Shea Stadium choked on their boos." As the ball sailed over, Pete Rose circled the bases, his right arm thrust defiantly in the air. Take that, New York! The Reds won, 2–1, tying the playoff and setting up a deciding game the next day.[17]

Unfortunately for Cincinnati, Jack Billingham was not sharp for that last game, while Tom Seaver was. The Mets got two in the first, the Reds answered with one run in the third, and then Rose doubled and scored a tying run in the fifth. The Mets got to Billingham, Gullett, and Carroll in the bottom of the fifth for four runs, and they added another in the sixth inning. Seaver kept the visitors off balance, while the Shea Stadium crowd of 50,323 became more and more unruly, as victory loomed. Play was halted three times for umpires and policemen to chase fans off the field. When Rose ran down a sixth-inning line drive into the left-field corner, a fan poured beer on him from the stands. In the ninth, with the smell of triumph in their nostrils, the fans surged into the box seats next to the dugout where Reds' executives and their wives were sitting. After the wife of the team physician was trampled and injured, Chief Bender ran out on the field and asked the umpires to stop the game while he led the Cincinnati delegation to safety.

With one out in the ninth, Rose drew a walk, and reliever Tug McGraw came in to get the last two outs. With the developing riot, the Reds players took up bats to make sure that Rose could get off the field when the game ended. When the final out was made, Rose dashed for the dugout as the fans poured onto the field. He knocked a few of them over as he made his way in, while the Cincinnati players used their bats to keep the fans out of the dugout. When the visitors in the gray uniforms were no longer available targets, the mob contented itself with trashing the field, stealing the bases, home plate, and the pitching rubber, even tearing out three sections of the outfield fence, oblivious to the fact that Shea would soon have to host the World Series. Sparky Anderson said, "I don't believe this can happen," while an editorial in the *Sporting News* excoriated the "hordes of vandals who swarmed out of the stands and engulfed the field." The whole affair was a disgrace to the city of New York as well as to the Mets' complacent management, but for the Cincinnati Reds, their season was still over. Once more, as in 1970 and 1972, a Reds team which may have been the best in baseball came up short.[18]

In November, Pete Rose received a letter from Chub Feeney, advising him that the National League had fined him and Bud Harrelson $250 each for their fight. Rose, as always, protested his innocence, wondering how a peacemaker like him could be punished. Johnny Bench had another take on Rose and the playoff fight. "As it turned out, his career really took off after that ruckus," Bench wrote. "The Harrelson thing made him—Big Pete, Little Bud, and the New York media blew it all across the country. . . . That was pure head-against-head stuff, with the crowd all over him, and still he came back."[19]

A few weeks later, Pete Rose got more headlines, when the Baseball Writers Association of America voted him the Most Valuable Player in the National League for 1973. It was not a landslide, but Rose edged out Pittsburgh's Willie Stargell by twenty-four points, getting twelve of the twenty-four writers' first-place votes. It was a ringing affirmation of Pete Rose's career, the more than 2,000 hits he had piled up, the way he played the game, and the super season he had put together in 1973.

Rose thanked the writers but said, "I've won three batting titles, two pennants, Gold Gloves and now this, the MVP award, but I haven't really won anything. I've never played on a world championship team and that is my goal." He added, "I wanted to get in the World Series so bad last year that I almost started World War III."[20]

There were, obviously, great hopes for the 1974 Reds over the winter, as well as much celebration of Pete Rose for the season just past. Gordy Coleman, the former first baseman who now headed the Reds' speakers bureau, said of Pete, "He's No. 14 on the scoreboard and No. 1 in the hearts of the fans." Harold "Pee Wee" Reese, the old Dodger shortstop, representing Hillerich and Bradsby, makers of Louisville Slugger bats, presented Rose with his third silver bat at the annual Ballplayers of Yesterday banquet.[21]

In one after-dinner speech, Rose said the Reds had "the nucleus of a dynasty," and Sparky Anderson said, "If we don't win this year, there's something wrong some place." Then, he added, realistically, "And, saying this, I know I'm placing my head right under the guillotine." The *Sporting News*, the Las Vegas bookies, and the baseball writers all picked the Reds to win.[22]

The Reds made one major trade for 1974, sending outfielder Bobby Tolan to San Diego for Clay Kirby, a pitcher with an 8–18 record in 1973. Trading Tolan was no surprise. The outfielder had been suspended at the end of the season and missed the playoffs because of his defiance of Anderson and Howsam in growing a beard. The Cincinnati club had its values, whatever one thought of them, and those who did not abide by them were expendable.

Pete Rose had little difficulty coming to terms with the Reds on a contract for $155,000 after his big year, "biggest raise I've ever gotten," he said. Then it became a matter of earning his money. In spring training, Rose injured his shin with a foul ball; when hemorrhaging, swelling, and an infection developed, he had to be scratched from the line-up. Troubled by the leg, he hit only .200 in spring training. "Just think," he proclaimed, "if I'd been a rookie this spring, I wouldn't have made the club."[23]

When the season started, Pete Rose played as if it were the previous October all over again. On Opening Day, against the Braves, he doubled with two out in the ninth to score George Foster with the tying run. His third hit of the game was a double in the eleventh inning. When Buzz Capra (no longer with the Mets) threw a pitch that bounced off the catcher's shinguard and rolled all the way to the Braves' dugout, Rose scored from second to win the game. By April 25, Pete's batting average was .353.

He then hit a dreadful slump and by May 22 was hitting only .268. He got it up a few points, but he could not seem to move that average much above .280. When he learned that he was one of the top vote-getters in the fan balloting for the All Star Game, Rose said that he would really be embarrassed if he was not hitting .300 when the game was played in Pittsburgh on July 23. He was voted to the team, batting .282 at the All-Star break.

Dick Young, the *New York Daily News* columnist, wrote, "Making a lot of money has taken the fun out of baseball for Pete Rose. Without knowing it, that's what he is saying." It happens all the time, Young said. "You make the big leagues. You have realized a dream. . . . Then, one day, you are making more money than you ever dreamed of. Suddenly, that means more to you than playing ball. . . . That is when, that is why, the fun goes out of it for the Pete Roses."[24]

It was amazing that Dick Young could see all this from his perch in New York City—just because Pete Rose was hitting only .280. But it was true that the money was coming to mean more and more to Rose. Johnny Bench would later describe Pete as "very money conscious." Rose even signed up to do a cigar commercial, although he did not smoke. Asked what that would do to his image, Rose responded, "I don't care about my image, not when the ad pays enough to put my boy through college."25

Pete's image had changed some from earlier in his career; he was often now a target for boisterous fans. In April, Rose was booed every time he came up at Candlestick Park in San Francisco, and three golf balls were thrown at him. In May, fans in the left field seats at Dodger Stadium hurled ice, chunks of wood, paper cups, and obscenities at Rose. In early June, when the Reds made their first visit to Shea Stadium since the 1973 playoffs, the Mets beefed up their security forces in the left-field stands. Rose said, "Nothing was thrown at me and I didn't hear one nasty word. They called me a hot dog and a bum, but I hear that every place."26

There were many, nevertheless, who would take issue with Dick Young and those obnoxious fans. Frank Dolson of the *Philadelphia Inquirer* wrote, "It's fun to watch the man play baseball. Fun to see one of the top-salaried players in the sport . . . charge through spring training of '74 with the enthusiasm of a youngster trying to make the team." Rose told him, "I think I get more out of my ability than anybody." In a world filled with athletes never quite living up to their potentials, Dolson said, "Pete Rose has squeezed out every ounce of God-given ability, including several ounces nobody suspected he had." Rose had proven "that a singles hitter could become a wealthy man."27

The Reds played pretty good ball through the first half of the season, but the Dodgers played a good bit better. At the beginning of July, Los Angeles came into Riverfront Stadium and took three out of four to take a lead over the Reds of nine and one-half games. The Reds knocked it back down to three and a half by the end of the month and two and a half by the end of August, but they were unable to get much closer. On September 14, the Reds beat the Dodgers twice to move within a game and a half, but the next day Jimmy Wynn hit a grand slam as Los Angeles won 7–1 to put the lead back at two and one-half games. And there it stayed.

On October 1, Walter Alston's Dodgers clinched the Western division when Cincinnati lost in Atlanta, and their final margin over the Reds was four games. There would be no postseason for the Cincinnati Reds in 1974. Pete Rose wound up the year hitting .284, ending a run of nine years of .300 or better averages. His hit total dropped to 185, although he managed to lead the National League in doubles and runs scored.

All in all, 1974 was a very disappointing season in the Queen City. At season's end, Sparky Anderson, who escaped the guillotine he had conjured up for himself, told Pete Rose to report for spring training at 190 pounds. Shortly before the end of the season, Rose had purchased a luxurious new home in the Walnut Hills section of Cincinnati, previously belonging to the late William Zimmer, former president of Cincinnati Gas and Electric Company, who had been one of the Reds' owners. In his new digs, Pete immediately went on a diet. Anderson had no doubt, though, that Pete would hit .300 in 1975. "Pride, that's why," he said. "All the great players have it."[28]

NOTES

1. *Sporting News*, March 17, 1973.

2. *Sporting News*, March 24, 1973.

3. Earl Lawson, "Reds' Rose Still Has Rifle Arm, Foes Discover," *Sporting News*, April 28, 1973. Rose said, characteristically, "I guess the players in the league don't read fielding statistics. They don't seem to know that I tied for the league lead in assists with 15 last year."

4. Earl Lawson, "Bench Bat Bringing Back Fond Memories," *Sporting News*, May 26, 1973.

5. Earl Lawson, "Joe Hums Tune to Pete's 2,000-Hit Lyrics," *Sporting News*, June 9, 1973.

6. *Sporting News*, August 11, 1973.

7. *Sporting News*, August 25, 1973. A few days later, Wagner turned in Bench for the same infraction. Perhaps he was simply concerned about the cost of those baseballs flying into the stands.

8. *Sporting News*, August 25, 1973; Earl Lawson, "Rose Wins Blue Ribbon in Red Show," September 1, 1973, 8.

9. *Cincinnati Enquirer*, September 18, 1973.

10. *Sporting News*, October 13, 1973, 5.

11. (Philadelphia) *Evening Bulletin*, October 4, 1973.

12. *Sporting News*, October 20, 1973.

13. Erardi, *Pete Rose*, 29; "When Bottle Flew from Shea Stands, Rose, Anderson, Other Reds Saw Red," *New York Times*, October 9, 1973.

14. Mark Heisler, "Rose after Brawl: 'Not a Dirty Player,'" (Philadelphia) *Evening Bulletin*; Murray Chass, *New York Times*, both October 9, 1973.

15. Jack Lang, "Mets Switch Roles with Reds to Win Flag," *Sporting News*, October 27, 1973, 3; Heisler, "Rose after Brawl: 'Not a Dirty Player'"; Reston, *Collision at Home Plate: The Lives of Pete Rose and Bart Giamatti*, 71.

16. Bud Harrelson, "Books: Who and Where Is the Real Pete Rose?" *New York Times*, September 28, 1975.

17. Bench and Brashler, *Catch You Later: The Autobiography of Johnny Bench,* 143; Mark Heisler, "Pete Rose Ends Boos," (Philadelphia) *Evening Bulletin*, October 10, 1973.

18. Bench and Brashler, *Catch You Later: The Autobiography of Johnny Bench*, 144–145; Mark Heisler, "Mets Fanatics 'From the Zoo' Tear Up Shea," (Philadelphia) *Evening Bulletin*, October 11, 1973, 35; *Sporting News*, October 27, 1973.

19. Bench and Brashler, *Catch You Later: The Autobiography of Johnny Bench*, 145.

20. Bob Hertzel, "Pete Rose Won't Rest on His MVP Laurels," *Cincinnati Enquirer*, November 22, 1973, 1-D.

21. *Sporting News*, February 2, 9, March 2, 1974.

22. *Sporting News*, January 26, February 9, 1974.

23. *Cincinnati Enquirer*, February 28, 1974; *Sporting News*, April 20, 1974.

24. Dick Young, "Money Dulls the Roses," *Sporting News*, July 6, 1974.

25. Bench and Brashler, *Catch You Later: The Autobiography of Johnny Bench*, 46; *Sporting News*, July 6, 1974.

26. (Philadelphia) *Evening Bulletin*, June 4, 1974.

27. *Philadelphia Inquirer*, March 13, 1974.

28. *Sporting News*, November 23, 1974.

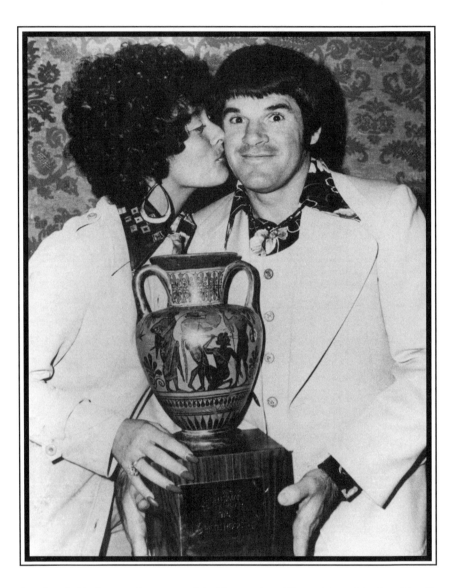

Pete Rose holds the 1975 Sportsman of the Year trophy while receiving a kiss from his wife Karolyn. © *Bettmann/CORBIS.*

THE BIG RED MACHINE

In his new house, Pete Rose played host to numerous teammates and ex-teammates who came to Cincinnati over the 1974–75 off-season, to the extent that some observers said the house amounted almost to a hotel. In the real hospitality business, Rose opened a restaurant in the western part of the city early in January, a twenty-four-hour operation called Pete Rose's Cake, Steak and Ribs. He joked that he needed a fallback with his coming salary cut.

Management had indeed asked Rose to take a sizable cut for his 1975 salary. Rose knew that his $160,000 pay level was based upon his consistent .300 hitting and that he had fallen off from that mark in 1974; he expected his pay to go down some. But he was not going to give up dollars without a struggle. Rose made noises about taking the club to arbitration over his contract, and he complained to Phil Pepe of the *New York Daily News*, "The thing that's strange is that if I broke my neck in the opening game of the season and missed the whole year they would have offered me a better contract. I believe I did the things I'm supposed to do. . . . I'm paid to get on base, score runs, be a leader. I did that."[1]

And he certainly intended to show in 1975 that his prior year's performance, which of course was not all that terrible, was an aberration. One national publication, after laying the Reds' 1974 finish at Rose's feet, wrote, "Pete will be 33-years old by mid-season and it isn't reasonable to believe that he can continue to be the player he was during the 1960s." Such a comment, along with the money, was just the sort of thing which pushed Pete, if indeed he needed any pushing.[2]

Rose bristled at suggestions that his physical condition was affected by his advancing age. "I miss .300 for the first time in ten years," he said, "and I'm suddenly out of shape and a 'fatboy.' Well, I didn't miss a game in 1974." The law of averages caught up with him, he contended. "You can't hit .300 every year," although he had never admitted that before. "I'm 32 and I feel good. I've had some good years and I think I have some good ones left."[3]

Negotiations for Rose's 1975 contract actually went more smoothly than he expected. On February 7, Pete said he was happy with the latest figures offered by the club and signed a contract calling for $155,000, a pay cut of $5,000, surely the best he could have hoped for. After settling with Howsam, Pete Rose was ready to go to work.

Rose, as usual, worked his tail off in spring training as he prepared for his "comeback" season, ironing out any possible kinks in his swing. 1975 loomed as a dogfight between Cincinnati and Los Angeles, with the experts split between the two clubs. The Cincinnati starting rotation looked solid, with Jack Billingham, Don Gullett, Clay Kirby, Fred Norman, and Gary Nolan, plus Clay Carroll ready to fill in where needed. Perez, Morgan, and Bench made up the heart of the line-up, along with Rose. Earl Lawson wrote, "Pride and a salary cut are motivation enough for Pete."[4]

The Reds sent the Dodgers a message in the opening series. They beat Los Angeles 2–1, in fourteen innings on Opening Day. A Riverfront Stadium crowd of 52,546 went wild, celebrating as Rose went 2 for 5. On April 9, Anderson's team scored two runs in the bottom of the ninth off Dodgers' reliever Mike Marshall to win, 4–3. And the next day, the Reds spotted Los Angeles five runs, then came back on two homers by George Foster to win, 7–6. Rose was 1 for 2 but was hit by a pitch in the eighth inning and scored the winning run on a double by Perez.

They could not keep up such a pace, of course, and by the end of the month were around the .500 level, although Rose, with 32 hits, had the best April of his career. Then Sparky Anderson made a move that solidified the Big Red Machine. For the first weeks of the season, John Vukovich, Darrell Chaney, and rookie Doug Flynn had played third base, depending on the opposing pitcher and Anderson's hunches. None of them provided much offense. On May 2, Sparky told Pete Rose that he would like him to move from left field to third base, permitting the Reds to get George Foster's potentially powerful bat into the line-up. Foster for Vukovich et al. looked like a pretty good trade, and Rose was enthusiastic about the switch.

"Pete created no problem," said Anderson. "He reacted just the way I knew he would." (Somewhere, Don Heffner read that and smiled sardonically.) Rose said, "I can play the position. I didn't do the job in 1966 because I really didn't have my heart in playing third. I didn't think it would help the club in those days." Now, he allowed, it was different. "I believe I can help the club by play-ing third."[5]

He went to work at being a third baseman in typical Pete Rose fashion. The first night he was to play the hot corner the game was rained out. Rose never-theless had the groundskeepers remove that part of the tarpaulin covering the third base area so he could take some ground balls.

In the middle of May, though, the Reds' offense faltered, and with Dan Driessen having fielding woes in left field, Anderson was ready to move Rose back. He was already moving Pete to left field and putting Vukovich at third base late in games in which the Reds held the lead. But he held off, and in late May, a seven-game winning streak drew the club close to Walter Alston's Dodgers. Anderson was pleased with the pitching of Gary Nolan and with the hitting of Foster, who was playing regularly with the shift of Rose to third base. Besides, Anderson said, "Pete has been doing a good job and from now on I plan to keep him at third the full game no matter what the score." When the Reds took over first place on June 2, Sparky told the reporters that four things had turned the Reds around: (1) Nolan's comeback, (2) the play of Ken Grif-fey, (3) Cesar Geronimo's defense in center field, and (4) the move of Rose to third base. Connie Ryan, the Atlanta manager, commented, "When Rose moved to third, he made that team."[6]

As June went on, the Reds increased their lead, and Rose continued to im-press Sparky Anderson. "He's come up with some real fielding gems," the man-ager said of his new third baseman, who was also hitting .319 by June 26. In June, the Reds won twenty-one of twenty-eight games, to take a firm grip on first place in their division.[7]

And they just kept winning, even though their southpaw ace Don Gullett was sidelined with a fractured left thumb. At the All-Star break, Anderson's club was twelve and one-half games in front of the Dodgers and cruising. Pete Rose was well over .300 and piling up base hits, and he went 2 for 4 in the All Star Game, along with a sacrifice fly in the Nationals' three-run ninth which won the game 6–3.

Sparky Anderson told the press, "I want to get out in front as far as we can," and his boys took him seriously. By August 18, they were seventeen and one-half games in front of the Dodgers, and Pete Rose was batting .324. Morgan, Perez, Bench, and Foster joined Rose in providing firepower for the Reds in a race that had been effectively over for several weeks. And, to top things off for Anderson, Gullett returned to the mound on August 18 and threw five score-less innings against St. Louis.

On August 17, Rose singled against Pittsburgh's Bruce Kison before a huge crowd at Riverfront for the 2,500th hit of his career. He recalled for the reporters that his first hit had come against Bob Friend of the Pirates, his 1,000th off Robin Roberts, then with Houston, and his 2,000th off Ron Bryant of the Giants. Teammate Terry Crowley said, "Pete is a hitting machine. I've never seen anyone who loves the game more."[8]

The Reds clinched the National League West on September 7 with an 8–4 win over the San Francisco Giants and finished with a 108–54 record, twenty games ahead of Los Angeles. Anderson of course pointed out to his players that their job was only one-third done, with the playoffs and World Series still ahead, but he also acknowledged that his 1975 club was probably the best in Cincinnati history. And it piled up its victory total without having a pitcher win more than fifteen games, a mark reached by Billingham, Gullett, and Nolan.

The Pittsburgh Pirates under manager Danny Murtaugh won the NL East with a 92–69 record. They came into Riverfront for the playoffs, and, as Bench said, "we did everything right from inning one." In Game 1, Don Gullett pitched a complete game 8–3 victory. Rose was 2 for 5. In Game 2, the Reds won 6–1 behind Fred Norman and Rawly Eastwick. Rose had one hit, a first-inning single ahead of a two-run homer by Perez.[9]

In the third game, in Pittsburgh's Three Rivers Stadium, the Pirates rookie lefthander, John Candelaria, took the mound on a day when he had everything working. He had 14 strikeouts and a one-hitter in the eighth inning as he faced Rose with a man on and a 2–1 lead. Rose took a 35-ounce bat to the plate, a heavier piece of wood than he normally used. He put it to good use, driving a fast ball deep into the left-field bleachers, and said later, "I don't think I ever hit one that hard from that side." Pittsburgh tied the score again, but the Reds came back to win, 5–3, with a Rose base hit in the midst of their winning tenth-inning rally.[10]

The Reds were riding high now as they prepared to meet the Boston Red Sox in the World Series. Rose looked at his Reds: "This is the most complete team. This team has the long ball, the defense, home run hitters, speed, good starting pitchers and the great bullpen. This is the best team we've had since I've been here." He and his teammates read all the stories about Boston's futility since 1918, when last the Sox won the Series—"the Curse of the Bambino"—and they expected to have little trouble with Darrell Johnson's team, which had defeated Oakland in the American League playoff. A rude awakening was in store.[11]

In the opening game, Anderson opened with Gullett against the fabled Cuban right-hander, Luis Tiant, whose pitching motion, in which he almost turned his back to the plate, troubled many hitters. The two pitchers matched scoreless innings for six frames before Boston exploded for six runs in the seventh. Rose was 0 for 4 while his teammates collected only five hits off Tiant, who won 6–0.

The Reds were down one, and some of their followers began to think that this team, good as it was, would never win a world championship.

Game 2 was played on a cold, rainy day in Fenway Park. The goofy Boston lefty Bill "Spaceman" Lee outpitched Billingham and had the Reds hitters baffled as he took a 2–1 lead into the ninth. Cincinnati had only four hits, two of them by Rose. Bench opened the ninth with a double, and right-hander Dick Drago replaced Lee. An infield single by Concepcion, a stolen base, and Griffey's double got two runs in for the Reds. When Rawly Eastwick set the Bosox down in order in the bottom of the ninth, the Reds were able to escape from Boston with a split.

Two days later, on October 14, the two teams engaged in a slugfest at Riverfront, with six home runs flying out of the park. A two-run shot by Dwight Evans of the Red Sox tied the game in the ninth inning. A tenth-inning bunt, however, proved to be decisive in the Reds' 6–5 win. Geronimo was on first with a single when little Ed Armbrister, pinch hitting for Eastwick, dropped a bunt in front of the plate. Armbrister then hesitated for a moment, so that when Boston catcher Carlton Fisk scrambled out to pick up the ball, he collided with the batter. With Armbrister in his way, Fisk's throw to second was wild, and the Reds wound up with men on second and third. The Red Sox protested bitterly—with good reason—to umpire Larry Barnett that Armbrister was guilty of interference, but Barnett, apparently misinterpreting the rules, refused to call it. Rose was walked intentionally, and Rogelio Moret fanned Merv Rettenmund for the first out, with the infield and outfield playing in. Joe Morgan then singled to center to win the game, though the Red Sox complained loudly that they had been robbed.

In Game 4, Tiant took the mound again for Darrell Johnson and struggled to a 5–4 win, pitching a complete game but throwing an astonishing 163 pitches to do it. With two Reds on in the ninth, Fred Lynn caught Griffey's ball at the wall after a long run and Tiant survived. Pete Rose had one of his team's nine hits off Tiant. The Series was tied once again, two games each.

The fifth game saw Tony Perez come out of the slump that had afflicted him throughout the World Series, as he slugged two home runs and drove in five to back up Gullett's fine pitching for a 6–2 Cincinnati victory. Pete Rose had a single and double in three official times at the plate.

There was a day off for travel to Boston on October 17, followed by three days of rain on which no baseball could be played. Dave Anderson of the *New York Times* talked to Rose in the hotel lobby after the first rainout, when he was champing at the bit to get back into action. "I played 13 years and 2,000 games to be in the situation I'm in now," he said. "Only one game to a world champion." He showed the writer the rings he had won for pennants in 1970 and

1972 and sneered, "These are disappointing rings." He explained: "These rings ain't got diamonds in them because we didn't win it all. I'm playing tomorrow's game for a diamond ring. I don't need the money. I need that diamond ring."[12]

Game 6 of the 1975 World Series was one for the ages. Nolan started against Tiant, and Lynn opened the scoring with a three-run home run in the first. Anderson's boys surged back with three in the fifth, two in the sixth, and another in the seventh to take a 6–3 lead. In the eighth, Boston put two men on—a single by Fred Lynn and a walk to Rico Petrocelli—and sent up pinch hitter Bernie Carbo, a former Red, with one out. On Eastwick's 2–2 fastball, Carbo sent a gigantic shot over the wall in center, and the Fenway fans were delirious as their team tied the score at six.

In the bottom of the ninth, the Red Sox loaded the bases with none out, and Lynn hit a fly ball to medium left. Foster caught it and then nailed Denny Doyle at the plate, trying to score after the catch. The Reds got the next out, and the game went into extra innings. When Rose came to the plate in the tenth, he remarked to Fisk, "This is some kind of ball game, isn't it?" "Yeah, it sure is," answered Fisk.[13]

In the eleventh inning, Rose, 2 for 5 up to then, was hit with a pitch. He was forced at second on a ball hit by Griffey. Joe Morgan then nailed a ball to deep right, an apparent home run, until Dwight Evans reached over the wall and pulled it in. Griffey was so far off first that he was easily doubled up. The Sox went down in the eleventh and the Reds in the twelfth, and Pudge Fisk led off for Boston in the bottom of the twelfth. Pat Darcy, on the mound for his second inning, tried to throw a fastball by Fisk, but the Boston catcher swung and got all of it, a drive high down the left field line. Fisk stood at the plate and waved at the ball, willing it to stay fair, and when it did—fair by the narrowest of margins—the Red Sox had their victory. The World Series was down to one final game.

Gullett and Lee were the opposing moundsmen in Game 7. Gullett, having control problems, gave up three runs in the third, two of them scoring on bases-loaded walks. Billingham came on in the fifth and kept the Red Sox quiet. In the sixth, Rose singled but was forced at second on a ball hit by Bench. It should have been a double play, but Pete took out second baseman Doyle, who threw the ball into the Boston dugout. Perez then hit a curveball over the left-field wall, and the score was suddenly 3–2. In the next inning, Rose singled home the tying run, and hearts grew faint in Beantown.[14]

In the ninth, with the score still tied, and a journeyman lefthander named Jim Burton on the mound for the Sox, Griffey walked and moved up on a sacrifice bunt and an infield out. With Rose coming up, the Red Sox brain trust chose to walk him, the man with more hits in the Series than anyone else. Morgan hit a dinky blooper to center field that dropped in as Griffey scored the fourth and winning Cincinnati run. Will McEnaney got three quick outs in the bottom of the ninth, and the Reds were World Champions. As Bench wrote, "We are finally number one, let the champagne flow."[15]

Pete Rose, with 10 hits in 27 times up, was voted the Most Valuable Player of the World Series. Former Phillies outfield star Rich Ashburn wrote, "It was fitting that Pete Rose should get the Most Valuable Player award in the Series. He symbolizes all the best of what a ball player should be, a great ball player in a great World Series." Rose himself paid tribute to the Sox: "I think the Cincinnati Reds are the best team going, but where does that leave the Boston Red Sox? . . . You win a championship off a team like Boston, and you can walk tall for a long, long time."[16]

Cincinnati's first world championship since 1940 was not the last achievement for the Reds in 1975. Joe Morgan won the league's Most Valuable Player award easily, followed in the voting by Greg Luzinski, Dave Parker, Bench, and Rose. Rose, in finishing fifth, received two and one-half first place votes, the half vote coming from hometown writer Bob Hertzel, who said he couldn't decide between Rose and Morgan so he split his vote between them.

Rose said he thought Morgan deserved the award, but he told writer Red Smith, "I thought I should have been second. . . . I'm not bitter, but I can't understand five guys leaving me off the ballot altogether."[17]

In late November Bob Howsam and his wife Janet took a Caribbean cruise along with Pete Rose, Johnny Bench, Tony Perez, broadcaster Marty Brennaman, Sparky Anderson, and their wives. It was a wonderful time to be a Cincinnati Red.

Over the winter Rose received the S. Rae Hickok belt as the Professional Athlete of the Year, nosing out golfer Jack Nicklaus for the honor. Pete and Karolyn, with their two children Fawn and Pete Jr., flew to New York for the presentation on January 8. Pete said that, even though he was booed at Shea Stadium, he loved coming to New York City. "Every time I come here," he said, "I'm either doing a commercial or getting something for free." The diamond-studded Hickok belt, with a huge buckle of gold and jewels, was said to be worth $30,000, so it was carefully placed in a locked case in Rose's home.[18]

A week or so earlier Rose was named by *Sports Illustrated* its Sportsman of the Year. Pete said he might not have deserved that particular nod "because I'm not a good sport. If I lose, I won't say anything bad about the other guys, but I won't go in their clubhouse to congratulate them." The *Sports Illustrated* article, celebrating baseball's "grandest season in years," began, "Saluting the sport as well as the man, we honor Cincinnati's Pete Rose, in whose person are combined so many of the qualities of excellence that merit his designation as Sportsman of the Year."[19]

The *SI* article quoted Jack Billingham, now a teammate, but an opponent back in 1961 in the Florida State League. "They couldn't believe he was for real," Billingham said of those minor league players. "They'd talk about him on buses. I'd hear all about this kid who runs out walks and never stops talking. Well, Pete's just the same now. He hasn't slowed up at all." Rose concurred: "I'm still just as enthusiastic about my job. Why shouldn't I be? For me, playing baseball for $3,000 a week is a license to steal." Ron Fimrite, author of the *SI* article, said, "No baseball player dedicates himself to his craft with more zeal than Pete Rose," and then concluded by quoting Reds' coach Ted Kluszewski. "Pete Rose," Klu said, "is an original. You won't see another like him in a thousand years."[20]

Rose came to terms with the Reds for 1976, settling on a contract in late March for $190,000. When the press asked him why he was not getting the $200,000 he had talked about, Rose replied, "If I wasn't happy with my contract, I wouldn't have signed it. I'm not saying I wouldn't have liked $200,000 if for nothing else than just the pride thing. But evidently someone upstairs thinks the other guys deserve more than me."[21]

He was, as always, ready to go with training for a new season. Unfortunately, in the latest round of the unending struggle between players and management, the owners decided not to open their spring training camps in the absence of an agreement with the players' union following the decision of arbitrator Peter Seitz in the Messersmith-McNally case. Seitz ruled that a player who played out his option year under the basic baseball contract became a free agent. Talks on a new agreement had broken down, and when the owners tried to overturn Seitz's decision by going to federal court, they were unsuccessful.

Rose was one of a handful of players who felt that union chief Marvin Miller was too hardline in his dealings with the owners. Asserting that some form of the reserve clause should be preserved, Rose said, "I don't like the way things get bitter and nasty every four years when basic agreement negotiations come around." A few players, of course, grumbled that Rose, with his big salary, could afford to look at ownership more benignly.[22]

A number of the Reds players went to Tampa nevertheless, arranging to work out on their own at a field near the club's spring training facility. Bench and Morgan did so, as did Pete Rose, who said, "I want to get all the work I can at third base." Consequently, when commissioner Bowie Kuhn directed the owners to open the camps, Rose and his teammates were quickly on hand.[23]

The Reds were looking forward eagerly to the new season, because they knew they had the best team in baseball and they wanted to demonstrate that fact once again. The baseball writers picked Cincinnati to win again, and Anderson's team started out by winning the first four games of the season. Bench and Perez struggled early, but Morgan and Geronimo got off to good starts, and Pete Rose was 9 for 16 in the opening series.

Late in April, with the Reds visiting Philadelphia, the great Phillies' third baseman Mike Schmidt talked about Rose to writer Jim Barniak: "I look at him and I say, now there is a hitter. If I could hit the ball the way I would like to be able to hit it, it would be exactly like him." Rose, in the meantime, looked at Schmidt and said, "Just to have his body, I'd trade mine and my wife's and throw in some cash."[24]

The next night, the Reds enjoyed a comfortable lead over the Phillies when Rose came to bat in the ninth inning. When the count reached no balls, two strikes, Phillies pitcher Tug McGraw came up and inside with a meaningful fastball and Rose had to hit the dirt. Pete was 31 for 65 at that point, everything was going his way, and he was not happy to have his equilibrium upset in such a manner.

When the Reds took the field, Rose started yapping at McGraw, in the home dugout. "I threw my arms in the air," Tug said, "as if to say, 'What's your beef?'" Rose made an obscene gesture toward the Phillies' bench, McGraw climbed a step closer to the field and shouted again, and Rose charged the dugout. Johnny Bench stepped in front of him before he could get there, but both dugouts emptied in time-honored baseball fashion, although nothing further transpired. McGraw later compared what he had done with the knockdown pitch to what Rose did with Bud Harrelson (McGraw's Mets teammate in 1973) as "trying to put some life in the team." He shrugged it off. "Aw, we're buddies," he said about Rose. "We've been around together."[25]

Because the Reds and Phillies were the preseason choices to win the two National League divisions, some observers saw this encounter as the start of the buildup for the playoffs. But there were still five months to go. Through May the Dodgers were running ahead in the west, even though Pete Rose was batting .335 as of June 1 and Foster won National League Player of the Month for May. Early in June, though, Cincinnati took over first place, this time for good.

In late June, Rose was featured by the *Chicago Tribune Magazine*. He told the writer the only thing wrong with baseball was "too many off-days. I gotta play every day." If he did not play baseball? "I dunno. But whatever it was, I'd be aggressive." And "the whole secret in baseball?" "All you have to do is keep from being hurt," he said.[26]

Rose was elected to the National League All Star team at third base, easily beating out Schmidt. He was joined in the starting line-up by four teammates,

Foster, Morgan, Bench, and Concepcion. In the game at Veterans Stadium in Philadelphia, Rose was 2 for 3, a single off Detroit's Mark Fidrych in the first and a triple off Tiant in the fifth. The NL won for the thirteenth time in fourteen years, because, as Rose claimed, "We come in and we have to play hard. . . . I don't believe you can turn it off and on." A reporter listened to him and, having seen the American League stars shrug off another loss, wondered how Pete Rose would react to thirteen defeats in fourteen years.[27]

As the Reds continued to build their lead over Los Angeles, Sparky Anderson decried the possibility of another romp as in 1975. "I don't think we'll ever lead the Dodgers by much more than five games the remainder of the season," he said. "Everything went right for us last year. This year we're not getting all the breaks."[28]

Hardly had Sparky uttered these words than the Reds built their lead to nine games, then up to thirteen games, with a four-game sweep of the Dodgers in early August. In the middle of the month, though, Pete Rose suffered through one of the worst slumps of his career, going 2 for 31, ending it with a bunt single against the Braves on August 16, the 2,700th hit of his career.

The Reds clinched the National League West on September 21 when Pat Zachry beat San Diego 9–1. After that game, Pete Rose led the league with forty doubles, as he bid to become only the fifth man in National League history to lead in doubles three years in a row. He added two more before the season ended, to win the title by four over Philadelphia's Jay Johnstone. Sparky Anderson said, "The way I figure it, Pete Rose gets 15 more doubles than he really should because of hustle." Rose himself, talking about doubles, said, "When you go for an extra base, you've got to make up your mind as soon as you leave home plate." "Look," he went on, "Joe Morgan steals bases on pitchers and catchers. I steal them on outfielders. If I see an outfielder is gonna have to make a perfect throw while he's on the run, I go for the extra base. Because not too often is he gonna make that perfect throw."[29]

The Reds won by ten games in the west, the Phillies by nine in the east, and expectations rose in the Quaker City with its first title of any kind since 1950. Rose said the Phillies were "tougher for us than the Dodgers and Pirates because they're more like us." They had the big bombers in Schmidt, Greg Luzinski, and Dick Allen, solid strength up the middle with Bob Boone, Dave Cash, Larry Bowa, and Garry Maddox, and strong pitching from Steve Carlton, Jim Lonborg, Jim Kaat, and Larry Christenson, plus a good bullpen.[30]

Cincinnati, though, was confident. Griffey, Rose, Morgan, Geronimo, and Foster all hit better than .300, and Foster and Morgan finished one-two in runs batted in. Pete Rose hit .323, led the league in hits (215), doubles (42), and runs (130), and finished second to Schmidt in total bases. The team led the league in runs, doubles, triples, home runs, batting average, stolen bases, fewest errors, and fielding average. It was truly a big red machine, looking forward eagerly to the postseason.

The much-heralded Phillies, as it turned out, did not offer much in the way of competition. The playoff series opened October 9 at Veterans Stadium and Don Gullett was simply superb. He pitched eight innings, giving up two hits and one run, and his teammates got him six runs, five off the Phillies' ace Carlton. Rose had three hits (two doubles and a triple), Foster hit a homer, and the Reds won easily, 6–3. Rose, always ready to stick in the needle, said, "Steve Carlton is their best. We beat their best, and that's got to make them think a little."[31]

In Game 2, the next day, the Phillies carried a 2–0 lead into the sixth inning, one run scoring on a mammoth upper-deck home run by Luzinski. Lonborg was working on a no-hitter for Philadelphia in the sixth when Concepcion walked and took second on a ground-out. Rose broke Lonborg's spell with a run-scoring single to right. When Griffey singled to center, Rose gambled on taking third, challenging Garry Maddox's arm; the throw by Maddox was late, and Griffey took second. Lonborg gave way to reliever Gene Garber, who walked Morgan intentionally to load the bases. In the key play of the series, Perez drilled a liner down the first base line that glanced off Allen's glove at first and scored two runs. The blow was ruled an error, much to the loudly expressed disbelief of Allen, and the Reds went on to a 6–2 triumph.

The next day a wire-service story surfaced, claiming that Rose was unhappy with the Cincinnati organization and would not mind being traded to the Phillies. Asked about it further, Rose said it was not the time or place to discuss such a thing. He said the wire-service writer asked him, while he was in the shower, if he was unhappy with the contract offer from the Reds. "I said, 'What offer? We haven't started talking yet.'" Rose explained. "Then he asked me if I was traded, where would I want to go? I told him I wouldn't mind going to the Phillies. They have the second best [behind the Reds] organization in baseball, and I could help them. I could play left field and Luzinski could take first base." "That," he added, "was the whole conversation." He admitted that his attorney, Reuven Katz, had talked about a new contract with the Reds a month earlier, but Rose would say no more about that.[32]

The whole business was about as inappropriate as it could possibly have been, given the circumstances, but the Big Red Machine took it in stride. Sparky Anderson, asked about it, laughed. Rose, he said, was a Cincinnatian, "and nothing, including money, is going to make him leave Cincinnati."[33]

The next day, at Riverfront, the Phillies carried a two-run lead into the ninth inning. Foster led off against big Ron Reed and belted a one-and-two pitch into the seats. Gene Garber came in for the Phillies, and Bench greeted him with a game-tying home run. When Concepcion followed with a single, Garber left in favor of Tom Underwood, who walked Geronimo. Ed Armbrister's bunt moved the runners up, and Danny Ozark ordered Rose walked. When Griffey's high bouncer skipped off first baseman Bobby Tolan's glove, Concepcion came in to score, and the Reds had the National League pennant.

Pete Rose looked at the American League playoff series, still in progress with the New York Yankees up two games to one over the Kansas City Royals, and offered his thoughts. "Personally," he said, "I'd like to play the Yankees. When I think of the World Series, I think 'Yankees.' When I was a kid, 'World Series' and 'Yankees' meant the same thing to me." He got his wish when a Chris Chambliss home run in the last inning of Game 5 gave the Yankees their first AL pennant since 1964.[34]

The Yankees put up even less of a struggle than the Phillies had. Cincinnati won Game 1 at home 5–1, behind Gullett's five-hitter. Perez and Morgan led the attack, while Rose was 0 for 2 with a walk and an RBI. In the second game, the Reds won 4–3 when Tony Perez doubled in Griffey with two out in the ninth, beating Catfish Hunter. Rose was 0 for 4.

At Yankee Stadium for Game 3, things went just about the same. Zachry and Will McEnaney stifled New York, and the Reds won, 6–2. Rose was 2 for 5, but he was overshadowed by designated hitter Dan Driessen, who had a single, double, and home run. The Reds completed their four-game sweep the next night, winning 7–2 behind two Bench home runs; Gary Nolan beat Ed Figueroa. Rose had a double in five at-bats. Wells Twombly, a Boston sportswriter, observed, "Other teams have been beaten in four games, but nobody has ever looked quite as awful as the Yankees."[35]

After going out in his final at-bat, Rose was trotting back to the dugout when Yankee pitcher Sparky Lyle said to him, "Great World Series, Pete." Rose was nonplussed. "I never met Sparky," he said. "I think it was a fine thing. I don't know if I could do that to someone who beat me. Maybe the next day, but not right there."[36]

In the fallout from the postseason, particularly the sweeps of the Reds against both the Phillies and Yankees, there was much talk of the Big Red Machine and its place among the all-time greats. Certainly the eight-man starting line-up rated with the best of all time, although the starting pitching, with no one in either 1975 or 1976 winning more than fifteen games, was downgraded. Sparky Anderson, however, defended his staff: "We get our pitchers out of there early," he said, "before they have a chance to get tired and become susceptible to injury. The records might not show it, but this is a solid pitching staff."

Plaudits also went to the Reds' big-league scouting, Ray Shore and Rex Bowen. They recognized that the catalyst for the Yankees' offense was fleet

Mickey Rivers, who hit .312 with many bunt singles during the regular season and stole 43 bases in 50 attempts. The scouts felt that Rivers had to be cut off. "Sparky told me," said Rose, "to play him in close, even if I had to shake his hand. You can't give him that bunt single, because if you do, he'll steal you blind and they'll have a big inning." With Rose playing way up from third base when Rivers batted, the Reds held Mickey to three singles in 18 at-bats, for a .167 average.[37]

Each Reds player's World Series share was $26,366.68, eclipsing the former record held by the 1973 Oakland Athletics. Joe Morgan repeated as the National League's Most Valuable Player, with Foster, Schmidt, and Rose following him in the balloting. Pete Rose, in the meantime, was celebrated in his home town. A local publication wrote that "the years of stardom have smoothed, or at least glossed over, many of the rough edges so visible in the man-boy who left western Cincinnati to travel to the Reds' rookie club in Geneva, New York in 1960."[38]

NOTES

1. *New York Daily News*, January 18, 1975.

2. Fred Down, *Major League Baseball, 1975* (New York: Pocket Books, 1975), 142–43.

3. Associated Press, (Philadelphia) *Evening Bulletin*, February 9, 1975.

4. *Sporting News*, April 12, 1975.

5. Earl Lawson, "Red Power Potential Rises with Rose at Third Base," *Sporting News*, May 24, 1975.

6. *Sporting News*, June 7, 21, 1975; Ron Fimrite, "Sportsman of the Year," *Sports Illustrated*, December 22–29, 1975, 50.

7. *Sporting News*, July 12, 1975.

8. Earl Lawson, "Pete Pedals Past 2,500," *Sporting News*, September 6, 1975, 11.

9. Bench and Brashler, *Catch You Later: The Autobiography of Johnny Bench*, 174.

10. Ray Kelly, (Philadelphia) *Evening Bulletin*, October 8, 1975.

11. *Sporting News*, October 9, 1975.

12. Dave Anderson, "The Cincinnati Kid," *New York Times*, October 19, 1975.

13. *Sporting News*, November 8, 1975.

14. On his game-tying hit, Rose said, "I was looking for a fast ball and got it. But I was worried about hitting it too hard and Fred Lynn catching it"; Ray Kelly, (Philadelphia) *Evening Bulletin*, October 23, 1975.

15. Bench and Brashler, *Catch You Later: The Autobiography of Johnny Bench*, 183.

16. Rick Ashburn, (Philadelphia) *Evening Bulletin*, October 23, 1975; *Sporting News*, November 8, 1975.

17. Red Smith, "When Pete Rose Sees His Uniform," *New York Times*, January 9, 1976.

18. Red Foley, "Diamond-Belted Rose Says Keep Clause," *New York Daily News*, January 9, 1976.

19. Smith, "When Pete Rose Sees His Uniform"; Fimrite, "Sportsman of the Year," 44.

20. Fimrite, "Sportsman of the Year," 46, 52.

21. Murray Chass, "No Revolution Planned by 3 Top Reds," *New York Times*, March 27, 1976, 45.

22. (Philadelphia) *Evening Bulletin*, March 8, 1976.

23. *Sporting News*, April 3, 1976.

24. Jim Barniak, (Philadelphia) *Evening Bulletin*, April 27, 1976.

25. Frank Bilovsky, "Rose 'Nudges' McGraw," (Philadelphia) *Evening Bulletin*, April 28, 1976. McGraw, of course, had been a member of the 1973 Mets.

26. Richard Dozen, "Scramblin' Rose," *Chicago Tribune Magazine*, June 27, 1976, 12.

27. Mark Heisler, (Philadelphia) *Evening Bulletin*, July 14, 1976.

28. *Sporting News*, August 7, 1976.

29. *Sporting News*, October 16, 1976.

30. Ibid.

31. *Philadelphia Inquirer*, October 10, 1976.

32. Ray Kelly, "Unhappy Rose Would Like Phillies' Money, Uniform," (Philadelphia) *Evening Bulletin*, October 12, 1976.

33. *Sporting News*, October 30, 1976.

34. (Philadelphia) *Evening Bulletin*, October 13, 1976.

35. Wells Twombly, *Sporting News*, November 6, 1976.

36. Dick Young, "Unexpected Compliment," *Sporting News*, November 6, 1976, 15.

37. Lowell Reidenbaugh, "Reds Tinged with Greatness, Says Sparky," *Sporting News*, November 6, 1976, 3.

38. J. M. Simon, "Pete Rose," *Entertainment Cincinnati*, October 18, 1976, 12.

END OF THE LINE IN CINCINNATI

Most of the news about Pete Rose early in 1977 concerned money. Somebody asked him what he did with his World Series check, and Pete responded, "I just endorsed the check and gave it to my CPA. And the CPA sent it on to the guy who handles my investments." He spent a good part of the off-season making commercials—for Zenith, Geritol, Swanson's Pizzas, Jockey shorts, and Aqua Velva.[1]

From there Rose headed into an epic battle with the Cincinnati Reds over his salary. On January 29, the club announced that Dick Wagner was taking over the job of general manager, with Bob Howsam staying on as president. Dick Wagner, it developed, had his own way of running a ball club. Beat writer Earl Lawson of the *Post* described Wagner: "He's tough, abrasive and often completely without tact and compassion." This was the man whose job it would be to tangle with a proud ballplayer who had never really understood why he was not the highest-paid player on his own team.[2]

Rose told Wagner that he wanted $400,000 a year; the club countered with an offer of $250,000, later raised to $325,000. As January passed into February, Rose let it be known that his negotiations with the club were going poorly. Asked if he would consider playing out his option, that is, playing the season under the "reserve" provision of his 1976 contract and then becoming a free agent, Pete answered, "If I can get almost double the money from some club that I'm making with the Reds, I don't see why I shouldn't."[3]

In December, Wagner had traded Tony Perez to Montreal, along with Will McEnaney, for a couple of pitchers. The deal solved two problems for the Reds;

Rose dives past George Brett of the Kansas City Royals in the 1976 All Star Game in Philadelphia. *National Baseball Hall of Fame Library, Cooperstown, N.Y.*

it cleared out one large salary and it also opened up the first base position for young Dan Driessen, who was coming into his own as a top-notch hitter. What Wagner overlooked was that in getting rid of Perez he had removed a chunk of the team's soul; Tony Perez was more than just home runs and RBIs to the Big Red Machine. "We were winners with him," Johnny Bench said, "for so many reasons people not close to the club would never see."[4]

The stalemate between Wagner and Rose continued into March. Pete went to Tampa and went through spring training with the club, although a tender right elbow kept him from his usual full schedule. With the Reds getting bad press around the Cincinnati area for what was regarded as a niggardly attitude toward their captain, Dick Wagner resorted to the unusual tactic of taking out full-page ads, in Cincinnati and Dayton newspapers, to set forth the club's side of the controversy. The ads portrayed Rose as greedy, and Pete responded angrily, telling reporters, "They're trying to force me out of Cincinnati." Relations between the Reds and their captain reached a new low.[5]

Wagner said, "There's no way we'll pay Pete Rose $400,000. . . . We have to decide whether one person is more important than the franchise, more important than the town, the ballpark and the ball club."[6]

Shortly before the Reds headed north from Tampa, Wagner announced that the club had withdrawn its "last offer" to Rose. Pete, through his attorney Reuven Katz, said his demand for an annual salary of $400,000, either for one, two, or three years, was not negotiable. He would stick with his number, except that it would automatically go up on Opening Day. Then, on April 5, Rose signed—a two-year contract calling for something between $700,000 and $800,000. But this was not $400,000 a year. What had happened?

When the team had arrived at the Cincinnati airport from spring training, Rose was surprised to see that his teammates were ignored by the writers, all of whom seemed to be interested only in Pete Rose's salary squabble. It was the big story in Cincinnati that April, with all the articles, management's newspaper ads, and some small businesses raising money to help the cheap Reds pay Rose's salary. The populace was definitely on Rose's side, but Pete saw Wagner digging in his heels defiantly.

The scene at the airport did it. "That was when I decided I had to do something," Rose told Atlanta newsman Furman Bisher. "I could see the same thing happening all around the league all season. Nobody would be interested in what I was hitting, what I thought about the race." He told Bisher, "I had to get out from under that."[7]

Rose quickly got in touch with Katz, and the deal was done. It was not a happy time for Rose, whose image as the dirty-uniform, headfirst-sliding hustler was morphing into one of a "money monger," as Bisher put it. Even Bench considered Rose "very money conscious," although he added that "nothing ever affects his playing or concentration." Pete Rose would remember Dick Wagner and this roughest of all dealings with the Reds' management. He was signed now until the end of the 1978 season, but he would remember.[8]

Cincinnati's 1977 season was nothing to remember. After the first two weeks of the season, the Reds were 4–8 and already trailed the Dodgers by five and one-half games. By the end of April, Dodgers catcher Steve Yeager told the reporters, "You guys can turn in your Cincinnati Reds tickets any time. They'll be lucky to finish third." Yeager said that trading Perez "just killed the club."[9]

Yeager was right. Rose started off hitting well, but the Reds lagged far behind Los Angeles. Just before the trading deadline, a flurry of deals sent Gary Nolan to the Angels, Rawley Eastwick to St. Louis, and Pat Zachry and three lesser lights to New York for pitching great Tom Seaver. It didn't do any good. Without Perez the team seemed to lack something essential.

Ron Cey of the Dodgers won the All Star Game voting at third base; Pete Rose, on the team as a reserve, did not enter the game at Yankee Stadium until the sixth inning. By the time the Reds split a double-header with the Cubs on July 27, they had to concede that they had little chance to catch Los Angeles. The Dodgers clinched the division title on September 20, and the Reds finished the season in second place, ten games back. Rose hit .311 for the year, with 204 hits. The only thing he led the league in was times at bat. It wasn't a bad year, but it was not what he had hoped for. He missed out on 100 runs, scoring 95, but he did have his best year in stolen bases, with 16, and he was on base 285 times. And by the end of the season, his 652 consecutive-games streak had tied the club record held by Frank McCormick.

Rose finished fifteenth in Most Valuable Player voting, which was won by Cincinnati's George Foster on the strength of his 52 home runs. No other Reds player finished in between Foster and Rose.

On January 20, 1978, the Greater Cincinnati Kidney Foundation held a thirty-five dollars per plate "roast" of the town's favorite son, the captain of its baseball team. Pete Rose sat through the barbs of Tommy Helms, Tony Perez, Sparky Anderson, Joe Morgan, Ken Griffey, and others. The next night Rose, Foster, and Tom Seaver were honored by a thousand guests at the annual Ballplayers of Yesterday dinner. Cincinnati was paying its respects to Pete Rose as he headed into the second and final year of his contract with the Reds.

In 1978, Rose was primed to break McCormick's team record for consecutive games on Opening Day, and not long thereafter he would pick up his 34th hit of the season, which would be number 3,000 for his career. Rose would become the thirteenth player in major league history to reach that plateau.

Anderson picked his Reds to win the National League West, as did the country's baseball writers and a poll of fans. The writers also picked Cincinnati to win the pennant and World Series. Seaver's presence on the pitching staff for a full season, added to the Reds' solid eight-man line-up, was a good part of the reason for Anderson's optimism and the opinion of the writers. Seaver gave Sparky the mound stopper he had never had, and Anderson figured the club could win a hundred games, which should be enough for the title.

Rose looked at the schedule and predicted he would get the 3,000th hit "sometime during the first week of May." He figured that 4,000 hits would not be possible, but he had his eye on Stan Musial's National League record of 3,630 hits. "I'd like that," he said, of becoming the senior circuit's all-time hit leader.[10]

Sure enough, on May 5, before 37,823 at Riverfront Stadium, Rose picked up two hits against Montreal's ace right-hander Steve Rogers; the second one was number 3,000. The Reds players rushed from the dugout while photographers swarmed around the Cincinnati captain. Rose hugged the Expos' first baseman Tony Perez, who had been with him in Geneva when he broke in back in 1960. "I saw Pete get his first hit in baseball," the smiling Perez said, "now I see him get his 3000th in the majors." The ovation went on for five minutes, and Rose said, "The longer and louder they cheered, the more choked up I got."[11]

The flurry over the momentous single was fine, but when the cheering died down things moved on. Two days later, Rose was suffering from influenza, and his consecutive-game streak ended at 678 games. The Reds were lagging in a struggle with Los Angeles for the lead in the National League West, as Seaver had a tough time notching many victories for Sparky Anderson. And in June, Pete and Karolyn Rose separated.

The break-up had been coming for some time, as Pete's extramarital dalliances became ever more flagrant. Rose regarded girls offering sexual favors as a perquisite of his ballplaying job, but he violated the unwritten rule that players played around on the road but not when they were at home. Karolyn was humiliated by the tales of Rose's infidelity that were circulating around Cincinnati, and she was unhappy at receiving phone calls at home from young women asking for her husband. The separation was temporary—she and Pete were back together after a few months—but it did not bode well for the couple.

By May 19, Rose had moved past Roberto Clemente and Al Kaline on the all-time hits list, and he was doing fine, even though the team was struggling. In June, Earl Lawson wrote that Rose "plans to come out soon with a chocolate beverage called 'Pete.' Already on the market are pewter statuettes, depicting Rose getting his 3000th hit. Other mementoes, commemorating the historic hit, now on the market are pewter ash trays, pewter mugs, and pewter medallions. One of the Cincy department stores has exclusive rights to 'I Love Pete Rose' T-shirts."[12]

In the meantime, Rose started something that would bring him far more renown than attaining 3,000 hits. On June 14, with his average at .267 after a 6 for 51 slump, Rose got a couple of hits against Dave Roberts of the Chicago Cubs. In the next game, on June 16, he picked up two hits against the Cardinals' John Denny. Over the next couple of weeks, Rose got at least one hit a game. On June 24 he had four base hits off the Dodgers' Bob Welch and three hits off Welch and a couple of relievers on June 30. By the time the All-Star break came along, after the games of July 9, Rose's hitting streak was up to twenty-five games, and it was starting to attract some attention.

Rose himself was feeling fine. "Going into the batter's box is fun again," he told a reporter. "My stroke is really good right now. I'm hitting strong from both sides of the plate and I'm seeing the ball real good."[13]

Rose won the third base position on the National League All-Star team in the fans' voting, and he was 1 for 4 in the game itself, played at San Diego. The squad from the senior circuit won, 7–3. Then it was back to business for Pete Rose.

He kept on hitting. On July 14, Rose got two hits against former teammate Pat Zachry, now pitching for the Mets, to tie the Cincinnati club record of twenty-seven consecutive games with hits, held by old-timer Edd Roush, who did it twice, and Vada Pinson. A single to center the next day against New York's Craig Swan gave Rose the Reds' record all to himself. Two games with Montreal, two with the Phillies, and Rose's batting streak was at thirty-three games.

The hits in Philadelphia were tough. On July 19, Pete came to bat 0 for 3 in the ninth inning with his team comfortably ahead. It's not considered good form to bunt in such a situation, but Rose was desperate for a hit and third baseman Schmidt was playing back, so he dropped one down and beat it out. The next night, against tough left-hander Jim Kaat, Rose was 1 for 5, an infield chop, but he was happy to get it.

On July 23, the Reds completed a three-game sweep in Montreal, and Rose had gotten his one or more hits in each game. Dick Williams, the Montreal manager, told a reporter that Rose was "one of the few guys I'd pay to watch play." And his old buddy, Tony Perez, now of the Expos, said, "The old goat. . . . I would like to see him get 60 in a row. I'm happy for him. . . . He go out every day and do job." Rose's streak was at thirty-six games, one shy of the modern (post-1900) National League record set by Tommy Holmes of the Boston Braves in 1945.[14]

The next night Holmes, now sixty-one years old and director of community relations for the Mets, was in Shea Stadium to watch Rose pound out two more hits to tie his record at thirty-seven games; Holmes said, "I have to honestly say, I hope he doesn't break it." On July 25, Holmes was present again as Rose singled to left off Mets pitcher Craig Swan, for his thirty-eighth straight game. Tommy Holmes came out to first base, presented Rose with the baseball he had hit, and shook his hand. He told the press, "Thank God for Pete Rose. Because of him, I got more recognition in the last week than I did when I set the record."[15]

Rose set his sights next on Willie Keeler's all-time National League record of 44 straight games, set in 1897. "What difference does it make that it happened before 1900?" Rose asked. "It's the all-time National League record and I'm a National Leaguer." Pete didn't share the statistician's distinction between records set before and after the turn of the century. The streak reached forty-one games when Rose hit in both games of a double-header in Philadelphia on July 28. In the nightcap of that twin bill, against lefty Steve Carlton, Rose was hitless in his first two at-bats, then dropped a bunt down the third-base line and beat it out when Schmidt was unable to make a play at first. Schmidt later claimed that he would have had Rose "if I get it in my hand and make a good throw," but it hopped off a seam in the artificial turf. Rose scoffed: "What seam? No way Mike throws me out."[16]

Hits in the two games of the Phillies double-header meant that Rose had passed Ty Cobb's forty-game streak and equaled George Sisler's run of forty-one in a row. Now there were only two streaks in major league history ahead of his, Keeler's forty-four games and Joe DiMaggio's fifty-six, set in 1941.

The next night, Rose wasted no time, singling in the first inning off of Jim Lonborg and then picking up two more hits in the game. The following night, going for game forty-three, Rose was hitless when he came to bat in the fifth against right-hander Larry Christenson. After Pete fouled off a bunt attempt, Phillies manager Danny Ozark told Schmidt to move in to guard against another one. Rose answered with a line drive past Schmidt that the third baseman might have caught had he been playing back.

As the streak rolled on, it was obvious that Pete Rose was having a glorious time. Not for him the pressure of having to perform day after day, night after night. He held a press conference every day, laughing and joking, and was completely accessible to wave after wave of writers, displaying what teammate Tom Seaver called "the patience of a saint." He took pleasure in pointing out that not once was his streak kept alive by a questionable decision of an official scorer. Rose's hitting streak became the feel-good story of the summer of 1978, and it drew big crowds everywhere Pete played.[17]

On the last day of July, the Reds were in Atlanta, and Rose kept his streak going by grounding a single to right field against knuckleballer Phil Niekro, the Braves' best pitcher, his third time up. Niekro, a local idol in Atlanta, had walked Rose in the first inning and was startled to be booed loudly by the 45,000 home-town fans in attendance. The hit off Niekro tied Keeler's string at forty-four games.

The next night, rookie southpaw Larry McWilliams took the mound for At-lanta. First time up, Rose walked, and the fans hooted. Next time at bat he hit a line drive up the middle that McWilliams speared at his ankle with a sensa-tional catch. Rose's third at-bat was a hard liner right at third baseman Bob Horner, and next time was a two-hopper to the shortstop. In the ninth inning, Rose came to bat with his team behind 16–4, and bearded relief pitcher Gene Garber, a junkballer, on the hill for the Braves. Six times earlier Rose had kept the streak alive with a hit his last time up.

Rose fouled off a bunt on the first pitch, then took two balls inside, as the crowd booed. A swing and a foul worked the count to two and two, and Gar-ber then struck Rose out swinging at a sidearm breaking ball. Garber leaped in the air, and the streak was over at forty-four games. An angry Pete Rose excori-ated Garber for not throwing him a fastball. "Most pitchers with a 16–4 lead just challenge you," he snarled. "They ain't out there inning-and-outing you, upping-and-downing you like it's the seventh game of the World Series." After the strikeout, he said, "I thought Garber had won the World Series. See him jump in the air?" Rose apparently thought he was entitled to hit the pitch he wanted, not the best pitch Gene Garber could throw, and he overlooked the no-tion that the notoriety of the streak permitted Garber to treat the at-bat as an important one, no matter the score. Rose's comments brought the feel-good story to a somewhat bitter end, with a dose of sour grapes.[18]

No matter how it ended, of course, Rose's hitting streak had been big news, good for baseball, good for men in their late thirties, good for attendance. And it seemed to come out of nowhere. One mathematician sat down later and fig-ured out that the chance of Pete Rose specifically having a forty-four-game hit-ting streak in 1978 was 1 in 5,159. The strikeout that ended the streak, it might be noted, was only Rose's sixth in forty-five games; he was out on an infield pop-up only once during the streak.[19]

While Rose was building up his streak, the Cincinnati Reds were in a tight race for first place in the west with Los Angeles and San Francisco. By the time the streak ended, Rose's batting average was up to .318 and he led the league in hits, runs, and doubles. As August passed, though, Rose's average tailed off, and the Dodgers moved into the division lead. By the end of the month, the Reds were in third place, seven games back, Rose was down to .300, and Sparky Anderson sat him down for a couple of games.

In September, Anderson's boys passed the Giants but they could not catch the Dodgers. They finished second, two and one-half games back. Rose wound up at .302, leading the league in doubles. With 198, he fell two short of his annual goal of two hundred hits, and he was a bit sore about it. Sparky Anderson pulled him out of the last game of the season in the seventh inning with the team three runs ahead. When the Braves tied the score and forced extra innings—the Reds won it in the fourteenth—Rose figured that he was cheated out of four more times at bat.

Looked at dispassionately, it was not a great season for Pete Rose. His average and totals were somewhat below what was expected of him, and he had not led his team into the postseason. He received only enough votes in MVP balloting to finish eleventh, with a fifth place vote the highest he got. Still, his forty-four game hitting streak had been the biggest baseball story of the year, and he had drawn many thousands of extra customers to ballparks around the league to see him. Late in September, he was honored with "Pete Rose Day in Washington," a ten-minute meeting with President Jimmy Carter in the Oval Office and a tumultuous reception on Capitol Hill.

As his contract with Cincinnati came to a close, Pete Rose was about to find out what he was worth on the open market. Rose and his lawyer Reuven Katz had approached the Reds early in the season to try to work out a long-term contract covering the balance of his career. They were spurned by Dick Wagner, who told Katz, "Reuven, it's the Reds' policy *never* to negotiate a contract during the season." Wagner never anticipated the kind of season Rose would have, and he would now have to negotiate in a completely changed atmosphere.[20]

There were skeptics. Earl Lawson wrote, "The reports are that Pete Rose may be in 'for a shock' when he participates in baseball's free agent reentry draft November 3. One club president," Lawson continued, ". . . was willing to bet that Rose again will be playing for the Reds in 1979. It was his way of saying that he believes Rose will learn that the best offer he can get will come from the Reds."[21]

He would soon find out.

NOTES

1. Earl Lawson, "Busy Rose Batting a Ton with TV Commercials," *Sporting News*, January 22, 29, 1977.

2. Earl Lawson, *Sporting News*, October 30, 1976; Bench and Brashler, *Catch You Later: The Autobiography of Johnny Bench*, 217.

3. Earl Lawson, " 'I May Play Out Option,' Rose Admits," *Sporting News*, February 26, 1977.

4. Bench and Brashler, *Catch You Later: The Autobiography of Johnny Bench*; 203.

5. Bruce Keidan, *Philadelphia Inquirer*, April 4, 1977.

6. Bob Hertzel, " 'Right or Rose,' the Reds Say No," *Cincinnati Enquirer*, March 30, 1977, C-1.

7. Furman Bisher, *Sporting News*, May 14, 1977, 6.

8. Ibid.; Bench and Brashler, *Catch You Later: The Autobiography of Johnny Bench*, 46.

9. *Sporting News*, May 14, 1977.

10. Earl Lawson, "Pete Programs 'It' for the First Week in May," *Sporting News*, April 15, 1978, 5.

11. *Cincinnati Enquirer*, May 6, 1978; Earl Lawson, "Pete's Next Goal: Musial's 3,630 Hits," *Sporting News*, May 20, 1978, 3.

12. Earl Lawson, *Sporting News*, June 24, 1978.

13. (Philadelphia) *Evening Bulletin*, July 10, 1978.

14. Frank Dolson, "All Baseball Talking Rose," *Philadelphia Inquirer*, July 24, 1978.

15. *Cincinnati Enquirer*, July 26, 1978; Phil Pepe, " 'Pete Made Me Big Leaguer Again'—Holmes," *Sporting News*, August 12, 1978, 6.

16. Jack Chevalier, "Pete's Mind on Keeler," (Philadelphia) *Evening Bulletin*, July 29, 1978; Bob Hertzel, "Rose Streak Reaches 41 as Reds Split with Phils," *Cincinnati Enquirer*, July 29, 1978.

17. "Rose One of a Kind," *Sporting News*, August 19, 1978.

18. Mark Heisler, "Rose Isn't Mellow the Morning After," (Philadelphia) *Evening Bulletin*, August 3, 1978; Bob Hertzel, "Braves Stop Rose's Streak at 44 Games," *Cincinnati Enquirer*, August 2, 1978. Garber was surprised that Rose was so "ungracious"; see Mark Heisler, "Rose's Streak Reaches End," (Philadelphia) *Evening Bulletin*, August 2, 1978.

19. Michael Freiman, "56-Game Hitting Streaks Revisited," *Baseball Research Journal* (2003), 15; *Cincinnati Post*, August 2, 1978. The algebraic acrobatics involved in such calculations are formidable, but it can be noted that the same article put the chances of Joe DiMaggio having a 56-game streak in 1941 at 1 in 9,545.

20. Rose and Kahn, *Pete Rose: My Story*, 193. Emphasis in original.

21. Earl Lawson, *Sporting News*, November 11, 1978.

TO THE PHILLIES

Shortly after the 1978 season, the Reds made what they called a "final offer" to Rose for a 1979 contract. Rose, announced Dick Wagner, "has been offered a two-year contract. . . . The highest ever extended a Reds' player." Reuven Katz, Pete's lawyer, however, calculated that his total compensation would still fall below that of Joe Morgan. Rose, saying, "I love this town, but evidently the people who run this ball club don't love me," rejected the offer.[1]

After the first game of the World Series, Katz telephoned Wagner with a counter-proposal, and a day later Wagner made a new offer, which Rose and Katz rejected on October 12. "Why don't they let me sit down and talk to Mr. Nippert?" Rose asked; Nippert was the club's majority stockholder and board chairman. "We're both life-long Cincinnatians." But Dick Wagner remained the Reds' negotiator, and he indicated that chances of signing Rose were "on the downward trend." Pete prepared for free agency.[2]

The first step in the free agency process in 1978 was the reentry draft, in which teams were allowed to put in a claim for the right to negotiate with a free agent. This draft, held on November 3, resulted in twelve clubs "drafting" Pete Rose, with Cincinnati also reserving the right to re-sign him.

The Reds, in the meantime, had been off on a month-long, seventeen-game tour of Japan, where Rose was the center of much attention from the baseball-avid Japanese. One club offered Rose a $700,000 playing contract, but Pete was not interested. He did pick up $60,000 in endorsements of Japanese products, and he told Sadaharu Oh, the Japanese slugger, "I will probably be playing with the Philadelphia Phillies next year."[3]

Pete Rose in the uniform of the Philadelphia Phillies. *National Baseball Hall of Fame Library, Cooperstown, N.Y.*

Six days after the team returned, on November 28, Sparky Anderson was stunned to learn he had been fired. "I had no idea it was coming," he told the press. Asked if Dick Wagner had given any reasons for the axing, Sparky replied, "He didn't give me none and I didn't ask for none."[4]

Reaction to the Anderson firing was generally negative in Cincinnati. Mayor Gerald Springer (later a controversial television talk show host) expressed a general view when he asked, "Have they gone bananas?" For Rose, the Reds' getting rid of Sparky Anderson was just about the last straw. He had nothing against John McNamara, Anderson's designated successor, but leaving the Reds looked a lot less difficult with his longtime manager gone.[5]

While Rose was in Japan, Ted Turner, the free-spending owner of the Atlanta Braves, contacted Reuven Katz with what Katz called "a proposal that I knew would make Pete happy." Turner's call relieved Katz of any concern that other owners would not outbid the Reds, and it made Atlanta the first stop on the tour which he was planning for Rose to make.[6]

Rose and Katz sat down one more time with Dick Wagner on November 26 but were unable to get a satisfactory offer from the Reds. "Wagner wished Pete well and Pete wished the Cincinnati Reds well," Katz said, "and that's the end of the negotiations with the Cincinnati Reds." Later, Wagner put another spin on the reason Rose's talks with the Reds never stood a chance. He told Roger Kahn, "The truth is that his marriage was breaking up. He was having serious woman trouble. Cincinnati was getting too hot for him." Rose, he said, "wanted to leave town." Rose vehemently denied this.[7]

By the time Rose returned from Japan, he and Katz had narrowed the list of teams seriously interested in Pete to the Atlanta Braves, St. Louis Cardinals, Kansas City Royals, Philadelphia Phillies, and Pittsburgh Pirates. Rose chartered a Learjet, Katz prepared a twenty-five-minute videotape of Pete Rose highlights, both on and off the field, and the two of them were off on a trip that would transform modern baseball. Katz told Rose, "Pete, get ready for the most fun you've ever had in your baseball career." One writer called it "a whirlwind search by Lear and limo, with heady surprises waiting" wherever they landed.[8]

They landed first in Atlanta, where Turner reiterated his offer of a million dollars a year for whatever length contract Rose might want. With that, the bar had been lifted considerably higher than where it had been set by Dick Wagner. On to Kansas City, where Ewing Kaufmann, the Royals' owner, offered a four-year contract which, with fringe options, would have reached about as high as Atlanta's. In addition, Kaufmann offered to throw in for Rose some oil investments.

Rose and his lawyer arrived in St. Louis and met with Cardinal owner Gussie Busch in the hospital, where Busch was being prepared for hernia surgery. "I'd have had a hernia, too," Pete quipped, "if I had to carry all that money he offered me." The salary offer was a little lower than the two previous ones, but it included a lucrative Budweiser distributorship. The next meeting was with Pirates' owner John Galbreath, who also owned the well-known Darby Dan horse-breeding operation near Columbus, Ohio, and knew of Rose's interest in race horses. Galbreath offered Rose $2 million for three years, as well as two highly regarded brood mares and the stud services of his best stallions.[9]

The last visit was to the Phillies, at the palatial home of owner Ruly Carpenter in Montchanin, Delaware. Rose all along had been partial to the Phillies. For several years, he had been quoted to the effect that if he ever left Cincinnati he would like to go with Philadelphia. Shortstop Larry Bowa and outfielder Greg Luzinski were good friends, and the club had a good offense. Even more, the Phillies had won the Eastern division for three straight years but had failed in the league championship series; the club needed something extra to take that final step—something Pete Rose was sure he could supply.

On November 30, Rose and Katz sat down with Carpenter to talk. They showed the Phillies owner their videotape, and Katz gave Carpenter an outline of the offers they had received, running into seven figures. "My God," said Carpenter. "That's a million dollars. We can't make an offer like that." The Phillies' offer was for $600,000 a year for three years, then $2.2 million for three years, with no horses, beer, or oil added in. Rose reluctantly rejected it, and Ruly Carpenter said, "Let's sit down and have lunch." After lunch, Rose, Katz, Carpenter, and general manager Paul Owens attended a previously scheduled press conference at Veterans Stadium, and Carpenter told the astonished reporters the Phillies had ended their pursuit of Pete Rose.[10]

Bill Giles, the Phillies' vice president, drove Rose and Katz on the short ride from the Vet to the Philadelphia airport, from which they would be flying on to another meeting with Galbreath. Giles, who had grown up in Cincinnati, where his father ran the Reds and was later National League president, was disconsolate. He had hoped and expected that Rose would become a Phillie, with all that that would mean to the team and to the team's attendance and impact on the city. It was a glum drive, Rose apparently just as dejected as Giles was. Giles asked, "Do you really want to play here? And will you take less money to play here than the other places?"

"Yes, I do and I would take less," Rose answered.

Katz asked Giles, "Can you rearrange the figures?"

"I think so," Giles responded. Just before he got on the plane, Katz nudged Giles, winked, and said, "You might not be dead yet. Talk to Ruly and get back to me."[11]

Part of the problem for the Phillies at this stage was the expectation built up

in the press and with their fans that Rose would in fact be coming to Philadelphia. Ray Didinger of the Philadelphia *Evening Bulletin* wrote that "for weeks
now, the fans have been drawing mental pictures of Pete Rose in a Phillies uniform. . . . They aren't gonna take this news very kindly. After three straight playoff blowouts, the fans are running out of patience, anyway." A couple of weeks
earlier, columnist Rich Ashburn said, "With Pete Rose, the Phillies have painted
themselves into a corner. The baseball fans of Philadelphia don't need another
letdown." Now they had one, and the howls of outrage and pain were heard
clearly in the Phillies' front office.[12]

With the flicker of encouragement given by Rose and Katz, Bill Giles came
back and told Carpenter, "Hey, Ruly, I think we've still got a shot." The solution, in Giles' mind, seemed to be an increase in television revenue that would
permit Carpenter to increase his offer. The club had recently signed a three-year
television extension with local station WPHL which gave the station the right
to televise seventy-five games for $1,350,000 a year and gave the baseball club
an even split of advertising revenues above a certain amount. Giles went to the
station executives and asked them to guarantee a flat $600,000 more in 1979
for the club from the advertising income. The people at WPHL, excited by the
prospect of Pete Rose and what he could do for their viewership, agreed, guar-
anteeing the $600,000 for all three years, not just one. With this extra revenue
in hand, Giles convinced Ruly Carpenter to up his offer.[13]

Carpenter called Katz on December 2 with his higher offer, and the next day
Katz called back to say that Pete Rose, who had talked in the meantime with
Larry Bowa, was going to be a Phillie. The contract that he signed on December 5 called for $905,000 the first year, $805,000 the second, and $705,000 the
third. For a fourth year, when Rose would be 41 years old, his salary would be
$565,000 with a bonus of $245,000 if he played in 125 games. A fifth year, on
the same terms as the fourth, was provided for but not guaranteed. One other
thing the Phillies gave Rose was the right to have his son Pete Jr. on the field
before games; Sparky Anderson had barred this, and it rankled Pete Rose.

Rose said that he was accepting the lowest of the five offers, but he was going
to the team he had preferred all along. "I wanted to play for the Phillies all
along," he said after signing. Besides, as Pete put it rather quaintly about the
money, "You could stack it all up and a show dog couldn't jump over it."[14]

When Rose signed with the Phillies, there was considerable speculation about
where he would play. There was talk that he would play third and Mike Schmidt,
the best fielder in the league at that position, would switch to second base. There
was a rumor, quickly squelched by Rose, that he would play second. Richie
Hebner, the incumbent first sacker, downplayed the coming of Rose, while some
observers saw Hebner going to second. Late in January, manager Danny Ozark

put out the word: "Pete Rose will be my first baseman in 1979 and, hopefully, for three years after that."[15]

Before the season started, the Phillies made a multi-player trade with the Cubs to bring them a top-notch second baseman, Manny Trillo, and they traded Hebner to the Mets. Rose spoke to the Philadelphia Sports Writers banquet and said, "I wish spring training started tomorrow."[16]

On playing first base, Rose said, "All you have to do is catch the ball. They tell me the toughest thing is catching high popups. I catch *them* in my hip pocket." Danny Ozark said Rose was a "way-below-average first baseman when he first got the glove," but he worked at it constantly until he became more than adequate.[17]

The Phillies started the season in great form, winning twenty-four of their first thirty-four games. The thirty-fourth game, though, was an historic 23–22 slugfest in Wrigley Field, Chicago, won by the Phillies on a Mike Schmidt home run. As if they were worn out by that game, they hit a bad stretch and lost sixteen of their next twenty-one games. The club dropped out of the division lead and fell to fourth place, although Rose helped it set a franchise attendance record with 2,775,011. The Phillies never really put it together after that, hampered as they were by numerous injuries. On August 31, general manager Paul Owens fired Ozark and named farm system director Dallas Green as the interim manager. The team played better for Green, but it still finished fourth. The only bright spots for the 1979 Phillies were big years by Schmidt and Rose. No one knew what to expect for 1980. All that was clear was that the key players on the Phillies team were getting older and were at, or possibly past, their primes.

Pete Rose had a very fine season on the baseball diamond in 1979; his year off the field was not nearly as good. In mid-February, a twenty-five-year-old divorcee from Tampa named Terryl Rubio filed a paternity action in Cincinnati against Rose. She said that she had been his mistress for three years and that he was the father of her ten-month-old daughter Morgan. Rose, she said, had "never denied that Morgan is his," and he had been sending her financial aid. When the checks stopped coming, she said, "He doesn't owe me a thing. But he does owe Morgan." So she filed suit.[18]

In late summer came his notorious *Playboy* magazine interview. The interviewers, Maury Z. Levy and a pretty blond free-lancer named Samantha Stevenson, were interested in talking about things that could create headlines, that would sell copies of the magazine, that would get Stevenson more assignments. She was not interested in how to go from first to third on a single to right or how to hit a slider. So she asked Rose to talk about drugs, about endorsements, about women in his private life.[19]

The series of interviews was supposed to be for twelve hours, but after eight hours Rose brought it to a close in a flurry of obscenities. Stevenson told Stan Hochman, a Philadelphia columnist, "I know Rose is going to say I did a hatchet job. But I worked hard, very hard, to make him sound decent."[20]

Stevenson asked Rose about "greenies," or amphetamine pills, legal only by prescription. Rose said he might have used them "last week," for dieting. She asked if he would use them for any other purpose? "There might be some day," he responded, "when you played a double-header the night before and you go to the ballpark for a Sunday game and you just want to take a diet pill, just to mentally think you are up."

Stevenson persisted: "You keep saying you *might* take a greenie. *Would* you? *Have* you?" Rose said, "Yeah I'd do it. I've done it."[21]

Rose soon denied that he had made the statement that he had taken "greenies"—"a damn lie," he called it—but Barry Golson, executive editor of *Playboy*, said he had replayed the tape of the interview and the quote was accurate.[22]

There was more fallout from the *Playboy* interview. Talking about why he was in so much demand for endorsements, Rose said, "Look, if you owned Swanson's Pizza, would you want a black guy to do the commercial on TV for you? Would you like the black guy to pick up the pizza and bite into it? Or would you want Pete Rose?" The Campbell Soup Company, which *did* own Swanson's Pizza, soon disassociated itself from Rose and reminded its customers that it had used as Swanson spokesmen such black athletes as Roosevelt Grier and Ed "Too Tall" Jones.[23] Rose, in his own book, admitted that "*Playboy* made me lose my cool. So there it is. I was bad."[24]

One last thing: on September 11, 1979, Karolyn filed for divorce in the Hamilton County Domestic Relations Court. The grounds were "gross neglect of duty," and she asked for an equitable distribution of property. The couple had apparently reconciled after the separation of the year before, which Karolyn thought perhaps had been a good thing "because I think it really reinforced our relationship." All seemed well when they moved into an apartment in downtown Philadelphia, despite the Rubio paternity suit and the other women who seemed always to be a part of Pete Rose's life.[25]

In August, however, during a Phillies' road trip, Karolyn flew to Cincinnati to check on their house. While there, she decided to have her physician check what she thought was a charley horse in her right leg. The doctor diagnosed a potentially dangerous blood clot, and Karolyn was admitted to Cincinnati's Christ Hospital on August 23. Heavily sedated and in serious condition, she remained hospitalized for more than two weeks, during which time she was ignored by her husband. "I didn't get flowers, and I didn't get a call or anything," she said. She knew, too, that Pete was squiring around Philadelphia a young blonde named Carol Woliung, a former Playboy Club bunny and now a Liberty Belle, one of the cheerleaders for the Philadelphia Eagles football team.[26]

Karolyn Rose said, much later, "I divorced Big Pete because he was flaunting his women, and I had to protect the kids, not because I didn't love him anymore." She sighed, "I waited long enough to decide. It was a very big decision for me." Pete said the secret to getting rid of unwanted wives was easy: "Hey, just give her a million dollars and tell her to hit the road." He did not contest the divorce, but the property settlement took a while: Pete's original offer, said Karolyn's lawyer, was "way low."[27]

NOTES

1. Earl Lawson, "Reds' Highest Offer Ever Too Small for Pete," *Sporting News*, October 21, 1978, 77; "Rose Rejects Reds Offer," (Philadelphia) *Evening Bulletin*, October 13, 1978.

2. Earl Lawson, "Dissatisfied Rose Prepared to Leave Reds," *Sporting News*, October 28, 1978, 25, 27.

3. Joseph Durso, (Philadelphia) *Evening Bulletin*, November 18, 1978.

4. Jerome Holtzman, "More than 40-Million Caught 'Baseball Fever,'" *Official Baseball Guide for 1979* (St. Louis: *Sporting News*, 1979), 324.

5. Ibid., 325.

6. Gary Caruso, "Braves Go High in Bidding for Rose," *Sporting News*, December 16, 1978, 45.

7. United Press International, "Rose Is No Longer Red," (Philadelphia) *Evening Bulletin*, November 27, 1978; Rose and Kahn, *Pete Rose: My Story*, 193–194.

8. *Cincinnati Enquirer*, March 4, 1981; Pete Axthelm, "Gilding the Rose," *Newsweek*, December 18, 1978.

9. Holtzman, "More than 40-Million Caught 'Baseball Fever,'" *Official Baseball Guide for 1979*, 304.

10. Rose and Kahn, *Pete Rose; My Story*, 205; Ray Didinger, "Pete's Flip-flop Started with Giles," (Philadelphia) *Evening Bulletin*, December 6, 1978.

11. Bob Hertzel, *Cincinnati Enquirer*, December 6, 1978; Didinger, "Pete's Flip-flop Started with Giles."

12. Ray Didinger, "Phillies are Rose-less and Red-faced," (Philadelphia) *Evening Bulletin*, December 1, Rich Ashburn, November 19, 1978.

13. Didinger, "Pete's Flip-flop Started with Giles."

14. Hertzel, *Cincinnati Enquirer*, December 6, 1978, March 4, 1981. As revised, the Phillies offer was no longer the lowest.

15. Jack Chevalier, "Ozark: It's Rose on First," (Philadelphia) *Evening Bulletin*, January 30, 1979.

16. Ibid.

17. Joseph Durso, "His Goal: To Get Team in Series," *New York Times*, March 1, 1979, B-10. Emphasis added. Bruce Newman, "He's the Phillie Fillip," *Sports Illustrated*, May 28, 1979, 22.

18. United Press International, "Divorcee: No $, so I Sued Rose," *Philadelphia Daily News*, February 21, 1979.

19. Maury Z. Levy and Samantha Stevenson, "Playboy Interview: Pete Rose," *Playboy*, September 1979. Stevenson herself had a few moments of fame years later when basketball star Julius Erving admitted that he was the father of her daughter, up-and-coming tennis player Alexandra Stevenson.

20. Stan Hochman, *Philadelphia Daily News*, July 31, 1979.

21. Levy and Stevenson, "Playboy Interview: Pete Rose," 108. Emphasis in original.

22. *Philadelphia Inquirer*, August 5, 1979. The disputed quote from the interview is used in Rose's own book; see Rose and Kahn, *Pete Rose: My Story*, 222.

23. Levy and Stevenson, "Playboy Interview: Pete Rose," 100–105; *Philadelphia Inquirer*, August 25, 1979.

24. Rose and Kahn, *Pete Rose: My Story*, 210.

25. Maury Z. Levy, "Karolyn," *Philadelphia Magazine*, June 1979, 221.

26. Rosemarie Ross, "Karolyn Files for Divorce," *Philadelphia Journal*, September 12, 1979; Pat Jordan, "War of the Roses," *Gentlemen's Quarterly*, April 1989, 327.

27. Jordan, "War of the Roses," 328; *Camden Courier-Post*, August 23, 1980; *Cincinnati Enquirer*, December 4, 1980.

ON TOP AGAIN

No one in Philadelphia criticized Pete Rose for his 1979 season, out loud. After all, he had 208 hits and batted .331, second in the league; stolen twenty bases; scored 90 runs; had the year's longest batting streak; and played a new position rather impressively. Not bad for a 38-year-old guy playing in a new town. There was, though, that business of expectations. The Phillies, their fans, and their writers had thought that Pete Rose was the guy to give the team the final push, the extra shove, to get it to the top. And that had not happened. The fourth place finish certainly could not be blamed on Rose, but the championship that had been expected had not materialized either. There was disappointment, whether merited or not.

The *Sporting News* named Pete Rose its Player of the Decade for the 1970s, and there was little dissent from the choice. Henry Aaron complained that he should have won the honor, but he had not even played after 1976.[1]

On the baseball field, 1980 did not look like such a fine time for Pete Rose and his teammates. Dallas Green, who stayed on as the Phillies' manager after his one-month trial in 1979, put the team through a grueling spring training. He stressed two themes—"We, not I" and "Grind it out!"—until his players were tired of hearing them, but Green knew that his collection of stars was nearing "now or never" time. He needed to get their attention. Pete Rose never required exhortations of that type, but he was unique.

Even with Green's prodding, the Phillies rode along for a good part of the season just a few games above the .500 level. A media flap over amphetamines prescribed by a Reading physician and delivered to the Phillies' clubhouse soured the players' relations with the press. A number of the Phillies' stalwarts, including Greg Luzinski and Garry Maddox, deeply resented the way they were handled by Dallas Green. The Phillies' clubhouse was not a happy place.[2]

Rose started the season in a batting slump, but in late May and June he pulled his average up substantially. Hitting slightly under .300 near the midway mark, Rose was helping out with his fielding and baserunning. Even with a broken toe and a hyperextended elbow, he stayed in the line-up. In May, against the Reds, Pete stole second, third, and home in one inning. Green contended that Rose was one of the three best fielding first basemen in the league. Still, it seemed that he could not transfer his drive and his work ethic to his teammates.

Early in August, the Phillies rolled into Pittsburgh for a four-game weekend series with the first-place Pirates. These were games the Phillies had to win to start their run at the Pirates, but instead they lost all four. Dallas Green blistered them in a closed-door meeting as quitters, and they limped out of Pittsburgh headed for Chicago. There, the players held a players-only meeting, pulled themselves together, decided "The hell with Dallas, let's win," and started playing for each other.[3]

From that time on, the Phillies staged a most improbable pennant drive, roaring through August and September, catching and passing the Pirates, and coming down to a final three-game series in Montreal tied for first place with the Expos. Their big hitter in this stretch was Mike Schmidt, enjoying the greatest season of his illustrious career, but every time one looked, there was Pete Rose, getting a hit or a walk, taking an extra base, just doing something to keep the pot boiling.

On Friday night in Montreal, Schmidt knocked in two runs with a home run and sacrifice fly, and pitchers Dick Ruthven, Sparky Lyle, and Tug McGraw made them stand up for a 2–1 win. The next afternoon, rain delayed the start of the game for three hours, and the game, when played, was no thing of beauty. Sure-handed Manny Trillo dropped an easy pop fly, bizarre baserunning turned a Luzinski two-run single into a double play, and the Phillies were down to their last out in the ninth when Bob Boone singled to turn a Rose walk into the tying run. In the eleventh, Rose led off with a single, his third hit of the game, and after an out, Schmidt hit a pitch from Stan Bahnsen into the seats for his 48th home run. When McGraw retired Montreal in the bottom of the inning, the Phillies were National League East champs.

One of the big contributors was 39-year-old Pete Rose, who hit .282 and led the league in doubles with 42. After the clincher in Olympic Stadium, Pete said, "It was a real three-ring circus." Though he missed the .300 mark for the first time since 1974, he said, "this makes it all worthwhile."[4]

Montreal was tough; the Houston Astros, winners of the Western division title, would turn out to be even tougher. Earlier, Rose had said, "Just get me to the playoffs and I'll take over from there." The night before the playoff series opened, Larry Bowa shouted across the Phillies' clubhouse to Rose, "OK, Pete. We're here now, it's time for you to do your thing."[5]

The first game went to the Phillies at the Vet, 3–1, behind Steve Carlton and McGraw. Luzinski's two-run homer erased an early Houston lead. It was a fairly routine ball game, no indicator of what was to come. Game 2 went to the Astros, 7–4, in ten innings. In the bottom of the ninth, score tied, the Phils' Bake McBride was on second when Lonnie Smith singled to right. McBride should have scored, but he was held up by third base coach Lee Elia and he never did score as the next two hitters went out. The Astros scored four runs in the tenth, to take a tied series home to Houston, where they had a spectacular record in 1980. Rose was 2 for 4 in each of the first two games.

In the Astrodome, the home team won the third game, 1–0, in 11 innings, when Joe Morgan, back in Houston, tripled to lead off the eleventh and his pinch runner scored on a sacrifice fly. Game 4 was one of the weirdest ever seen: it had a ball hit to the mound, caught or trapped by Houston pitcher Vern Ruhle, and called, in succession, safe, a triple play, and, finally, a double play, with both managers protesting the game. It had a Houston run taken off the board because the runner left third too soon, and a trapped ball by the Astros right fielder turned into a double play by a blown umpire's call. The Astros tied the game at 3–3 in the ninth, bringing on extra innings once again.

With one out in the tenth, Pete Rose singled into center field. Schmidt flied out, but Luzinski, batting for McBride, hit Joe Sambito's pitch to the left-field wall. Left fielder Jose Cruz made a poor throw to Rafael Landestoy, the cutoff man, as Rose came barreling around the bases. Elia waved him on at third as Landestoy made a low throw to the plate. Catcher Bruce Bochy bobbled the short hop, reached for it, and was leveled by Rose, coming in high with a forearm shiver to Bochy's head.

"The throw wasn't a good one," Rose recounted. "It would have been hard for anybody to handle it. So I went in any way I could. . . . I didn't mean to knock the guy over. I was just trying to get to the plate, to do something."[6]

Rose's run was the winner in the Phils' 5–3 victory, which knotted the series going into the decisive fifth game. For that crucial contest, the starting pitchers were future Hall-of-Famer Nolan Ryan for Houston and rookie Marty Bystrom, a September callup who had won five straight games, for Philadelphia.

Pete Rose made two sensational fielding plays in the fifth inning, and a *Bulletin* writer said, "This was Rose's kind of ballgame." Still, it looked like another heartbreak for the fans of Philadelphia when Houston scored three runs in the seventh to take a 5–2 lead. Only six outs left and Ryan on the mound.[7]

Larry Bowa led off the eighth with a single, and Ryan misplayed Boone's bouncer to the mound into an infield hit. Greg Gross bunted for a hit to load the bases. As Rose came to bat, Mike Schmidt heard Pete taunting Ryan, "We're coming to get you" and "You ain't getting me out, Nolan." Rose, after being fooled and just ticking a 3–2 pitch foul, walked on the next pitch to force in a run and get Ryan out of the game.[8]

Two outs followed before Del Unser's single and Trillo's triple gave the Phillies a 7–5 lead. The Astros came back with two to tie, and the game—as might be expected by then—went into extra innings. In the tenth, a double by Unser and a single by Maddox gave the Phillies another lead, and Dick Ruthven made it stand up for an 8–7 triumph. The Phillies had won the pennant, their first since 1950, and only the third in their existence.

The American League pennant winner, the Kansas City Royals, came into Philadelphia to open the World Series two days later, as Dallas Green looked over his overworked pitching staff for a possible starter. With few options, he settled on Bob "Whirlybird" Walk, a rookie who had come up from Oklahoma City in mid-May and won eleven games. Walk had not pitched in the Houston series, so he was well-rested for his start against Kansas City's twenty-game-winner Dennis Leonard.

Walk gave up a couple of two-run homers, but the Phillies came back with two runs in the third. With two outs, though, the bases were empty when Rose came to bat. With a one-ball, two-strike pitch, Leonard plunked Rose on the right knee, although the Royals suspected that Pete put his knee in harm's way intentionally. When Leonard threw over to first, Rose shouted at him, "You better worry about Schmidt. I ain't gonna steal no bases. He can tie the game with one swing." After Leonard walked Schmidt, it was Bake McBride who hit one over the right-field wall, and suddenly the Phillies were one up. They stayed one up for a 7–6 victory.

Game 2 went to the Phillies 6–4, on a four-run eighth inning against the Royals' star reliever Dan Quisenberry. Kansas City slugger George Brett had to leave the game after the sixth inning, suffering from a bad case of hemorrhoids, which produced a spate of tasteless jokes from the assembled sportswriters. The third game, in Kansas City a couple of nights later, went to the Royals, 4–3, in ten innings, with Brett—"my problems . . . all behind me"—doing major damage with a double and a home run.

In Game 4, the Royals came out slugging against Larry Christenson and had five runs in the first two innings. In the fourth inning, Dickie Noles, pitching for the Phillies, let go a fastball to Brett that just missed the Kansas City third sacker's head, sending him sprawling. Royals' manager Jim Frey charged out of the dugout, shouting at the umpires, shouting at Noles, pleading for justice to be done. Soon Rose and Frey, the two Western Hills alumni, were screaming at one another, face to face, as Pete defended his pitcher. "People say I should mind my own business," Rose said later. "But that's one of my young pitchers out there. . . . He don't know what to do. He's never been in a World Series before. He's never seen a manager come out hollering like that."9

Noles later denied throwing at Brett, though few believed him. What was quite noticeable, though, was that after the knockdown pitch the Royals seemed more tentative at the plate, and their hitting tailed off through the rest of the Series. They won Game 4 5–3, with the runs they already had, but they had only tied the World Series, two games apiece.

The fifth game went to Philadelphia, 4–3, on two runs in the ninth on hits by Schmidt, Unser, and Trillo. The Royals left thirteen men on base, including three in the ninth when Tug McGraw fanned Jose Cardenal to end the game. The Phillies headed home with a 3–2 lead in the Series and Steve Carlton ready to go in Game 6.

With 65,838 victory-starved fans in the Vet, Carlton gave the Phillies seven scoreless innings and his teammates gave him a 4–0 lead. Rose and Schmidt drove in runs in the third inning, and they scored two more in the fifth and sixth. Pete had three hits in four appearances in the game. Carlton tired in the eighth as Kansas City scored one run, but McGraw got out of the inning with the bases loaded. In the ninth, with the mounted police and guard dogs ringing the field, McGraw again loaded the bases with a walk and two singles. It was at this point that Frank White hit a pop-up that bounced off Bob Boone's mitt, only to be gathered in by the ever-alert Pete Rose. When McGraw fanned the next hitter, Willie Wilson, the Phillies were World Champions for the first time in their ninety-seven-year history. That, more than a few people thought at the time, was why they had signed Pete Rose.

Garry Maddox talked about Rose's influence: "But if anyone was 'waiting to see,' they have now seen it, in the way he took over down the stretch and in the playoffs. He's a great player and he inspires guys."10

After that there was nothing to do but savor the parade down Broad Street the next day before huge throngs of happy Philadelphians, past the Vet, down into a packed Kennedy Stadium. Later, Rose told a writer, "The greatest spectacle I have ever seen and the most awesome thing I've ever seen was the parade the day after we beat Kansas City. . . . There were a million people and they all had the same smile on their faces."11

NOTES

1. (Philadelphia) *Evening Bulletin*, January 31, 1980. Aaron had said, "As for player of the decade, I think the things I achieved overshadowed anything anyone else did."

2. A *Trenton Times* article on July 8 said eight Phillies, including Rose, were to be questioned by Pennsylvania drug authorities about prescriptions written by Dr. Patrick Mazza. Rose tried to pass it off by saying, "I don't know anybody in Trenton. I don't know anybody in Reading. I don't even know any doctors in Pennsylvania, the whole state." (Philadelphia) *Evening Bulletin*, July 9, 1980. It would later develop that this was not quite true.

3. Frank Dolson, *The Philadelphia Story: A City of Winners* (South Bend, IN: Icarus Press, 1981), 268–269. On Green's tirade, Rose said, "I've never heard anything like it," and he added, "From that day on I think it was a different, more-dedicated team"; Hal Bodley, *The Team That Wouldn't Die: The Philadelphia Phillies, World Champions, 1980* (Wilmington, DE: Serendipity Press, 1981), 96.

4. Jack Chevalier, "Phillies Clubhouse Bubbles Over," (Philadelphia) *Evening Bulletin*, October 5, 1980.

5. Bodley, *The Team That Wouldn't Die: The Philadelphia Phillies, World Champions, 1980*, 49, 111.

6. Mark Whicker, "A Daring Dash by Rose Pushes Series to the Limit," (Philadelphia) *Evening Bulletin*, October 12, 1980.

7. Jack Chevalier, "Boone and Rose Play Major Roles," (Philadelphia) *Evening Bulletin*, October 13, 1980.

8. *Philadelphia Inquirer*, August 25, 1989.

9. Stan Hochman, "A Subtle Playoff Influence on Phils," *Philadelphia Daily News*, October 21, 1980, 70.

10. Ibid.

11. Bodley, *The Team That Wouldn't Die: The Philadelphia Phillies, World Champions, 1980*, 116.

CHASING MUSIAL . . . AND COBB

After the 1980 season ended, the domestic relations court in Hamilton County, Ohio, cleaned up the last pieces of the Rose marriage. Karolyn had been granted a divorce on July 31 after testifying that for sixteen years Pete's "girlfriends" had plagued her marriage. The divorce itself was uncontested, but the property settlement took some work.[1]

After five meetings with the judge and innumerable conferences between counsel, the settlement was ironed out late in the fall and approved by the court in early December. Karolyn received the home in Cincinnati worth $300,000, the Rolls Royce, $105,000 cash, and alimony over thirteen years reportedly amounting to $1.2 million. Pete would pay $600 a month child support for Fawn and Petey. There had been an interim order issued permitting Petey to attend the World Series; Karolyn had objected to this only because Fawn, as usual, was not included.[2]

With Karolyn dealt with and Carol Woliung well-settled in as his new girlfriend, Pete Rose was ready to set out on his next challenges: another title for the Phillies and Stan Musial's National League record for career base hits. At the close of the 1980 season, Rose had 3,557 hits, which left Musial's lifetime total of 3,630 well within reach. One of the reasons Rose had turned down Kansas City's free agency offer in 1978 was that the Royals were in the wrong league for his pursuit of Musial's mark. Now Pete was ready to go after Stan the Man.

First, though, came the disposition of the case of the Reading doctor and the amphetamines. At a preliminary hearing on January 7 before a Reading district justice, several Phillies players and their wives stoutly denied having anything to do with Dr. Mazza. Pete Rose, asked under oath if he had ever used "greenies," responded innocently, "What is a greenie?" to the astonishment of everyone who had read his *Playboy* interview. Mazza testified that "Pete was having trouble with his weight and he needed some help with his 38-year-old body," in explaining why he had prescribed the drugs for Rose. At a resumed hearing on February 4, however, pitcher Randy Lerch admitted receiving the amphetamines, and the case against Dr. Mazza broke down. All charges were dismissed, and the Phillies players involved came out looking like liars who were willing to let a friend face criminal charges so they could avoid a little embarrassment.[3]

With Dallas Green persuaded by Ruly Carpenter and Paul Owens to stay on one more year as manager before returning to the front office, there was speculation that Rose stood next in line for the job. He allowed that he had some interest in it. For 1981, Green would still be in the dugout. After that would be a question.[4]

Rose was optimistic about the new season. "I think our team is going to be so strong it's going to be scary," he exclaimed. "We've got to be better than last year. . . . I'm not saying we're a cinch, but we don't have the question marks we had at this time a year ago." Besides, he said, "this team knows it can win the big games now. It knows the feeling of winning a pennant, a playoff, a World Series. . . . All those things have to help us mentally."[5]

When the season got underway, the Phillies played well, with Schmidt and Rose both setting a torrid pace. Montreal once again appeared to be the club's main competition, with the St. Louis Cardinals also hanging close to the top. Looming over everything in baseball, however, was an impasse on a new contract between the owners and the players' union, with a strike deadline fixed for May 30. As Rose piled up the hits, he approached ever closer to Musial's mark.

Pete Rose was enjoying his pursuit of the National League hits record. He knew that he would catch Musial sooner or later. "There's no pressure in this thing," he told the press in mid-May. "Even if there's a strike at the end of the month, they won't call off baseball forever." The strike deadline, as it happened, was pushed back to June 12. As he got closer, Rose said, "It's fun going after the record."[6]

On the evening of June 10, a crowd of 57,386 showed up at the Vet, with Pete Rose owning 3,629 hits, needing one to tie Musial's mark, two to break it. Stan himself was in a box seat by the Phillies' dugout, and Nolan Ryan was on the mound for Houston. In the first inning, Ryan fell behind, two and one, then came in with a fastball "out over the plate and he hit it clean," Nolan said. The single to left center tied the record. But Nolan Ryan was going to be no one's patsy. "I was into it," he said later. "I'm sure my concentration was as keen against him as it was all night. I pitched him the last three times up as well as I've ever pitched anybody in three straight at-bats."[7]

In those three at-bats, in the third, fifth, and eighth, Rose struck out three times. After that, Ryan aggravated an old back injury, and the Phillies scored five runs against the Astro bullpen to win the game 5–4. Rose admitted, "I was a little embarrassed about striking out three times."[8]

The win gave the Phillies a record of 34–21, and a game and a half lead over the Cardinals. At the time, no one realized the significance of that game and a half, but all knew there would be no more baseball for a while. The players' strike started, and its end was nowhere in sight. The Phillies players scattered, and Pete Rose went home to Cincinnati, to find places where he could work out—batting cages where he could hit baseballs, tennis courts where he could play sets.

Rose was officially tied with Musial for the National League record, but there were still two men ahead of him in total hits, Henry Aaron, whose 3,771 total included those from two seasons in the American League, and Ty Cobb, whose 4,191 was still off in the distance. Aaron was certainly catchable, but every game Pete Rose lost to the strike in 1981 meant a lost opportunity to close that gap on Ty Cobb.

At last, on July 31, the strike was settled, having endured for fifty days. The lords of baseball decreed that the first post-strike activity would be the annual All Star game, on August 9 in Cleveland. Then the season would resume, but with this difference: the team leading its division when the strike began was declared the winner of the first half of the season and would play a division series at the end of the year with the team winning the second half of the season. So that game and a half lead for the Phillies meant they were already in the post-season; August 10 to the end of the year was essentially meaningless for them. Unfortunately, many of them played it that way.

Rose played first base for the National League All Stars, going 1 for 3 as the Nationals won 5–4 on Mike Schmidt's eighth-inning home run. Then it was back to business, with the Phillies entertaining St. Louis, 60,561 fans, and old Cardinal Stan Musial, waiting in a box seat for his record to fall. In the first inning, Rose's bouncer to short was misplayed by Garry Templeton for an error. Unfortunately, the man in charge of fireworks for the evening set them off at that point; he thought Bill Giles had yelled, "Go, go!" when he had really shouted "No, no!" Even Rose on first base laughed when the fireworks went off prematurely.[9]

In the third, Cardinal hurler Bob Forsch speared Rose's sharp ground ball, and in the fifth Pete bounced out to the second baseman. In the eighth inning, though, with reliever Mark Littell now on the hill for the Redbirds, Rose grounded a ball between Templeton and third sacker Ken Oberkfell into left field, and the celebration began. Musial came out to first base to hug the new record-holder, 3,631 colored balloons were released, and the fans went wild, chanting "Pete, Pete, Pete!" for a full five minutes. The scoreboard flashed the information that Rose needed only 560 hits to pass Cobb. And in the clubhouse after the game, Rose took a call from President Ronald Reagan. It was a grand way to start the second half. What came after was not so beautiful.

The Phillies never hit their stride after the break. They won twenty-five and lost twenty-seven the rest of the way, to finish third in the second half and third overall in their division for the year. Schmidt and Rose hit well, Mike winning his second straight MVP award and Pete batting .325 for the year, leading the league in hits with 140. Rose tacked on 66 more hits after the record-breaking one, to finish the year with 3,697. But the pitching, aside from Carlton's, was spotty, the hitting was marginal, and the team effort lackluster.

But the Phillies were in the playoffs, to play Montreal, the "champs" of the second half. To illustrate just what a terrible mistake the split season was, the best records for the season in the two National League divisions were those of St. Louis in the east and Cincinnati in the west. Neither team happened to win a half-season championship so neither was in the playoffs.

The Phillies lost the division playoff to Montreal, three games to two, and the fans of Philadelphia, turned off by the strike and the arbitrary way their team was declared a "champion," took little interest in the proceedings. Rose did all right with 6 hits in 20 at-bats, one of them a double, but it was a tough way to end a bad year for baseball.

During the playoffs, Dallas Green accepted a job as general manager of the Chicago Cubs, and on November 4 former Phillies catcher Pat Corrales was named the club's new manager. Bill Giles was putting together a group to purchase the Phillies from the Carpenter family; baseball's new economics had disillusioned Ruly and his father, former president Bob Carpenter. He was asked about Rose. "I've talked with Pete about it," Giles replied. "If I have the ballclub, I'd like him to be my manager sometime. But I don't think even he can play and manage at the same time." He went on: "It wouldn't be fair to him because he still has a shot at Ty Cobb's record." This was fine with Rose: "All I'm interested in is playing first base," he said.[10]

The year 1982 got off to a sour start as far as Pete Rose was concerned, when he injured his back playing tennis with Reuven Katz on February 15. He aggravated the injury by continuing to exercise and was confined to bed on the twenty-fifth. He sat out most of the spring training games, but he was in good shape by Opening Day and continued a consecutive-games streak which was then over 500.

The season was a moderately successful one for the Phillies. They finished second in the east, trailing the Cardinals by three games, with a record of 89–73. But it could have been much better. On September 14, after Steve Carlton had beaten the Cardinals, Pat Corrales' team had a one-game lead. But losses in the next two games pushed them behind St. Louis, and they never caught the Redbirds again. Pete Rose saw his batting average slip to .271, and the press started wondering about keeping him in the line-up day in and day out.

A big event for Rose during the '82 season came on June 22, when he doubled off of John Stuper of the Cards. It was base hit number 3,772, moving Rose ahead of Aaron, leaving only Cobb still ahead of him. For the year Pete had 172 hits, so he was still 322 behind the old Tiger.

After the season, Rose signed on as an off-season sportscaster for WKRC-TV, Channel 12 in Cincinnati, for a minimum of twenty-five appearances over the fall and winter. Peter King, the radio and television writer for the *Enquirer*, watched him a couple of times, then wrote, "He is good, and fun to watch." Pete, asked about his interviewing technique, said, "I ask questions that I, as a sports fan, want to ask. . . . I usually just ask what comes in my mind." It was a popular show, and Rose was back in Cincinnati's good graces.[11]

The 1983 season was a peculiar one, for the Phillies and for Pete Rose. Before the start of spring training, the club had picked up Joe Morgan in a trade with the Giants and Tony Perez as a free agent. The reunion of the Big Red Machine in Phillies pinstripes attracted a lot of press attention. With four other players over 38 years old on the roster, the club found itself tagged the "Wheeze Kids" (a play on the "Whiz Kids" nickname of the 1950 Phillies).

There was concern over Rose's .271 average the year before. Morgan felt he could help. "I know Pete as well as I know anybody," Joe said. "I know when to kick him in the rear, and I know when to pat him on the back." Talk about resting him bothered Rose; "I'll rest plenty when I'm dead," he scoffed. Corrales said he would talk to Pete about reduced playing time; "somebody's going to have to do it sometime," he said.[12]

For most of the season, the Phillies played about even with the rest of the division, no better and no worse. They played dull baseball, and the fans were turned off. Tony Perez hit well in the beginning of the year, but Rose seemed to be slipping badly and Morgan hit hardly at all. The players were unhappy with Pat Corrales, and on July 18 he was fired, although the Phillies were in first place at the time, albeit just one game above .500 with a 43–42 record.

General manager Paul Owens came down to the dugout as the new manager, and the team started playing better—much better. It won forty-seven and lost thirty the rest of the way and won the division with a big September. The Phillies won eleven games in a row and fourteen of the last sixteen, clinching the division on September 28.

The way they won it was curious. Joe Morgan had a very productive September. He wound up hitting .230 for the season, but most of his offense came in the last month. Rose, on the other hand, spent a good part of the last month on the bench. A rookie first baseman named Len Matuszek, ironically a product of Moeller High in Cincinnati, was brought in as a September callup, and his .275 hitting, with 4 home runs and 16 RBIs, was a key part of the September surge. With the offense of Matuszek, there was little need of Pete Rose and his .245 batting average, with no home runs at what was supposed to be a power position. For the season, Rose had 121 hits, so he was still 201 behind Cobb.

Matuszek was ineligible for the postseason games because he had come up too late, so Rose was restored to first base for the National League playoffs against the Los Angeles Dodgers, who had beaten Philadelphia eleven out of twelve in the regular season. But these were the playoffs, and the old records were meaningless. The Phils won the opener in LA 1–0, on a Schmidt home run, as Carlton and reliever Al Holland shut down the Dodgers on seven hits. Rose was 1 for 4.

In Game 2, the Dodgers' Mexican lefthander Fernando Valenzuela stopped the Phillies 4–1, Pete Rose going 0 for 3. Game 3, back in Philadelphia, was won by the Phillies 7–2, as a big home run by Gary Matthews supported the complete game hurling of rookie Charles Hudson. Rose, with three singles, looked more like himself.

Finally, Carlton won the fourth game, 7–2, on another big homer by Matthews, and the Phillies had themselves the fourth pennant in their 100-year history. Tom Lasorda's Dodgers went home, and it was on to the World Series for Paul Owens and his surprise winners, against the Baltimore Orioles.

Rose was 2 for 5 in the final game, giving him a .375 average for the series, although Dave Kindred of the *Washington Post* said the average was misleading, "built on infield choppers and humpbacked liners." Rose, he wrote, "has lost bat speed."[13]

The first game of the World Series, played in Baltimore's Memorial Stadium on a rainy night before 52,204, was a pitching duel between the Orioles' Scott McGregor and John Denny, the Phillies' nineteen-game winner who would win the Cy Young trophy that season. Denny gave up a home run to Jim Dwyer in the first but then shut down the O's. Home runs by Morgan and Garry Maddox ultimately gave the Phillies a 2–1 victory. Rose's single was one of only five

Philadelphia hits. Game 2 went to Baltimore 4–1, as soft-tossing Mike Boddicker held the Phils to three hits. Rose wore an 0-for-4 collar.

For the third game, in Veterans Stadium, Paul Owens felt he had to shake up his slump-ridden line-up. With Rose batting .125 for the Series, he decided to replace him on first base with Tony Perez, who had had good numbers in the American League against Orioles' starter Mike Flanagan. Owens gave Rose the courtesy of telling him personally, and Rose reacted badly. He went on ABC television for a pregame interview with Howard Cosell, saying, "It's embarrassing. It's not the way baseball is played." He said he was hurt by the benching, as if the benching of a .125 hitter who hit .245 for the year was a cataclysmic occurrence.[14]

Because of the fuss Rose made, veteran writer Bob Burnes said, "the resulting flap put unnecessary pressure on Perez, and the rest of a discordant team reacted unfortunately." It was, Burnes wrote, "the one really smart move" Owens made in the Series, and it backfired because of Rose's truculence and sulking.[15]

The Phillies lost that third game 3–2, when Owens left Carlton, bothered by an achy back, in one batter too long, and shortstop Ivan DeJesus booted a ground ball while the eventual winning run scored. Rose pinch hit for Joe Lefebvre in the ninth inning and grounded out. Pete was back in the line-up for the fourth and fifth games and had two hits in each, but the Phillies went down meekly in both to lose the Series, four games to one. Rose wound up with a .313 average for the Series, but the Phillies were devastated by Schmidt's 1-for-20 performance and a team batting average of .195.

After Rose's act with Cosell, there were not many Phillies fans who were surprised when the club released him on October 19, three days after the end of the World Series. "Pete wants to play every game," said Bill Giles, "and we could not assure him he would play every game with the Phillies." Rose responded, "I don't like to play part-time. . . . I'm sure there are some teams out there who want me." It was rumored that the Braves, Royals, Pirates, and Yankees were interested in Rose, but Reuven Katz said, "Any rumor is a false rumor. We haven't had any conversations with anyone." Pete Rose, obsessed with his pursuit of Cobb's record, said money was not his main objective now; "we'll just go back to Cincinnati and anticipate the phone calls and make sure the phone's on the hook every ten minutes."[16]

Five years after his earlier venture into free agency, Pete Rose would find the calls much fewer this time around.

NOTES

1. *Cincinnati Enquirer*, August 1, 1980.

2. (Philadelphia) *Evening Bulletin*, January 1, 1981; October 21, 1980.

3. (Philadelphia) *Evening Bulletin*, February 5, 1981; "The Continuing Saga of Dr. Mazza and His 'Good Friends,'" *Sports Illustrated*, February 16, 1981, 11. Those involved were Rose, Lerch, Steve Carlton, Larry Christenson, former Phil Tim McCarver, and two wives, Jean Luzinski and Sheena Bowa.

4. Milton Richman, "Pete Rose Wants to Manage Phils," *Philadelphia Journal*, February 19, 1981.

5. *Cincinnati Enquirer*, February 8, 1981; Jack Chevalier, "For Mister Optimism, 40 is just a number," (Philadelphia) *Evening Bulletin*, April 7, 1981.

6. Mark Whicker, (Philadelphia) *Evening Bulletin*, May 14, 1981; *Cincinnati Post*, June 3, 1981.

7. Rick Ostrow, "Ryan Earns Decision in His Duel with Rose," (Philadelphia) *Evening Bulletin*, June 11, 1981.

8. *Cincinnati Enquirer* and (Philadelphia) *Evening Bulletin*, both June 11, 1981.

9. *Cincinnati Post*, August 11, 1981.

10. Bill Fleischman, "For Now, Rose Will Manage to Play," *Philadelphia Daily News*, October 12, 1981, 85.

11. Peter King, *Cincinnati Enquirer*, December 5, 1982.

12. Steve Wulf, "In Philadelphia, They're the Wheeze Kids," *Sports Illustrated*, March 14, 1983, 33.

13. *Cincinnati Enquirer*, October 12, 1983.

14. Henry Hecht, "Take a Seat, Pete," *New York Post*, October 15, 1983.

15. Robert L. Burnes, "Rose's Pouting Put Damper on Phillies' Chances," *St. Louis Globe-Democrat*, October 18, 1983, 2D.

16. Associated Press, "Rose Released by Phils," *New York Times, Cincinnati Enquirer,* and *Cincinnati Post*, all October 20, 1983.

RETURN TO CINCINNATI

In March 1982, Reuven Katz had hired a New York marketing agency called Robert Landau Associates "to market the phenomenon called Pete Rose to the corporate world." Motivational pep talks were priced at $50,000, while for $250,000 a company could have a whole year of Pete for the works: pep talks, corporate spokesman, personal appearances, print ads and television commercials. In the meantime Pete Rose needed a job.[1]

The offers were not flooding in. Rose's desire to play every day reduced the market substantially; a .245 hitter who would be 43 years old in April was a questionable commodity, regardless of his pursuit of Ty Cobb's record. The Reds, under considerable pressure from their fans to bring Pete back, made it clear they would not sign him as an everyday player.

Finally, in January 1984, it became apparent that the Montreal Expos were the only club with serious interest in Rose. There was debate even in Montreal about signing him. One Expos official said the fans were about 50–50, the media 40–60 against, and the club itself about 50–50. "But Mr. [Charles] Bronfman [the owner] is part of the 50 percent who want Pete," he said, so the Expos signed him to a one-year deal on January 20.[2]

Rose told the Expos that he no longer demanded to play every day. If he was hitting well he wanted to play, and if not he would understand. Pete told the press when he signed, "I think if the season started tomorrow, I'd be in left field. I don't think they got me to sit on the bench." He added that the Expos had not yet won a championship, and "I think I can add that ingredient that's been missing."[3]

During the winter, Rose reluctantly agreed with those who said that at his age he should undertake a "sophisticated offseason conditioning program." After going through all sorts of tests at Ohio University, Pete worked out a program with Reds' trainer Larry Starr. Pete cut out red meat and then went to work with Starr. To no one's surprise, Starr commented that Rose "has approached his program with a level of intensity most players can't handle."[4]

So Pete Rose was in good shape as the season opened. He purchased a new home for $530,000 in posh Indian Hill, on the eastern side of Cincinnati. The Expos came to the Queen City for their third series of the new season on April 9, and at 8:30 on the morning of the 11th, Rose married Carol Woliung in a private ceremony at the home of Reuven Katz.

In the first seven games of the season, two in Houston, three in Atlanta, and two in Riverfront Stadium, Rose had nine of the ten hits he needed to reach 4,000. Cincinnati's fans turned out in full force on April 11 to see the newly-wed reach another milestone, but Reds pitcher Bruce Berenyi walked Rose four times, and manager Bill Virdon replaced him with a pinch runner in the eighth. The fans booed, but the big hit would come in Canada, not Cincinnati.

On April 13, the Expos played their home opener against the Phillies before 48,060 fans. Rose reached left-hander Jerry Koosman on a fastball away for a double down the right field line and became only the second major leaguer ever to accumulate 4,000 hits.

Rose began the year in left, with Al Oliver the regular at first base, but it soon became evident that his throwing arm was not up to the demands of the position. He became an occasional starter at first base and a pinch hitter, as the Expos languished in fifth place. There was no longer a Rose magic touch to make a contender into a winner. Pete was hitting just .259, with 72 hits, when Montreal traded him on August 15 to his hometown Reds, for infielder Tom Lawless.

Reuven Katz had initiated discussions with the Reds, at Rose's suggestion, when he ran into Bob Howsam at a wedding reception. The Reds were looking for a new manager, Rose was willing (as long as he could be a player-manager), and John McHale, the Expos' general manager, was happy to make a trade.

In Cincinnati, of course, this was the story of the year. "PETE COMES HOME" was the huge headline in the *Enquirer*, when Howsam introduced Rose as the club's new manager, replacing Vern Rapp. Rose would continue as a player, but Howsam said, "Pete is coming mainly to be the manager, and also pinch hit and fill in a few times."[5]

Later, Howsam said that when Rose told him, "I can still do the things I could do ten years ago, but I can't do it every day," that was what he wanted to hear in order to bring Pete back. The Reds set no limits on Rose's playing time, but Howsam made it clear Rose "would not abuse his office," as writer Tim Sullivan put it, "to aid his pursuit of Cobb." Perhaps not, but Rose played first base in twenty-three of Cincinnati's remaining forty-one games, pinch hitting in three others. He hit .365 for the Reds, though, so no one complained.[6]

In his first game back, on August 17, the Reds had to delay the start of the game for ten minutes to accommodate the crush at the ticket windows for the largest crowd since Opening Day. In the first inning, with Gary Redus on second, Rose lined a run-scoring single to center. When Cubs' center fielder Bob Dernier fumbled the ball, Pete kept going and slid headfirst into third base, as the fans screamed. He scored shortly after and later in the game picked up a run-scoring double. Pete truly was back. When a reporter asked if bringing him back was a publicity stunt for the Reds, Rose said, "If it is, it's a damn good one, don't you think?"[7]

The Reds, nineteen games under .500 when Rose took over, had a good September and went 19–22 overall under Pete's leadership. Rose felt that the atmosphere and attitude on the team had changed; "I think guys are having fun again." Pete had fun in the club's last game, on September 30, when Houston's Jose Cruz and Jerry Mumphrey collided in the outfield, letting Rose's ball drop for his 726th double, putting him one up on Musial for two-base hits by a National Leaguer.[8]

Rose took a pay cut, down to $225,000, for 1985. This figure was still a good one for a manager who figured to play only occasionally. But Rose, who batted .286 for the year in 1984, felt he would play more than that. Nineteen eighty-five, after all, was the year in which he hoped to break Ty Cobb's record. When the season started, Pete was just ninety-four hits away. Besides, he was starting his first full year as a manager with a clean slate. With a pitching staff led by Mario Soto, Jay Tibbs, and lefty reliever John Franco, with reliable hitters like Dave Parker, Cesar Cedeno and Eric Davis, youngsters like Nick Esasky and Ron Oester, and a couple of relics from the Big Red Machine in Dave Concepcion and Tony Perez, the Reds looked as if they could be a threat in the Western division. Pete Rose hoped the Cobb chase would not be too much of a distraction.

Pete was ready. In October 1984, he had hired Taft Merchandising, a local group, to handle promotions connected with the Cobb pursuit, and the Taft people were eager to help Pete cash in. William Hayes, Rose's man at Taft, said Rose represented "longevity, continuity, dedication, enthusiasm." There would be ceramics, silver and gold medallions, key chains, T-shirts, trading cards, and more, all with Rose's name or likeness and some reference to Ty Cobb. Pete had signed up with baseball writer Hal Bodley to do a day-by-day diary of the season; it would come out before the end of the year and be called *Countdown to Cobb*. All he needed now was those 94 hits, then one more to break the record.[9]

Pete told a reporter, "There are those who say I'm an egomaniac. But seeing records within reach is an incentive." He went on to comment on the Hall of Fame: "If I don't get into the Hall of Fame on the first ballot, I don't want to get in at all," ignoring some pretty fine ballplayers who were not elected their first year eligible. (The year before, when a Montreal writer had referred to him as a "potential Hall of Famer," Rose cut him short: "Hey, I ain't no *potential* Hall of Famer, pal!")[10]

The season opened on April 8, at Riverfront Stadium, with the Expos furnishing the opposition, in front of a new ballpark record crowd of 52,971. The day was a great success, even though it drizzled and snowed off and on, for the Reds won 4–1, behind Soto, and first baseman Pete Rose had a single and double in three tries.

After a day off, Montreal beat the Reds, 4–1, with Rose picking up one single against Bill Gullickson, and the team headed for New York, where the Mets took three in a row from it. Rose was 4-for-12 in the series, but the Reds totaled only thirteen hits in the three games. They went to Atlanta and took off on a seven-game winning streak.

As Rose's forty-fourth birthday neared, a reporter asked Ted Williams about him. "I've seen a lot of better hitters than Rose," said the old Red Sox slugger. "I can name you 15 right now. But he's durable, versatile, grindy, a great contact hitter. He's made a lot of adjustments. He's smart."[11]

The 1985 Reds were far superior to the 1984 version of the team. With top-notch pitching from Soto, rookie Tom Browning, and reliever Ted Power, and great hitting from Dave Parker, they stayed in contention for most of the season, chasing San Diego the first part of the year, then the Dodgers, who eventually started widening the lead on them. Through it all, the constant was the struggle of Pete Rose for those 95 hits he needed to pass Ty Cobb. He was pretty much a left-handed hitter now, platooning himself with Tony Perez at first base.

Rose was hitting in the .260s, so he was not handicapping the team much with his presence in the line-up, though his extra-base power was just about gone. One thing he was concerned about was the possibility of another lengthy strike. The owners and the players' union engaged in another long and fruitless negotiation, and on August 6 the players went out on strike again. After two days, however, Commissioner Peter Ueberroth managed to get the two sides into agreement, and the strike ended.

As September began, Rose needed eight more hits to break Cobb's record. On Sunday the first he picked up two singles as the Reds beat Pittsburgh and Rick Rhoden at Riverfront. The next day he went 0 for 3 and the countdown remained at six. Rose said he asked Parker before the game whether the Cobb chase was a distraction to the Reds players. "No way," Parker said. "The guys are liking it. What they don't understand is how you're able to handle it so well." They did not realize that the public attention and scrutiny were like mother's milk to Pete Rose.[12]

Rose did not play against the Cardinals on September 3, but he got a hit off of lefthanded reliever Ken Dayley at Busch Stadium the next day. The fifth was an open date, but it was filled by the action of the Cincinnati City Council, which voted 6–3 to change the name of Second Street, which went past Riverfront Stadium, to Pete Rose Way, despite a cost of between five and ten thousand dollars to mount thirty-five new street-level signs and replace a dozen large highway signs on downtown interstates. Councilwoman Marian Spencer, one of three Charter Party members to vote against the change, said she was against naming streets for living persons "because living persons can sometimes commit embarrassing acts after they are honored."[13]

On September 6, at Wrigley Field, Pete hit a single and his second home run of the year. After an 0-for-4 the next day, Rose figured he would take Sunday the eighth off because lefty Steve Trout was scheduled to go for the Cubs. That seemed all right, because with two hits to tie and three to break Cobb's record, it looked as if they would come at home in Cincinnati. But Trout fell off his bicycle Saturday night, injuring himself, and the Cubs started right-hander Reggie Patterson instead. So Rose put himself into the line-up.[14]

Pete was concerned, because none of his family members were at Wrigley that day, nor was owner Marge Schott or Commissioner Ueberroth. What he did not know was that ex-wife Karolyn was there, just in case he should break Cobb's record in Chicago. In the first inning Pete singled to center. After grounding out in the third, he singled to right in the fifth, for career hit number 4,191, tying Cobb, setting off a great ovation from the 28,269 fans. In the seventh he hit a hard shot that shortstop Shawon Dunston handled, and in the ninth he struck out against Lee Smith. The game was called a 5–5 tie for darkness after nine innings, but the hits counted.[15]

On Monday, September 9, back in Cincinnati, Rose kept himself on the bench against San Diego lefty Dave Dravecky, and on Tuesday, with 51,045 people at Riverfront, he went 0 for 4 against Lamar Hoyt and Lance McCullers. The next night, September 11, the crowd was a bit smaller, 47,237, but the anticipation was just as great. Rose didn't keep them waiting long.

Batting with one out in the bottom of the first against Padres righthander Eric Show, Rose lined a 2–1 slider softly into left center field for his 4,192nd hit. As the crowd cheered and cameras flashed all around the ballpark, with security guards and off-duty policemen fanning out down the foul lines, with Show coming over to shake his hand, Pete Rose stood on first base, thought about his father and Ty Cobb, and then began to weep. He clutched first-base coach Tommy Helms, his old roommate and teammate from as far back as Tampa, around the neck and shoulders and sobbed. "I don't know what to do," he said. Then his son Petey came out from the dugout to receive a hug from his dad. His teammates from the Big Red Machine, Perez and Concepcion, still teammates, lifted Rose to their shoulders. Marge Schott came out and a red Corvette with Ohio license plate "PR 4192" was driven onto the field. Eric Show sat down on the mound while all this was going on.[16]

Eventually the game was resumed, and Rose got a triple and a walk following the historic hit. He scored both runs as the Reds behind Browning and Power beat San Diego 2–0. After the game Pete got a phone call from President Ronald Reagan and received from Schott a silver punch bowl, tray, and twelve cups, each engraved with a highlight from Rose's career.

The Reds, though, were still nine games behind the Dodgers. They kept battling, as Pete Rose had taught them, and finished second, five and one-half back. They were not eliminated from the race until October 2, and they were six and one-half games ahead of third place Houston and San Diego. Rookie Tom Browning was the club's first twenty-game winner since 1970, and Power and John Franco were solid in the bullpen. Rose finished the season with a .264 average and 107 hits—not bad for a 44-year-old player-manager.

As the season neared its end, there was talk about Pete Rose as the National League Manager of the Year, for transforming the dismal 1984 Reds into 1985's pennant contenders. That honor eventually went to the Cardinals' Whitey Herzog, but there was recognition of the solid job Rose had done. In addition, he was named by the *Sporting News* its Man of the Year.

On October 31, the Reds gave Pete a three-year contract paying him a million dollars a year in 1986 and 1987 and no less than $750,000 in 1988, to be adjusted so that Rose received at least $1 more than any other manager. "He will be," said Reds general manager Bill Bergesch, "the highest paid manager in the game." At the press conference announcing the new contract, Rose said first base was not set for 1986. "It will depend on whether or not one of our young outfielders can do a better job than Tony [Perez] and I can do at first," he said, in which case Nick Esasky would move from left field to first base.[17]

NOTES

1. Robert Raissman, "The Selling of Pete Rose," *Cincinnati Post*, July 9, 1983, 7-B; *Cincinnati Enquirer*, August 7, 1983.

2. *Cincinnati Enquirer*, January 20, 1984.

3. *Cincinnati Enquirer*, January 21, 1984.

4. *USA Today*, December 14, 1983.

5. Greg Hoard, "Pete Comes Home," *Cincinnati Enquirer*, August 16, 1984. Dick Wagner, fired by the Reds in 1983, described Howsam's decision as "an interesting marketing move."

6. *Cincinnati Enquirer*, August 17, 1984.

7. Ibid.

8. *Cincinnati Enquirer*, October 1, 1984.

9. Richard Alm, "Rose's Run for a Record: Everybody's Cashing In," *U.S. News and World Report*, September 2, 1985.

10. *Dayton Daily News*, April 7, 1985; *Cincinnati Enquirer*, April 15, 1984. Emphasis in original.

11. *Cincinnati Enquirer*, April 14, 1985.

12. Pete Rose, with Hal Bodley, *Countdown to Cobb: My Diary of the Record-Breaking 1985 Season* (St. Louis: The Sporting News, 1985), 192.

13. *Cincinnati Enquirer*, September 6, 1985.

14. Rose, with Bodley, *Countdown to Cobb: My Diary of the Record-Breaking 1985 Season*, 196.

15. *Cincinnati Enquirer*, September 4, 1985.

16. *Cincinnati Enquirer*, September 12, 1985; Lew Moores, "Head-first History," *Cincinnati Post*, September 12, 1985; Rose, with Bodley, *Countdown to Cobb: My Diary of the Record-Breaking 1985 Season*, 202.

17. Greg Hoard, "New Pact Makes Pete Highest Paid Manager," *Cincinnati Enquirer*, November 1, 1985, D-1.

A troubled Pete Rose as manager of the Reds. © *Bettmann/CORBIS.*

TROUBLE

The three years that followed for Pete Rose seemed to move on two tracks: the public track of Rose as manager of the Reds, and the seeming disintegration of Rose's private life.

After the exhilarating performance in 1985, there was great hope that Cincinnati would be in the race all the way in 1986, with division and league titles leading to the World Series. Rose looked forward to the race. He admitted, during the winter, "I'll be 45 next month. Baseball is a young man's game." But, "If you can attack it with the same enthusiasm as a kid and don't worry about getting dirty and sliding headfirst and having fun, there's no reason why you should get old."[1]

Nevertheless, Rose started the year on the disabled list with a stomach disorder, and the club took an early nosedive. By May 10, the Reds were 6–19, ten games out of first place. Not until late August could they reach the .500 level, at 62–62, and they were never in contention. Rose moaned, "I preached and preached and preached during spring training the importance of a fast start. I thought we were ready. I don't know what happened. . . ."[2]

What happened was an offensive failure at the beginning of the season combined with uncertain starting pitching all year long and a weak bench. From June 29 on, though, with Dave Parker, Eric Davis, and Buddy Bell contributing to a revived attack, the Reds won 56 and lost 35. They finished second again, with 86–76, but they were ten games behind the division champion Astros. By the end of the year, the club roster was considerably younger than it had been at the start. A rookie named Barry Larkin had replaced Concepcion at shortstop, and Tony Perez was switched from the active roster to the coaching staff.

Rose himself hit only .219 with but 52 hits. On August 14, he picked up what was to be the last hit of his career, a single against San Francisco's Greg Minton. It was Pete's 4,256th. Four days later, the Padres' Goose Gossage struck Rose out in his last plate appearance. From then on he stayed on the bench. On November 11, the Reds released Pete as a player, opening up a roster spot. But no one thought he was through quite yet. "I don't know when," Rose said, "but I'll probably play again."[3]

He never did. In 1987, Pete Rose was strictly a manager and—for a while—a very successful one. On May 29, after a 13–6 win at Pittsburgh put the Reds in first place, they stayed on top all the way into August. They were still in first when they arrived in San Francisco on August 7, but four straight losses to the Giants knocked them back, and a record of 9–20 for the month killed their chances. A good September enabled Cincinnati to finish second for a third year in a row, with a record of 84–78, six games back of the Giants.

Late in August, the Reds lost three straight one-run games in Pittsburgh. Marge Schott helped things along, telling the press, "The only good thing about this is that if we don't win, it's not my fault. It's Bergesch's and Pete's fault. They run the baseball." Bergesch, fired as general manager on October 12, summed up the season: "Little by little we deteriorated and we lost our spirit. We went through the motions. No heart."[4]

On December 7, at the annual baseball meetings in Dallas, Rose officially retired as a player. "I thought I already was retired," he said. "I mean, I didn't play all last year and I wasn't on the roster. I don't really see the need to make an announcement that I'm retired." No problem, said Marge Schott: "It's over. He's the manager now. He's definitely not a player."[5]

The Reds once again got off to a slow start in 1988, running fourth with a 35–42 record through the end of June. An ugly incident on April 30 marred the season for Pete Rose. In a Saturday night game at Riverfront with the Mets, there were a number of bad scenes in a tense, close game—several disputes with umpires and a batter hit after Rose directed his pitcher to throw at him. Then, with the score tied in the ninth inning, a Mets runner at second with two out, New York's Mookie Wilson hit a hot smash that shortstop Barry Larkin grabbed in the hole. His long throw to first was wide, and first sacker Nick Esasky pulled his foot off the bag to reach for it just as Wilson arrived. After a split-second delay, umpire Dave Pallone called the runner safe. Esasky, oblivious to the baserunner rounding third and heading home, went after the umpire, screaming his objection to the call. Then Rose raced onto the field, beside himself with anger, shouting that Pallone's delay had given the Mets the tie-breaking run.

Pallone pointed out that it was Rose's first baseman whose mental lapse had permitted the run to score.

Dave Pallone was not your usual kind of umpire. He had come to the National League in 1979 when the regular umpires had gone on strike, and he was still regarded as a "scab" by the rest of the men in blue. He was not a particularly good umpire. Pallone was also gay. Although this was not public knowledge at the time, there were enough baseball people who knew it, including Pete Rose; Pallone believed Rose had been spreading word of the umpire's sexual orientation around the league. And Pallone, in his career, had had special problems with the Cincinnati Reds.

Rose, in continuing his profanity-laced argument with the taller umpire, was jabbing his finger in Pallone's face. "It's your fault!" screamed Rose. "You stole the goddamn game from us! You waited too goddamn long!" Pallone waved his finger in Rose's face, and then Rose gave him a hard shove backward with his forearm. Pallone thumbed him out of the game and turned to walk away, when the Cincinnati manager pushed him again.[6]

Matters nearly got out of hand at that point, as garbage, golfballs, empty bottles, and other assorted trash was hurled from the stands onto the field. Those fans with transistor radios were further incited by the inflammatory rhetoric of the Reds' radio announcers. The crew of umpires left the field until order had been restored some fifteen minutes later.

Rose later claimed that Pallone's finger had struck him under the eye. After the game Pete showed reporters what one writer called "a strange and suspicious abrasion near his eye." Pallone claimed that Rose had done this himself, for effect. In any event, the new president of the National League, A. Bartlett Giamatti, recently arrived from the hallowed halls of Yale University, imposed a drastic punishment upon Rose: a thirty-day suspension and a fine of $10,000. Calling the incident "disgraceful," Giamatti said, "The National League will not . . . countenance any potentially injurious harassment, of any kind, of the umpires." Pallone was fined $1,000 for participating in the argument, instead of turning his back and walking away.[7] It was Pete Rose's introduction to Bart Giamatti.

Rose missed the month of May with his suspension, and June was little better for the team. After that, however, the Reds turned things around and won fifty-two games, losing just thirty-two the rest of the season. What it got them was their fourth straight second-place finish, with an 87–74 record, seven games behind the Dodgers.

As Rose's active career moved slowly and haltingly toward its end, especially after his return to Cincinnati, Pete needed something to keep his competitive juices flowing. He found it in a pastime which had always been a part of his life but which became an ever larger part. From his early years, when his father introduced him to pari-mutuel wagering at River Downs, Rose had enjoyed gambling—a day at the ponies, picking a few possible winners, the rush of seeing his choice vindicated. Now the gambling became more of a necessity, more compulsive, and he found more chances to bet on than just horses. Football, basketball, jai alai, dogs, even baseball, any kind of sporting event, along with the horses—all of these represented opportunities for Pete Rose to gamble.

In his big home in Indian Hill, Rose had a first-floor den with a forty-inch television set, and two nineteen-inch TVs on the side, so he could watch three different games at a time, keeping track of who—or how much he—was winning or losing. His bets kept getting larger and larger, and, because the bookies he placed them with always had the house's edge, and a lot of Pete's bets were not so smart, his losses mounted as well.

One biographer wrote that virtually everyone who had anything to do with him agreed that "Pete Rose's gambling had become pathological by 1985." At different times he owed bookies, some of whom had ties to the mob, "hundreds of thousands of dollars." Rose needed lots of cash.[8]

He found a partial answer to his problem in baseball card and memorabilia shows. Especially after the great amount of publicity surrounding his pursuit and passage of Cobb's hit record, Pete Rose was a hot item on the autograph circuit and in great demand. Rose had for a long time had a custom of asking for payment for such appearances in cash, possibly because of a youth in which he never had much of it, and this custom now became a matter of necessity. He could sit at a table in a large room where a card show was in progress, sign whatever was put in front of him, smile for the fans with their little box cameras, and walk out after several hours with a paper bag full of bills, in amounts as high sometimes as $20,000. He would take the bag home and stash it somewhere in his house, using the cash later on to pay off some of his gambling debts.[9]

The gambling wins and losses, the autograph show payoffs—these were all "off the books," because they were in cash. With no record of them, Rose felt no need of telling the IRS—or Reuven Katz—about them. If a show promoter insisted on paying by check, Rose would have him write a check or checks—they had to be under $10,000, the minimum that banks had to report to the government—with blank or fictitious payees, which Rose or one of his flunkies could present at a racetrack where they would be accepted, because they were from Pete Rose.

As his gambling activity mushroomed out of control, Rose developed a coterie of unsavory associates. He started with a kid from Massachusetts named Tommy Gioiosa, who met Rose through young Petey. In Florida, during spring training in 1977, Petey approached Gioiosa and asked him to play catch. Gioiosa did so, and again the next day, and soon he found himself in the good graces of Petey's mother and father. This led to an invitation to visit in Cincinnati, and soon after Gioiosa moved into the Rose home. As Pete's marriage broke apart, Gioiosa became more and more a part of Rose's life.

An infielder at Massasoit Junior College, Gioiosa soon found himself holding the Pete Rose baseball scholarship at the University of Cincinnati, at the personal request of the scholarship's donor. Gioiosa tried to do everything the same way his idol did, but when Rose got him a tryout with the Baltimore Orioles in 1982, he failed to make the team. His baseball dream shattered, Tommy Gioiosa latched onto his benefactor ever more closely. One of the ways he helped out was by signing Rose's name on baseballs, cards, posters, and other memorabilia.

When Tommy Gioiosa took up weightlifting and bodybuilding at Gold's Gym in Cincinnati, where he was hired as manager in 1985, he introduced Rose to a whole new set of friends, and Pete picked up a few on his own. There was Donald Stenger, a part-owner of the gym and a major distributor of cocaine in Cincinnati. There was Mike Fry, Stenger's partner and another drug dealer. And Paul Janszen, another bodybuilder and drug runner, who was always around. Gioiosa too got into the drug racket. Mike Bertolini was a memorabilia dealer and gambler from Brooklyn. There was Dennis Walker, a wheeler-dealer from Medford, Oregon, who dealt in securities of a bank he ran in the island-nation of Tonga, in the South Pacific. And there were the bookmakers: Joseph Cambra, from Fall River, Massachusetts, convicted of illegal bookmaking in 1986, whom Rose once called "my number one friend"; Ron Peters, a restaurant man, cocaine dealer, and bookie from Franklin, Ohio, north of Cincinnati; and Richard Troy, known as "Val," with connections to the Bonnano mob family.[10]

Walker, the Oregon man who opened a National Sports Hall of Fame in Medford, bought Rose's Hickok Award belt from Pete, $20,000 in cash, the rest in $50,000 worth of Tongan securities maturing two years later. Rose, double-crossing his partner, secretly had the precious stones removed from the belt and replaced with fake gems. Two years later, when the Tongan securities matured, Rose found to his dismay that they were worthless.

More and more, the Reds players and coaches were disturbed by the unsavory-looking men who seemed always to be hanging around the manager's office. "I was scared," said one former Red. "I didn't like the kind of people Pete had around him." There had been an edict from the commissioner's office in 1985 barring "nonessential" people from the clubhouse, but Rose violated it flagrantly. As Pete's gambling debts mounted, and as the lowlifes who seemed to be his closest companions got into trouble on their own, matters were coming to a head.[11]

NOTES

1. *USA Weekend*, February 28–March 2, 1986.

2. Hal McCoy, "Early Losses Kill Reds' Hopes," in *Official Baseball Guide, 1987 Edition* (St. Louis: The Sporting News, 1987), 59.

3. Ibid., 61.

4. Hal McCoy, "Unarmed Reds Fall Hard," in *Official Baseball Guide, 1988 Edition* (St. Louis: The Sporting News, 1988), 145.

5. *Cincinnati Enquirer*, December 8, 1987.

6. Reston, *Collision at Home Plate: The Lives of Pete Rose and Bart Giamatti*, 231. Rose says he "bumped" Pallone; see Rose and Kahn, *Pete Rose: My Story*, 230.

7. Reston, *Collision at Home Plate: The Lives of Pete Rose and Bart Giamatti*, 232–233.

8. Ibid., 211.

9. In 1981, Rose was paid $46,197.54 in cash by the Mizuno sporting goods company in Japan and failed to declare the cash on his customs declaration. Five years later, Reuven Katz paid for him a fine of half the undeclared amount. A Mizuno official said, "He personally requested that he be paid in cash"; see Neff and Lieber, "Rose's Grim Vigil," 59.

10. Quote on Cambra, also called "a very dear and a very close friend of mine," from letter, Rose to John Scarpellini, March 24, 1987, in John M. Dowd, *Report to the Commissioner*, 1989, Exhibit 67.

11. Neff and Lieber, "Rose's Grim Vigil," 58.

PETE'S DOWNFALL

One day in mid-February 1989, Pete Rose poked his head into the office of general manager Murray Cook at the Cincinnati training complex in Plant City, Florida. He had to fly to New York on February 20 to meet with Commissioner Ueberroth, so he needed the day off. "I do recall the old antenna going up," Cook said later. "I knew something was up because you don't get called into the commissioner's office just to chat. And the only thing it could have been in Pete's case, it had to be something to do with gambling."[1]

Both Ron Peters and Paul Janszen had offered to sell their stories of Rose's gambling to *Sports Illustrated*, which turned them down but then began its own investigation. News of this inquiry had inevitably reached the commissioner's office, which started to look into it as well.

Ueberroth told the press about the Rose visit: "There's nothing ominous and there won't be any follow-through," which was a bit disingenuous, to say the least. Rose met with Ueberroth, the lame-duck commissioner, and his designated successor, National League president Bart Giamatti. One of the questions Ueberroth asked was, "Did you bet on baseball?" When Rose answered, "No," the commissioner said, "That's good enough for me."[2]

But it wasn't good enough for the incoming commissioner. Giamatti discussed the apparent Rose problem with Fay Vincent, who would become his deputy commissioner. Vincent recommended an outside investigator and suggested John M. Dowd, a Washington attorney with a good reputation for solid investigations. On February 23, Dowd accepted the assignment and went right to work.

At issue, of course, was whether Rose had broken Major League Rule 21, a copy of which is posted in every major and minor league clubhouse. Rule 21 provides that any person betting on a baseball game is subject to a one-year suspension, while any person betting on a game in which he has a duty to perform—play, coach, manage, etc.—faces permanent suspension.

Dowd and his investigative team interviewed forty witnesses, the principal ones being Paul Janszen and Ron Peters. Dowd also took a 359-page deposition from Rose himself on April 20–21. Peters, the bookmaker, and Janszen, the bodybuilder who was a close associate of Rose, testified at length about Pete's betting habits, his losses, and the huge debts he ran up. Tommy Gioiosa refused to cooperate with Dowd, but Janszen and Peters made it clear that Rose had bet on many baseball games, including those of the Reds while he was their manager. Peters and Janszen had no love for one another; Janszen's testimony had helped convict Peters in the latter's legal scrape, but their testimony about Rose fit together. The secondary witnesses interviewed by Dowd corroborated much of what Peters and Janszen said, as did numerous pieces of documentary evidence, like betting slips in Rose's handwriting, telephone records, and several tape-recorded conversations.

There were, of course, no witnesses presented by Pete Rose, nor was Rose's counsel able to cross-examine Dowd's witnesses. These procedural safeguards were to be available in the hearing that Rose was to be given.

On May 9, 1989, Dowd presented his 225-page report to Giamatti along with seven volumes of exhibits and supporting documentation. Dowd summarized his findings: "The testimony and the documentary evidence gathered in the course of the investigation demonstrates that Pete Rose bet on baseball and, in particular, on games of the Cincinnati Reds Baseball Club, during the 1985, 1986 and 1987 baseball seasons."[3]

Dowd dealt specifically with the trustworthiness of the depositions of the three principal witnesses he heard, providing extensive analyses of their testimony. He found both Peters and Janszen worthy of belief in view of the independent corroboration of their testimony. And, as he made his way meticulously through Rose's deposition, which he clearly believed to be a pack of lies, Dowd wrote, "It is difficult to square Rose's sworn testimony with the sworn voluntary testimony of other witnesses, and the betting records in Rose's handwriting and the handwriting of others."[4]

On May 11, a copy of the report and the exhibits was delivered to Rose's attorney. Giamatti said that Rose "is owed, in my opinion, an opportunity to review the report and its accompanying materials, and thereafter to respond to me if he wishes to do so." He set a hearing date for May 25 in his office, later changed to June 26 at Rose's request.[5]

In the meantime, however, Bart Giamatti had done an unwise thing that was about to cause him a great deal of unnecessary trouble. John Dowd had assured Ron Peters that if he cooperated in the investigation, Dowd would do what he could to help Peters at his sentencing for the two felony charges of drug dealing and tax evasion, to which he had pled guilty. Accordingly, Dowd prepared a letter to U.S. District Court Judge Carl Rubin, describing "the significant and truthful cooperation" of Peters and saying he was "satisfied Mr. Peters has been candid, forthright and truthful."[6]

The letter went out to Judge Rubin on April 18, 1989, bearing, however, Giamatti's signature, not Dowd's. Because Dowd had interrogated Peters and had reviewed all the additional evidence that he felt corroborated Peters, Dowd should have signed the letter, not Giamatti.

In addition to being a jurist who resented such interventions in the sentencing process, Judge Rubin was a Cincinnati Reds fan, a great admirer of Pete Rose, and a lifelong friend of Reuven Katz. He immediately recognized the letter as an indiscretion that could prove helpful to Rose. He called Katz to his office to show him the letter and then turned it over to the press, saying it was "evidence . . . of a vendetta against" Rose.[7]

On June 19, a week before the rescheduled hearing before Bart Giamatti, Rose's attorneys filed suit in the state court in Cincinnati; the defendants were the commissioner, Major League Baseball, and the Cincinnati ball club. The pleading demanded that Giamatti be replaced by "an impartial decision-maker" because of the commissioner's "displayed bias and outrageous conduct," as demonstrated in the letter to Judge Rubin. It requested that Giamatti be enjoined from holding a hearing and that the Reds be barred from taking any action against Rose. The suit was a direct challenge to the commissioner's historic role.[8]

The matter of a preliminary injunction came before Judge Norbert A. Nadel, who just happened to be running for reelection in Cincinnati. Nadel convened a special Sunday session of court, permitted national television of the proceedings, and granted Rose the preliminary injunction he requested. Most lawyers, who knew that judges hardly ever intervene in administrative hearings before they take place, were dumbfounded by Nadel's ruling, even though it was easily recognized as a "hometown decision" for Rose.

Over the next couple of months, Giamatti moved successfully to have the case transferred to federal court, and Rose lost an appeal of that ruling. The public perception of the matter was that Pete Rose would do anything, including destroying the historic authority of the commissioner of baseball, to prevent a hearing on the charges against him. Giamatti continued to insist that he had not prejudged Rose and could hold a fair and unbiased hearing.

Throughout the summer, Rose's attorneys explored with Fay Vincent, the deputy commissioner, the possibility of some sort of settlement. They were adamant that there be no admission that Rose had bet on baseball, despite the overwhelming evidence to the contrary in the Dowd Report.

Finally, the impasse was broken. Late in the afternoon of August 23, Rose's lawyers and the lawyers for the commissioner completed the settlement agreement that they had struggled with for most of the summer. Then Pete Rose left to fly to Minneapolis to appear on the Cable Value Network's "Sporting Collections Show," peddling autographed bats, balls, and jerseys.

The next morning, Commissioner Giamatti held a press conference at the New York Hilton to announce and distribute the five-page settlement document. Rose had given up his right to a hearing, accepted a permanent suspension from baseball, dropped the legal action filed earlier, and waived any right to bring any further actions against the commissioner or baseball. The agreement acknowledged that the commissioner had treated Rose fairly and that he had "a factual basis to impose the penalty." The final terms, one writer concluded, "amounted to Rose's unconditional surrender."[9]

Giamatti told the assembled writers, "One of the game's greatest players has engaged in a variety of acts which have stained the game, and he must now live with the consequences of those acts."[10]

The crucial part of the settlement agreement for Pete Rose was the following: "Nothing in this agreement shall be deemed either an admission or a denial by Peter Edward Rose of the allegation that he bet on any Major League Baseball game." It was, in effect, a plea of *nolo contendere*, but it was what Rose insisted upon. The strange feature was that he then accepted the harshest punishment in baseball's arsenal.[11]

In addition, when Giamatti was asked, in his press conference, whether he believed Rose had bet on baseball, he replied, "I am confronted by the factual record of the Dowd report. And on the basis of that, yes, I have concluded that he bet on baseball." On the Reds? "Yes," said Giamatti.[12]

Asked about Rose's possible reinstatement, the commissioner said there was a standing rule on the subject. This was Rule 15(c), which permitted application for reinstatement one year from the date of placement on the Ineligible List. Asked what Rose had to do, Giamatti said, "It isn't up to me. It is up to Mr. Rose to reconfigure his life in ways I would assume he would prefer."[13]

Pete Rose held his press conference at Riverfront Stadium at 10 A.M. He began by saying, "As you can imagine, it's a very sad day. I've been in baseball for three decades, and to think I'm going to be out of baseball for a very short period of time hurts." He contended that the settlement was fair, "especially in the wording that says there's no finding that I bet on baseball." And, defiantly, he added, "Regardless of what the Commissioner said today, I did not bet on baseball."[14]

Rose said he had no doubt he would be reinstated and that he had no gambling problem; "I won't be seeking help of any kind." A writer asked him, "If you are innocent why did you agree to this?" Pete thought for a long moment before stepping aside to let Katz answer for him with a statement that never answered the question. Then Rose left to go back to Minneapolis for another night of hawking memorabilia on the Cable Value Network.[15]

The baseball world was shocked nine days later to learn that A. Bartlett Giamatti had died of a heart attack at his summer home on Martha's Vineyard. Some said that the Rose affair had killed him, but there was little doubt that his heavy smoking and unhealthful lifestyle did him in. Still, for someone with a bad heart, the intense pressure of the Rose business could have done no good.

The Reds had managed to keep somewhat free of the distractions of their manager's troubles, and as late as June 10, 1989, they were in first place in their division. Then they began to fall back, and were in fourth place with a record of 61–66 when Rose was removed from his job. With Coach Tommy Helms serving as interim manager, the Reds went 14–21 the rest of the way, finishing in fifth place.

In the months after Rose's suspension took effect, he continued in the news. On November 8, he revealed on the *Donahue* television show that he was undergoing counseling for what he now admitted was a gambling "problem." He had consulted Dr. James Randolph Hilliard, chairman of the psychiatry department at the University of Cincinnati, only because he figured that some kind of counseling was essential to a reinstatement application. When Hilliard told him he had a problem, what the doctor called "a clinically significant gambling disorder," Rose resisted at first but finally faced up to it. He admitted that he had been undergoing treatment, but he declined to detail his rehabilitation any further than that.[16]

On February 1, 1990, Tommy Gioiosa was sentenced to five years in prison by U.S. District Judge S. Arthur Spiegel for transporting cocaine and for conspiring to hide some of Rose's gambling winnings from the IRS. That evening, television network ESPN ran an interview that a local broadcaster had taped with Gioiosa, in which Rose's former housemate said he saw Rose betting on baseball games. "I've sat in his office and watched him bet on baseball games," said Gioiosa, "including the Reds and many other baseball teams." He also said that he had refused to participate in Dowd's investigation because "I knew I would have to tell the truth." At that point, he had still wanted to protect Rose. When Rose declined to give Gioiosa any support in his trial, not even showing up in the courtroom at the end, Gioiosa decided to end his silence.[17]

The courtroom Pete Rose had shunned when Tommy Gioiosa was sentenced was the same one he himself stood in six and one-half months later after he had pled guilty to not reporting $354,968 in income from memorabilia sales, card show appearances, and gambling. He had underpaid his federal income tax by $162,000 from 1984 to 1987. Rose stood before Judge Spiegel and said, "Your Honor, I would like to say that I am very sorry. I am very shameful to be here today in front of you." He admitted that in the last year and a half he had lost his dignity, his self-respect, his fans, and some friends. "I really have no excuses," he said, "because it's all my fault."[18]

Judge Spiegel sentenced Rose to five months in prison, three months in a halfway house, one thousand hours of community service, and a fine of $50,100. On August 8, Rose arrived in an unmarked prison van at the federal minimum security prison at Marion, Illinois, ironically the hometown of Ray Fosse. Rose worked in the welding shop at Marion for eleven cents an hour. The prison guards called him "Pete," but he was still patted down six times a day and strip-searched once a week. Discharged from prison in January, he reported to the halfway house in Cincinnati to complete his sentence and work off his community-service obligation at five inner-city schools.[19]

NOTES

1. *Cincinnati Enquirer*, February 18, 1990.

2. *Cincinnati Enquirer*, February 22, 1989; February 18, 1990.

3. Dowd, *Report to the Commissioner*, 3. Dowd found that Rose made 412 bets on baseball games, including 52 on Reds games.

4. Ibid., 205, 216.

5. Clifford Kachline, "The Unusual and Unexpected Became the Norm in Tragic '89," *Baseball Guide 1990 Edition* (St. Louis: The Sporting News, 1990), 16.

6. Jerome Holtzman, *The Commissioners: Baseball's Midlife Crisis* (New York: Total Sports, 1998), 251.

7. Ibid., 252. Rubin subsequently recused himself from the Peters sentencing proceedings.

8. Ibid.

9. Holtzman, *The Commissioners: Baseball's Midlife Crisis*, 254; Sokolove, *Hustle: The Myth, Life, and Lies of Pete Rose*, 277.

10. *Cincinnati Enquirer*, August 25, 1989.

11. "Rose Is Out!" *Cincinnati Post*, August 24, 1989.

12. Holtzman, *The Commissioners: Baseball's Midlife Crisis*, 254; *Cincinnati Enquirer*, August 25, 1989. In the final negotiations for the settlement, Reuven Katz had wanted it understood that the agreement would speak for itself, with no further comment by

the principals. Vincent had turned him down, saying that the Commissioner might want to speak out about it.

13. *Cincinnati Enquirer*, August 25, 1989.

14. Ibid.

15. Holtzman, *The Commissioners: Baseball's Midlife Crisis*, 255; Charles Leerhsen, "The End of the Affair," *Newsweek*, September 4, 1989, 58–59.

16. Tim Sullivan, "Rose Treated for Gambling," *Cincinnati Enquirer*, November 9, 1989, A-1.

17. Greg Hoard, "Gioiosa Claims Rose Bet on Reds," and Hoard, "Gioiosa on His Silence: I Didn't Want to Lie," *Cincinnati Enquirer*, February 2, 1990, D-1 and A-1. Eleven years later, in the September 2001 issue of *Vanity Fair* magazine, Gioiosa expanded on his story, telling about his placing of bets for Rose and his signing of Rose's autograph on memorabilia items. He even charged that Rose, late in his career, had used a corked bat. Buzz Bissinger, "A Darker Shade of Rose," *Vanity Fair*, September 2001, 311, 318.

18. Tim Sullivan, "Rose: Prison, Then on with His Life," *Cincinnati Enquirer*, July 20, 1990, A-1.

19. *Cincinnati Enquirer*, January 8, 1991.

THE HIT KING

One of the things Pete Rose did after being banned from baseball was to hire a publicist named Barbara Pinzka to help brighten the dark image that the gambling, the suspension, the tax evasion, and the jail term had created. He also published another autobiography—his third or fourth, depending on how one classified his earlier efforts. This one was written by a writer named Roger Kahn, famous for his earlier work on the 1950s Brooklyn Dodgers, *The Boys of Summer*. Although titled *Pete Rose: My Story* and bylined "Pete Rose and Roger Kahn," the book was written in the first-person by Kahn, with numerous quotes from Rose.

The book, which came out in the fall of 1989, was begun before the gambling investigation mushroomed into a national story, but it contained all Rose's defenses, as well as Kahn's averments of belief in Pete's denials. Still, Rose and his people were not happy with the work or with Kahn. Pinzka told Michael Sokolove, "The book wasn't what we thought it was going to be."[1]

In early 1991, a special committee of the Hall of Fame board in Cooperstown recommended to the full board a rule change that barred from consideration for Hall membership all persons on baseball's permanent suspension list. The vote of the special committee was 7–3, and when the full board approved the change on February 4, Pete Rose's 1992 eligibility for election was wiped out.[2]

Late in 1990, Rose put his Indian Hill home in Cincinnati up for sale, as well as his place in Plant City, Florida, near the Reds' spring training camp. Reuven Katz confirmed to the press that Pete was building a new home in Boca Raton, Florida. On July 23, 1991, Rose said goodbye to his hometown in a twenty-minute press conference. "No one's forcing me out of Cincinnati," he said. "I'm not leaving Cincinnati because I'm running from anything. I just think it's a lot easier at this time for my young children [Tyler, 6, and Cara, 2] to grow up in a place other than Cincinnati."[3]

The years after the move passed with the usual run of autograph shows, personal appearances, and denunciations of the Dowd Report. When Fay Vincent succeeded Bart Giamatti as commissioner, Rose's reinstatement chances did not look very good, and indeed no application for it was made. "I'm not looking to apply to be turned down," Rose said, while a Cincinnati sportswriter noted that "Vincent has thus far gone out of his way to discourage Rose from applying for reinstatement." Rose's usual denunciation of the witnesses to his gambling as "convicted felons" was undercut by his own felony conviction.[4]

Vincent was forced out by the owners in 1992, and Milwaukee Brewers owner Allan "Bud" Selig took over as interim commissioner; several years later, Selig was elected as baseball's ninth commissioner. Rose finally applied for reinstatement in 1997.

When filing his application, Rose called the Dowd Report an unbalanced investigation. John Dowd responded that "Pete Rose has had more due process than any human being out there." He continued: "When I completed my report, we gave Pete and his lawyers the chance to take the testimony of all witnesses they wanted. They declined." As to Rose's claim that Giamatti's press conference statement violated the settlement agreement, Dowd said, "I was in the room with Reuven Katz and Bart when Bart told Katz he would not agree to refrain from public comment."[5]

Bud Selig, for his part, told a service club audience in Madison, Wisconsin, early in 2000, "Pete did accept a voluntary lifetime suspension from Dr. Giamatti. There hasn't been any new evidence since then."[6]

Over the years, however, pressure built up from the public to offer Rose some sort of relief. In 1999, baseball chose its All-Century team, which was unveiled at Game 2 of the World Series in Atlanta. Rose's ineligibility was waived for the occasion, and he received a great ovation when he appeared on the field. When NBC sportscaster Jim Gray ambushed Rose with a hostile live interview on the field on national television, Pete garnered a great deal of sympathy. Opinion polls showed Rose's reinstatement gaining in support, although many Hall-of-Famers, led by Bob Feller, were strongly opposed to Rose getting back in the game.

At a meeting in Bud Selig's Milwaukee office on November 25, 2002, Rose confessed to the commissioner that he had bet on baseball, including Reds games. The process that was then put in motion, apparently to lead to Pete's reinstatement, was to include a meeting of Selig with the fifty-eight living members of the Hall of Fame on January 17, 2003. That meeting was cancelled, and the process apparently halted, because of a couple of items that came to light in January: one, an IRS tax lien placed on Rose's new home in Sherman Oaks, California, for more than $150,000 of unpaid 1998 taxes; and, second, reports of Rose gambling in a couple of the big Las Vegas casinos.[7]

On January 8, 2004, a new book by Rose, *My Prison Without Bars*, done with a writer named Rick Hill, made its appearance, with a flurry of interviews and a lengthy *Sports Illustrated* excerpt. In the book Pete Rose admitted publicly what he had been steadfastly denying for years.

The reaction was not what Rose expected. There was resentment at the timing of the release, clearly aimed at blanketing the news of the 2004 Hall of Fame election results. And there were some Rose partisans who were disappointed at what Pete said. It was obvious that he had decided to say whatever had to be said to get himself reinstated; what he regretted most was not the gambling but getting caught. There was little evidence of real contrition in the book. "Right or wrong," Rose had decided, "the punishment didn't fit the crime—so I denied the crime." He concluded, "I'm sorry it happened. . . . Let's move on."[8]

Joe Morgan said he felt Rose's admission lacked sincerity, and he decried Pete's trying to cash in on his confession with a book. Ferguson Jenkins, previously a supporter, wrote Rose, "Knowing what I know now, I will never support your reinstatement to the game or your bid for the Hall." Even Mike Schmidt, Rose's staunchest supporter, looked at the reaction to Rose's admission and said, "It doesn't look good; it's taken a turn for the worse." He added, "I haven't heard anything good, but I hope the commissioner is reserving judgment. I've heard some of the worst references about Pete." Tom Verducci of *Sports Illustrated* wrote, "Rose and his advisers bungled his first and possibly last chance to return to the game he loves."[9]

So there it stands. Rose's 1997 application for reinstatement has still not been acted upon. Rose's admission seems to bring him squarely under Rule 21 and its provision for a permanent suspension. It is also a confession of lying for fourteen years—not an attractive posture. So baseball, the commissioner, and Pete Rose stand in a sort of uneasy equilibrium. Perhaps a solution would be to let the suspension stand but ask the Hall of Fame board to revoke its 1991 ineligibility rule, so that Rose could be elected to the Hall on the basis of his play.

We are left with the record that Rose made on the baseball diamond. Nobody played in more games, appeared at the plate more often, or had more base hits than Pete Rose. He won three batting titles, two Gold Gloves for outfield play, an MVP award, and three World Series rings. He stands as a monument to longevity, for his twenty-four years played permitted him to become the "Hit King," as he modestly markets himself. His lifetime batting average of .303 is sixty-four points below that of Ty Cobb's .367, but Rose persevered until he had overtaken Cobb's record number of hits.

What is most striking about Pete Rose the player, of course, is that he was almost entirely self-made. He was not big and strong, or fast, or possessed of a great arm. What he had was fierce determination. He took excellent care of his body; he did not smoke and only rarely drank—usually a slug of champagne at championship celebrations. His body then permitted him to go on and on, well past the age when most ballplayers call it a career.

He loved playing baseball, and he always played it hard. "Charlie Hustle" he was tagged early, and he never stopped hustling. The image of Pete Rose diving headfirst into third base is one of the strongest reasons that so many fans continue to support him, despite the evidence of his gambling. Few fans recognize the corrosive effect that gambling has on the integrity of the game; Pete's paid his debt, they feel, for a few bets. Off the field he may have been crude, or money-hungry, or arrogant; he may have been a terrible husband and not much of a father. But on the field, where the fans saw him in action, Pete Rose was an indomitable figure, the kind of ballplayer the fans know every player should be but so few are.

Writer Red Smith once said that "Pete Rose has an almost lascivious love of baseball . . . [playing] with total, intense dedication, relishing every moment." Johnny Bench, whose relationship with Pete Rose has been up and down over the years, wrote about him, before the gambling: "Rose is also Rose. Sometimes I get so pissed off at him I want to shoot him. It's usually about nothing in particular, but he's got a square jaw and a square head and both match his personality. The way he thinks things should be is the way he has them. Period. But how that man loves the game of baseball. And not too many people play it better than he does."[10]

NOTES

1. Sokolove, *Hustle: The Myth, Life, and Lies of Pete Rose*, 153.
2. The seven voting for the change were Bobby Brown, Chub Feeney, Lee MacPhail, John McHale, Charles Segar, Robin Roberts, and Buck O'Neil. Voting no were Jack Lang, Phil Pepe, and Ed Stack. Bill White and Whitey Ford abstained.
3. *Cincinnati Enquirer*, July 24, 1991.
4. *Cincinnati Enquirer*, June 12, 1992.
5. *Cincinnati Enquirer*, September 27, 1997.
6. *Cincinnati Enquirer*, February 17, 2000.
7. The 1998 tax claim was subsequently settled.

8. Pete Rose, with Rick Hill, "Pete Rose's Confession," *Sports Illustrated*, January 12, 2004, 80, 82.

9. "Schmidt, Morgan Speak out about Rose's book," *Philadelphia Inquirer*, January 9, 2004, 23; "Rose Loses Hall of Famer's Support," *Philadelphia Inquirer*, January 15, 2004; Tom Verducci, "Still Hazy after All These Years," *Sports Illustrated*, January 19, 2004, 21.

10. Red Smith, "The Leader of the Phils," *New York Times*, October 20, 1980, C-9; Bench and Brashler, *Catch You Later: The Autobiography of Johnny Bench*, 45–46.

THE LEGEND OF PETE ROSE

Pete Rose recognized early on the value of a strong and positive public image. One of the first friends he made when he came to the Cincinnati Reds was Earl Lawson, the baseball beat writer for the *Cincinnati Post* and, not so incidentally, the man who wrote the weekly Reds reports for the *Sporting News*. Lawson saw a colorful and talented rookie who was in the process of taking a job away from an established regular, and he knew immediately that he had a story that would have far more appeal than the usual dry spring training fare. And for years after, Lawson wrote more about Pete Rose than about any other Reds player.

It was not just Earl Lawson, however, who spotted Pete Rose as a good story. Over the course of his career, Rose was usually the most accessible of ballplayers, always good for a quote on the game just played, or on anything else about baseball. The writers, deadlines looming up before them, knew that their best course was to walk over to Pete Rose's locker for a wrap-up to the day's story, rather than to take a chance that something quoteworthy might come out of some other player. Rose was also willing to talk for publication to non-baseball media, such as *Playboy*, sometimes to his regret.

Rose was able to parlay running to first base after a walk, headfirst slides, and the "Charlie Hustle" image into a public perception that has lasted over the years. Obviously, without his reliable .300 hitting and his steady accumulation of base hits, Rose's image would have been of little more value than that of a flash in the pan like Super Joe Charbonneau. That image, though, combined with Rose's actual accomplishments, created a public persona that has, to a considerable degree, outlasted even the negative publicity of his gambling, suspension, and tax troubles. Thousands of baseball fans, not just in Cincinnati, but all over the United States, have supported Pete Rose through his years of banishment. The lords of baseball seemed astonished to observe the adulation given Rose on those rare ceremonial occasions when he was permitted on the field with other icons of the game.

Contemporaneous newspaper reports have been called "the first drafts of history," and it is those newspaper reports that have served as a resource of first resort for this work. The two Cincinnati dailies, the *Enquirer* and *Post*, the three Philadelphia dailies, the *Inquirer*, the *Bulletin* (no longer published), and *Daily News*, and the *Sporting News*, the baseball weekly, have been full of information on Pete Rose and his career, usually as it unfolded. In addition, *Sports Illustrated* also covered Rose's doings on a fairly regular basis. Articles from other papers, particularly the *New York Times*, have also been of assistance.

Someone has said that Pete Rose has had more written about him than any other baseball player. Whether or not this is so, there is no lack of material on the kid from Anderson Ferry. Some of it is furnished by Rose himself, as in his *Playboy* interviews; some of it by his first wife Karolyn, who talked about Pete both before and after the breakup of her marriage, with notably different emphases. Some of it is even supplied by Fawn and Pete Jr., his children by Karolyn, as in the long *Gentleman's Quarterly* article by Pat Jordan in 1989, in which the dominant note is one of disappointment that their father was not the father they had hoped he would be. Pete Jr., said of his father, "My relationship with him is more player-manager. . . . I wish he'd made time for me when I was growing up," while Fawn said, "I love my dad but I don't respect him" and called him "the world's worst father."[1]

There has been no lack of established writers weighing in with their opinions about Pete Rose. George Will in his book *Bunts* discussed the clash between Rose and Giamatti and decried Rose's "extreme willfulness." Hal Bodley in his book on the 1980 Phillies as well as in the work he co-authored with Pete, *Countdown to Cobb*, dwelled on "his run-at-all-times enthusiasm, gung-ho belly slides and aggressiveness in all phases of the sport."[2] Newspaper columnists Jerome Holtzman, Bob Broeg, Red Smith, and Frank Dolson have all written extensively over the years about Pete Rose, generally in admiration of his unrelenting hustle and drive. Bill James, in his updated *Historical Baseball Abstract*, devoted thousands of words to tearing down the Dowd Report and finding Rose innocent of betting on baseball, a conclusion which became a trifle embarrassing once Rose himself confessed.[3]

It was not, of course, just the written word that helped to shape Pete Rose's public image. The growing influence of television spread Pete's face and story to an ever-widening circle of fans. As Rose stretched a single into a double because of an outfielder's indifference, the fan watching in Peoria or Mahanoy City thought to himself, "That's the way to play!" And when Rose did it again a few innings later, that fan was confirmed as a Rose devotee. Pete Rose crashed into Ray Fosse in front of millions of All Star Game viewers who said to themselves something like, "That son of a gun doesn't think this is a meaningless exhibition game! He wants to win!"

Rose also wrote, or put his name to, a number of books, some for children, or for aspiring ballplayers, or for adult fans, and these books contributed more to the Rose legend, although not as much as the daily newspaper and television reports. Further, a number of his teammates—Joe Morgan, Mike Schmidt, Johnny Bench, Frank Robinson, and his manager Sparky Anderson—wrote memoirs that described Pete Rose, his drive, his hustle, and his will to win. Finally, the Internet is full of Rose material, although more of it, sadly, is on the Dowd Report and his suspension from baseball than on his playing career.

With the exposure of his gambling problems in 1989, the Rose legend took on a darker hue. The series of articles about the investigation in *Sports Illustrated* soon led to national coverage of the ongoing probe and legal struggle. Three books that came out between 1989 and 1991—Pete's autobiography written with Roger Kahn, *Pete Rose: My Story*; Michael Sokolove's highly critical *Hustle: The Myth, Life, and Lies of Pete Rose*; and James Reston Jr.'s *Collision at Home Plate*, a dual biography of Rose and Bart Giamatti—laid out the Rose story in considerable detail from three widely divergent points of view. Rose's own book, of course, denied everything, while Sokolove's detailed the various charges against Pete with considerable specificity. Reston's tale of the conflict between Rose, always pushing the envelope, and the commissioner, devoted to the rules for an orderly society, had something of the air of a Greek tragedy about it.

Previously uncritical Rose fans found it necessary to join one of two camps: that of those who still believed that a superstar was being persecuted by an overreacting baseball hierarchy, or that of those who agreed with Giamatti that Pete Rose had seriously tarnished the game. Although the opinion of the former group was for a long time clearly the majority view, the largely negative reaction to Rose's January 2004 "confession" and publication of *My Prison Without Bars* seemed to swell the ranks of the latter group and, perhaps for the first time, to turn public opinion against Rose.

My Prison Without Bars has a curiously whining tone to it, as if all the world, for some reason, was out to get Pete Rose. Prison, it develops, was not a nice place. John Dowd and Fay Vincent were nasty people, although, of course, they turn out to have been correct. Rick Hill, the ex-Hollywood screenwriter and actor engaged to put Rose's thoughts into cogent prose, seems to have just missed coming up with a flavor that might genuinely have engaged the reader's sympathy for the book's embattled hero. The reader comes away from the book with the feeling, "Well, he says he did this and this and this, but he doesn't really think he did anything wrong—except get caught." *My Prison Without Bars* was, as several commentators noted, an opportunity for Pete Rose which he flubbed.

Rose's fate sometimes seems to be entwined with that of Joe Jackson, the hard-hitting outfielder who was suspended for life by Commissioner Kenesaw M. Landis in 1920 for his part in the Black Sox scandal of the 1919 World Series. Rose and Jackson are the two men on the "permanently ineligible" list who are for that reason barred from Hall of Fame consideration. This pairing seems a little rough on Rose, because betting on games, serious as it may be, is still far removed from taking a bribe to throw the World Series.

What is certain is that the Legend of Pete Rose has not yet been chiseled in stone. Future actions by the commissioner, the Hall of Fame board, the writers, even the Veterans Committee may reshape that legend to some degree. Every time Pete Rose opens his mouth in public or talks to a writer there is a chance of some change. What is clear is that Peter Edward Rose is still news, still a big story, many years after the last swing of his bat.

NOTES

1. Pat Jordan, "War of the Roses," *Gentleman's Quarterly*, April 1989, 276, 279, 329.

2. Rose, with Bodley, *Countdown to Cobb: My Diary of the Record Breaking 1985 Season*, 15 (in a section written by Bodley).

3. Bill James, *The New Bill James Historical Baseball Abstract*, 787–92.

APPENDIX: PETE ROSE'S CAREER AND WORLD SERIES STATISTICS

CAREER STATISTICS

Year	Club	League	G	AB	R	H	2B	3B	HR	RBI	BA	PO	A	E	FA
1963	Cinci. Reds	NL	157	623	101	170	25	9	6	41	.273	360	366	22	.971
1964	Cinci. Reds	NL	136	516	64	139	13	2	4	34	.269	263	301	12	.979
1965	Cinci. Reds	NL	162	670	117	209	35	11	11	81	.312	382	403	20	.975
1966	Cinci. Reds	NL	156	654	97	205	38	5	16	70	.313	409	374	18	.956
1967	Cinci. Reds	NL	148	585	86	176	32	8	12	76	.301	287	93	11	.971
1968	Cinci. Reds	NL	149	626	94	210	42	6	10	49	.335	270	20	3	.990
1969	Cinci. Reds	NL	156	627	120	218	33	11	16	82	.348	317	10	4	.988
1970	Cinci. Reds	NL	159	649	120	205	37	9	15	52	.316	309	8	1	.997
1971	Cinci. Reds	NL	160	632	86	192	27	4	13	44	.304	306	13	2	.994
1972	Cinci. Reds	NL	154	645	107	198	31	11	6	57	.307	330	15	2	.994
1973	Cinci. Reds	NL	160	680	115	230	36	8	5	64	.338	343	15	3	.992
1974	Cinci. Reds	NL	163	652	110	185	45	7	3	51	.284	346	11	1	.997
1975	Cinci. Reds	NL	162	662	112	210	47	4	7	74	.317	161	230	14	.973
1976	Cinci. Reds	NL	162	665	130	215	42	6	10	63	.323	115	293	13	.969
1977	Cinci. Reds	NL	162	655	95	204	38	7	9	64	.311	98	268	16	.958
1978	Cinci. Reds	NL	159	655	103	198	51	3	7	52	.302	135	256	15	.961
1979	Phil. Phillies	NL	163	628	90	208	40	5	4	59	.331	1429	93	10	.914
1980	Phil. Phillies	NL	162	655	95	185	42	1	1	64	.282	1427	123	5	.997
1981	Phil. Phillies	NL	107	431	73	140	18	5	0	33	.325	929	91	4	.996
1982	Phil. Phillies	NL	162	634	80	172	25	4	3	54	.271	1428	123	8	.995
1983	Phil. Phillies	NL	151	493	52	121	14	3	0	45	.245	827	74	10	.983
1984	Mont. Expos	NL	95	278	34	72	6	2	0	23	.259	349	44	6	.976
	Cinci. Reds	NL	26	96	9	35	9	0	0	11	.365	181	9	2	.990
	1984 Totals	NL	121	374	43	107	15	2	0	34	.286	530	53	8	.983
1985	Cinci. Reds	NL	119	405	60	107	12	2	2	46	.264	870	73	5	.995
1986	Cinci. Reds	NL	72	237	15	52	8	2	0	25	.219	523	43	6	.990
Major League Totals (24 seasons)			3562	14053	2165	4256	746	135	160	1314	.303	12394	3349	213	.987

World Series Record

Year	Club	G	AB	R	H	2B	3B	HR	RBI	BA
1970	Cinci. Reds	5	20	2	5	1	0	1	2	.250
1972	Cinci. Reds	7	28	3	6	0	0	1	2	.214
1975	Cinci. Reds	7	27	3	10	1	1	0	2	.370
1976	Cinci. Reds	4	16	1	3	1	0	0	1	.188
1980	Phil. Phillies	6	23	2	6	1	0	0	1	.261
1983	Phil. Phillies	5	16	1	5	1	0	0	1	.312
World Series Totals		34	130	12	35	5	1	2	9	.269

A = assists; AB = at-bats; BA = batting average; E = errors; FA = fielding average; G = games; H = hits; HR = home runs; PO = put-outs; R = runs; RBI = runs batted in; 2B = doubles; 3B = triples

SELECTED BIBLIOGRAPHY

BOOKS

Allen, Dick, and Tim Whitaker. *Crash: The Life and Times of Dick Allen*. New York: Ticknor and Fields, 1989.

Anderson, Sparky, *They Call Me Sparky*. Chelsea, MI: Sleeping Bear Press, 1998.

Anderson, Sparky, with Dan Ewald. *Sparky!* New York: Prentice-Hall, 1990.

Bench, Johnny, and William Brashler. *Catch You Later: The Autobiography of Johnny Bench*. New York: Harper and Row, 1979.

Bodley, Hal. *The Team That Wouldn't Die: The Philadelphia Phillies, World Champions, 1980*. Wilmington, DE: Serendipity Press, 1981.

Dolson, Frank. *The Philadelphia Story: A City of Winners*. South Bend, IN: Icarus Press, 1981.

Down, Fred. *Major League Baseball, 1975*. New York: Pocket Books, 1975.

Erardi, John G. *Pete Rose*. Cincinnati: The Cincinnati Enquirer, 1985.

Gorman, Tom, as told to Jerome Holtzman. *Three and Two!* New York: Charles Scribner's Sons, 1979.

Gregg, Eric, and Marty Appel. *Working the Plate: The Eric Gregg Story*. New York: William Morrow and Co., 1990.

Holtzman, Jerome. *The Commissioners: Baseball's Midlife Crisis*. New York: Total Sports, 1998.

Morgan, Joe, and David Falkner. *Joe Morgan: A Life in Baseball*. New York: W.W. Norton and Co., 1993.

Reston, James, Jr. *Collision at Home Plate: The Lives of Pete Rose and Bart Giamatti*. New York: Edward Burlingame Books, 1991.

Robinson, Frank, and Berry Stainback. *Extra Innings*. New York: McGraw-Hill, 1988.

Rose, Pete. *The Pete Rose Story: An Autobiography.* New York: World Publishing, 1970.

Rose, Pete, with Hal Bodley. *Countdown to Cobb: My Diary of the Record-Breaking 1985 Season.* St. Louis: The Sporting News, 1985.

Rose, Pete, and Peter Golenbock. *Pete Rose on Hitting: How to Hit Better Than Anybody.* New York: Perigee Books, 1985.

Rose, Pete, with Bob Hertzel. *Charlie Hustle.* Englewood Cliffs, NJ: Prentice-Hall, 1975.

Rose, Pete, and Roger Kahn. *Pete Rose: My Story.* New York: Macmillan, 1989.

Schiffer, Don. *Major League Baseball 1964.* New York: Pocket Books, 1964.

Schmidt, Mike, with Barbara Walder. *Always on the Offense.* New York: Atheneum, 1982.

Sokolove, Michael Y. *Hustle: The Myth, Life, and Lies of Pete Rose.* New York: Simon and Schuster, 1990.

Will, George F. *Bunts: Curt Flood, Camden Yards, Pete Rose, and Other Reflections on Baseball.* New York: Scribner, 1998.

ARTICLES

Alm, Richard. "Rose's Run for a Record: Everybody's Cashing In." *U.S. News and World Report*, September 2, 1985.

Bell, Marty. "The Sport Interview: Pete Rose." *Sport*, April 1979.

Bissinger, Buzz. "A Darker Shade of Rose." *Vanity Fair*, September 2001.

Director, Roger. "The Devil and Charlie Hustle." *Inside Sports*, May 1982.

Dolson, Frank, and Bob Broeg. "Does Pete Rose Deserve a Spot in Hall of Fame?" *Baseball Digest*, December 1989.

Dowd, John M., Esq. *Report to the Commissioner.* 1989.

Dozer, Richard. "Scramblin' Rose." *Chicago Tribune Magazine*, June 27, 1976.

Fimrite, Ron. "Sportsman of the Year." *Sports Illustrated*, December 22–29, 1975.

Freiman, Michael. "56-Game Hitting Streaks Revisited." *The Baseball Research Journal*, 2003.

Jordan, Pat. "War of the Roses," *Gentleman's Quarterly*, April 1989.

Kaplan, Jim, and Steve Wulf. "They're Playing the Sweet Swing Music of the 40s." *Sports Illustrated*, July 19, 1982.

Levy, Maury Z. "Karolyn." *Philadelphia Magazine*, June 1979.

Levy, Maury Z., and Samantha Stevenson. "Playboy Interview: Pete Rose." *Playboy*, September 1979.

Lewis, Allen. "How the Big League Teams Shape Up for 1967," *Baseball Digest*, April 1967.

———. "Why the White Sox and Reds Will Win." *Baseball Digest*, April 1965.

Lieber, Jill, and Craig Neff. "The Case against Pete Rose." *Sports Illustrated*, July 3, 1989.

Lyon, Bill. "Pete Rose at 38: 'I'll Keep Hustling until I Keel Over.'" *Philadelphia Inquirer Magazine*, April 18, 1979.

Neff, Craig, and Jill Lieber. "Rose's Grim Vigil." *Sports Illustrated*, April 3, 1989.

Newman, Bruce. "He's the Phillie Fillip." *Sports Illustrated*, May 28, 1979.

Peebles, Dick. "This Was One Hit Pete Rose Didn't Get." *Baseball Digest*, September 1978.

Posner, Gerald. "Say It Ain't So, Pete!" *Penthouse*, September 1989.

Ribowsky, Mark. "Playboy Interview: Pete Rose." *Playboy*, May 2000.

Rose, Karolyn, with Fred D. Cavinder. "Bed of Roses." *Discover*, January 28, 1979.

Rushin, Steve. "Morganna: The Final Kiss-off." *Sports Illustrated*, June 30, 2003.

Saidt, Bus. "Pete Rose: Player of the Decade." *Baseball Magazine*, April 1980.

Sheed, Wilfred. "Pete Rose: The Sweet Smell of Excess." *Family Weekly*, May 6, 1979.

Siller, Philip. "The Truth about Pete Rose." *The Baseball Research Journal*, 2000.

Simon, James Michael. "Pete Rose." *Entertainment Cincinnati*, October 18, 1976.

Wulf, Steve. "For Pete's Sake, Look Who's Back," *Sports Illustrated*, August 27, 1984.

———. "In Philadelphia, They're the Wheeze Kids." *Sports Illustrated*, March 14, 1983.

Zumsteg, Derek, "Evaluating the Dowd Report," *Baseball Prospectus*, October 31, 2002.

NEWSPAPERS AND MAGAZINES

Akron Beacon-Journal
Baseball Digest
Cincinnati Enquirer
Cincinnati Post
Cincinnati Post and Times Star
Los Angeles Herald-Examiner
Louisville Courier-Journal
Newsweek
New York Daily News
New York Post
New York Times
Philadelphia Daily News
(Philadelphia) *Evening Bulletin*
Philadelphia Inquirer
St. Louis Globe-Democrat
Sport
Sporting News
Sports Illustrated
Syracuse Herald-American
USA Today
US News and World Report

INDEX

About the Author

DAVID JORDAN is president of the Philadelphia Athletics Historical Society and also lectures frequently on both baseball and the Civil War. He is the author of *Occasional Glory: The History of the Philadelphia Phillies; The Athletics of Philadelphia: Connie Mack's White Elephants, 1901–1954*; and *A Tiger in His Time: Hal Newhouser and the Burden of Wartime Baseball.*